WITHDRAWN

THE POLITICAL DILEMMAS OF MILITARY REGIMES

322.5
P759c

The Political Dilemmas of Military Regimes

edited by Christopher Clapham and George Philip

BARNES & NOBLE BOOKS
Totowa, New Jersey

©1985 Christopher Clapham and George Philip
First published in the USA 1985 by
Barnes & Noble Books
81 Adams Drive
Totowa, New Jersey 07512

Library of Congress Cataloging in Publication Data
Main entry under title:

The Political dilemmas of military regimes.

    Contents: The political dilemmas of military regimes/
C. Clapham and G. Philip—Portugal / I. Campbell—Greece /
T. Veremis— [etc.]
    1. Civil-military relations—Addresses, essays,
lectures. 2. Military government—Addresses, essays,
lectures. I. Clapham, Christopher S. II. Campbell, Ian,
1938-   . III. Philip, George D.E.
JF195.C5P65 1985   322'.5   84-18414
ISBN 0-389-20533-8

Printed and bound in Great Britain

CONTENTS

The Authors
Acknowledgements

ALLEGHENY COLLEGE LIBRARY

85-6255

THE AUTHORS

J. 'Bayo Adekanye is Senior Lecturer in Government at the University of Ibadan, and in 1982-83 was Visiting Fellow at the Centre for the Study of Arms Control and International Security, University of Lancaster. He is the author of Nigeria in Search of a Stable Civil-Military System (1982), and of numerous articles on civil-military relations.

Christopher Clapham is Senior Lecturer and Head of the Department of Politics, University of Lancaster. He is the author of Haile-Selassie's Government (1969) and of numerous articles on Ethiopian politics, as well as Third World Politics (1984).

James Dunkerley works at the Latin America Bureau, London, and is an Honorary Research Fellow of the Institute of Latin American Studies, University of London. He is the author of The Long War : Dictatorship and Revolution in El Salvador (1982), and of Rebellion in the Veins : Political Struggle in Bolivia, 1952-82 (1984).

Barry Green researches in Indonesian politics at the University of Queensland, Australia.

Bener Karakartal took his first degree and doctorate in Paris, and taught at the University of Paris-X (Nanterre), before becoming Professor of Politics and International Relations at the University of Istanbul. He has written on political parties and military government in Turkey.

Guillermo Makin took his first and second degrees in political science at Universidad del Salvador, Buenos Aires, and is currently working on Argentine

Politics at Cambridge. He has published articles in *International Affairs*, *Government & Opposition*, and elsewhere.

George Philip is Lecturer at the London School of Economics and the Institute of Latin American Studies, University of London. He is the author of *The Rise and Fall of the Peruvian Military Radicals 1968-76* (1978) and of *Oil and Politics in Latin America* (1982), and is currently writing a book on the military in Latin America.

Gowher Rizvi lectures in Imperial and Commonwealth History at the University of Warwick. He is the author of *Linlithgow and India 1936-1943* (1978) and editor of *Imperialism and Decolonization* (1984), and is currently writing a history of the British Empire 1760-1960.

Ulf Sundhaussen teaches Asian politics at the University of Queensland, and in 1981-82 was Visiting Professor at the University of Saarbrucken. He is the author of *The Road to Power : Indonesian Military Politics 1945-1967* (1982), and of many other studies of Indonesian politics.

Thanos Veremis received his doctorate in politics and history from Oxford, and is currently Lecturer in Modern Greek History at the Panteois School of Political Science, Athens. In 1983-84, he was a visiting scholar at the Center for European Studies, Harvard University.

Peter Woodward worked with V.S.O. in Sudan and taught at the University of Khartoum, before becoming Lecturer in Politics at the University of Reading. He has edited the memoirs of Sir James Robertson, *Transition in Africa* (1974), and written *Condominium and Sudanese Nationalism* (1979).

ACKNOWLEDGEMENTS

This book originated in workshops held under the auspices of the European Consortium for Political Research in Aarhus (Denmark) in 1982 and Freiburg-im-Breisgau (West Germany) in 1983, in which all of the authors took part, except for James Dunkerley, Barry Green and Thanos Veremis. We would like to thank the Consortium and all the other participants, and especially Ian Campbell (University of Warwick), who helped to organise the workshops and provided valuable comments on the draft chapters. The text of this book has been produced on a BBC Microcomputer, and our thanks are due to Karen Skinner, Fiona Hayter and Susan Riches, of the Department of Politics, University of Lancaster, for word-processing the successive drafts.

THE POLITICAL DILEMMAS OF MILITARY REGIMES

Chapter One

THE POLITICAL DILEMMAS OF MILITARY REGIMES

Christopher Clapham and George Philip

THE PROBLEM OF MILITARY REGIME SUCCESSION

The basic problem about military regimes is one not
of how they can gain power, but of what they can do
with it. A military coup, like an election victory,
installs a new government and helps to define a
pattern of opposition and support which will
constrict its political options. But as time goes
by, the way in which a government gained power takes
second place to the problem of how it is to keep it,
and it is at this point that the most distinctive
dilemmas of military regimes become apparent.
Firstly, they must reconcile continuing control over
the military with a measure of acceptance from civil
society. Military regimes need not be popular, but
they do need to command obedience on the basis of
more than simple coercion; even though legitimacy
(i.e. de jure acceptance from civil society) is not
always necessary, a degree of political (and not
just military) organisation certainly is. Secondly,
they must devise some institutional structure,
whether formally of a military or a non-military
kind, through which this political settlement can be
maintained. This book is about how they seek to
resolve these dilemmas.
     If these basic dilemmas are common to all
military regimes, there are nonetheless important
differences, stemming both from the kind of military
involved and from the kind of civil society which it
is governing. Military organisations derive from an
enormous range of cultural and historical
circumstances, and vary widely in internal
structure, political outlook, and social
composition. The regimes which they form may have
very different relationships with their ´parent´
militaries, stay in power for longer or shorter

1

periods of time, and display sharply contrasting
degrees of internal stability. Most disruptively of
all, from the viewpoint of comparative political
analysis, they swiftly become enmeshed in the
ordinary business of government (economic
management, international relations, the immediate
need to cope with specific local crises and
circumstances) and in the process come to look
increasingly like national governments concerned
with the problems of their own particular states,
decreasingly like any general category of ´military
regime´. It is therefore not too surprising that
militaries exhibit for instance no distinctive
uniformities in economic policy, save for a tendency
to spend more on the army itself, or that there is
quite a high level of variance in their
international alliance pattern and ideological
stance.(1) Soldiers are not inherently either
conservative or radical. Military leaders may be
old conformists from the top of the hierarchy, or
young firebrands from the bottom. They may come
from privileged or from disadvantaged sections of
indigenous society, or even from outside the society
which they govern altogether. They may be
anti-Communist or anti-American, or simply forced
into dependence on one external backer or another by
the immediate demands of their own international or
domestic political difficulties.

But these differences help to provide varying
answers to what are fundamentally the same questions
about the relationship between the military
organisation and the world of politics. These
questions often resolve themselves into a specific
dilemma between alternative patterns of
institutionalisation and demilitarisation.
Institutionalisation involves the maintenance of the
military leadership in power, coupled with attempts
to entrench its position and broaden its support by
seeking alliances with civilian political groups
which are then subordinated to it. Demilitarisation
conversely involves the withdrawal of the military
from direct control of government, whether
voluntarily in favour of some designated civilian
successor, or involuntarily under varying degrees of
pressure or compulsion. While these are in
principle choices open to all military regimes, the
constraints within which such choices have to be
made, the success which they achieve, and especially
the patterns of succession of one form of regime by
another, make possible a comparative political
analysis which goes beyond the simple codification

of the attitudes of the regimes themselves.

The reason why these problems are constant, common to all militaries, is because no military regime, even in the simplest political system, is able to maintain an uncomplicated unity of military and political command, either by itself or in conjunction with the civil bureaucracy, in anything but the short term: a matter of some two or three years at most. This is not primarily the result of the military´s supposed lack of ´legitimacy´, a problem very easily exaggerated in weakly institutionalised political systems where there are few if any generally shared assumptions about the proper means of acquiring and exercising political power: and these are, after all, the political systems in which military intervention is in any event most likely to occur. It is much more the result of the straightforward problems of political management. The very short term does not usually create much difficulty. Often the army or some group within it takes over as the result of a crisis which may well lead to its intervention being greeted with relief. Even when it isn´t, there is rarely any other source of organised force (apart from divisions within the armed forces themselves) which is immediately capable of resisting it. The problems arise during the subsequent period, during which the regime has to devise policies to cope with whatever crisis prompted its intervention, together with the further issues raised by the intervention itself, or thrown up in the ordinary course of events. Such policies inevitably arouse opposition and define support: a natural process no different for military rulers than for any other form of government. In the case of military governments, however, this process is almost certain to raise the question of the status of the regime itself, both within the military and in the wider political society, and to confront the regime wih the need to formulate some kind of longer term political or constitutional programme.

In formulating such a programme, the military quickly comes up against the limitations imposed by its own values and structures; at the same time, the political analyst comes up against the corresponding problem of whether there _are_ structures and values, common to all militaries, which can be used to provide a general rationale for the behaviour of military regimes. We would start by expressing a firm preference for structural over attitudinal considerations. Without committing ourselves to any general opinion on the relative importance of cultural as against institutional variables, there are two specific reasons for emphasising the structural element in this case. First, in the military more than in almost any other form of social organisation, deliberate attempts are made to inculcate values appropriate to the structures already established; values may therefore be seen as following from structures, rather than vice versa. These notably include the authoritarian attitudes derived from military hierarchy, the associated ´military virtues´ of discipline, efficiency and esprit de corps, the core value of nationalism, and the shared attitudes which arise in particular military institutions from the physical proximity of its members and their isolation from the rest of society. Secondly, however, what is important is the extent to which these military values are inculcated, rather than any substantial variance in the values themselves. Even military structures cannot be relied upon to entrench military attitudes, and competing values may intrude from the social group identities and cultural characteristics of the society. If soldiers cannot be relied upon to hold the values commonly attributed to them, then such values readily turn into stereotypes which may be misleading as guides to actual behaviour.(2)

The structural characteristics of the military do however have some value in defining the political options which it is able to accept. The most important of these is its status as part of the permanent state bureaucracy, which provides it with a set of political and economic interests from which it is extremely difficult for any military regime to escape. The military maintains the state, and the state maintains the military. A military coup is, prima facie, the capture of control over the state by its own employees: that is why it is so easy. A military regime will from this viewpoint have interests in common with the civilian bureaucracy, and be inherently opposed to any measure which would threaten the state´s control over the resources which it needs to maintain itself. A secondary though still important structural feature is the command hierarchy itself, which defines a mode of operation of an extremely constricting kind. It allows some scope for political discussion and compromise within the military leadership, usually confined to a peer group of officers of roughly similar rank, and some opportunity for co-opting

4

other groups and interests to support the regime; but it allows little capacity for handling political organisation beyond a very limited level.

Despite the enormous variations between military regimes, therefore, they do face a common political problem: that of combining their need to preserve the interests derived from their position in the state apparatus, with the inherent limitations in their capacity for political organisation. This problem is equally evident in the experience of such widely differing regimes as those of Chile and Ethiopia, and is also common to former guerilla liberation armies, such as those of Algeria or Guine-Bissau, once these come to inherit state power. This lands them in dilemmas which are likewise characteristic and recurring, even though the precise forms which these take, and the practical options which are open, will vary from case to case.

TERMS AND VARIABLES

In order to start working out some of the characteristic patterns of political settlement by military regimes, it is necessary to define three sets of variables. The first set consists of those key civil-military variables which provide the most important influences on the structure and nature of military regimes. The second set consists of military regime types, while the third consists of different forms of political outcome. Even though we do not subscribe to any rigidly causal view of comparative political explanation, we regard the key variables as providing powerful constraints which help to account for the type of regime, and subsequently to produce discernible patterns of regime succession, while allowing some measure of autonomous political choice.

The Key Civil-Military Variables

The main constituents of the set of key variables will be familiar to any student of civil-military relations, derived as they are from the structure of the military, the structure of civil society, and the nexus between the two. Moving from the most specific and military-related variables, to the more general and civil society-related ones, these are:

The unity of the military command structure. The most basic distinction here is between armies that behave like armies (that is to say, according to an official stereotype of discipline, hierarchy and established procedures) and ones that do not. This may broadly be associated with a geographical continuum stretching from the ´professionalised´ militaries of South America and Europe (including Turkey) at one end, through those of the Middle East, Central America and South-East Asia, to institutionally weak African militaries at the other. This should not be taken to imply any geographical causation, and takes no account of wide variations within each zone, such as those produced in Portugal by the effects of conscription and colonial war. Low unity is indicated by the prevalence of coups and coup attempts by junior officers and other ranks, and by intra-military killings, as in Nigeria (1966), Ethiopia (1974-78), and Bangladesh (1980); it may also, paradoxically, be a feature of highly personalist long-term dictatorships, such as that of Somoza in Nicaragua. High unity is conversely indicated by the absence of these phenomena even in military regimes subjected to high political stress, such as Chile since 1973 and Turkey since 1980. The ability of military regimes to change leaders without bloodshed under high political stress, as in Argentina (1982), is evidence of high unity rather than low, and helps to indicate the way in which unity constrains the leaders of military regimes, as well as the lower ranks.

Differentiation of the military from civil society. This criterion concerns the permeability of the boundary between the military and civilian politics, and is particularly important in cases where the military seeks to play the role of arbiter between contesting civilian political groups, or to withdraw intact from government in favour of a civilian regime. It does not correspond nearly as closely as the ´unity´ criterion to any general level of ´development´, but may be influenced both by the structure and experience of the military, and by general social factors. Professional armies will tend to be more differentiated than conscript ones, and deliberate measures may be taken to increase differentiation through the introduction of military schools and higher education colleges, and the inculcation of a distinctly military ideology. While foreign training missions may thus increase differentiation, as in South America in the early twentieth century, extensive external dependence is likely to reduce it, especially (as in Iran or Ethiopia) by raising doubts both in the army and outside about its relationship to the core value of nationalism; analoguous problems may be one legacy of military defeat, as in the Egyptian army after 1948 or the Portuguese in the 1970s. Ethnic and regional divisions provide an obvious threat to differentiation, especially once immersion in politics leads soldiers to be regarded as spokesmen for their own local interests. Class divisions on the other hand are much less of a threat, and it is possible as in South America for military regimes to defend established class interests without becoming permeated by their civilian suppporters. Indeed, in a more general way, differentiation may only be possible in a country large and developed enough to sustain a substantial professional middle class.

Level of perceived threat from civil society. This is an explicitly subjective variable, but nonetheless a very important one in determining the military's relationship with civilian political groups. At its most intense, a sense of threat may provoke measures of extreme repression, while threat at a lower level influences both the military's capacity to withdraw from office and its need to select and influence a successor regime. Threat is a reflection of two elements. The first is the military's awareness of values or interests which it regards as central to its own position; these may be associated with nationalism (especially when the army represents a core governing group opposed by centrifugal forces), with class interests, or with the internal unity and differentiation of the military itself. The second is its estimate of the strength of autonomous political organisations whose goals clash with these interests. In a rough and ready way, then, threat expresses the military's felt need for political involvement, and indicates the way in which, and level at which, involvement will take place.

Level of autonomous political organisation. Autonomous political organisations are ones which are capable of maintaining themselves over time without direct access to the coercive and distributive powers of the state, and if need be in opposition to them. The level of autonomy reflects both the scope of such organisations, in terms of the range and number of the people whom they incorporate, and their intensity, in terms of organisational effectiveness and membership commitment. This variable derives entirely from civil society, but tends to vary in line with 'development' criteria in the same way as military unity, while differentiation and threat, being derived from the relationship between civil and military, do not. Autonomous political organisation nonetheless strongly influences the possibility of combining civil and military elements within a single regime, as most clearly instanced by the difference between Argentina, where autonomous political organisations inhibit the formation of civil-military coalitions, and Brazil, where the comparative weakness of such organisations facilitates them.

These variables naturally shift over time in any given case, and are inter-related with one another. Most obviously, unity affects differentiation, and autonomy affects threat. Since we are not in any event concerned to develop a causal or mechanistic model of military regime succession, this does not worry us. Our concern, rather, is to develop criteria which will be helpful in organising and appraising alternative patterns of relationship between military regimes and their civilian allies, rivals or successors.

Types of Military Regime

Our second group of variables then consist of military regime types, being on the whole derived, with some modification, from Huntington's well-known categories.(3) It is not necessary to specify types of regime for every possible combination of our four initial variables, partly because these are interrelated as already noted, partly because some combinations do not commonly occur, or where they do occur (e.g. high unity, differentiation and autonomy, low threat) do not give rise to military regimes. The types which we feel it useful to distinguish are the following:

Veto Regimes. These correspond closely to Huntington's category, and are characterised by high unity, fairly high differentiation (though allowing for association between the military and privileged or centralist political groups), high threat, and medium or high autonomy. This is, of course, a recipe for military regimes of the most systematically repressive kind, as in Chile and Argentina, since it pits the military directly against strongly organised civilian political structures. Where, as in Turkey perhaps, the military is more differentiated (in the sense of not being inherently committed to either right-wing or left-wing political parties), and the perceived threat against which the military decided to intervene is one to civil society rather than to the military as such, the degree of repression is unlikely to be so intense, and the regime comes closer to the moderator type.

Moderator Regimes. These most closely correspond to Huntington´s ´guardian´ type, and are characterised by fairly high (though variable) unity and differentiation, combined with fairly low threat and moderate autonomy. Classically, this is the case of the professional military which feels itself obliged to ´step in, to sort out the mess´ created by factious politicians, and after a period of ´corrective government´ to hand over to a cleaned up civilian political system. Moderator regimes may be found in societies at varying levels of social and economic development, and be drawn both from the small ex-colonial armies of West Africa considered in Adekanye´s chapter, and from the much larger and more institutionalised armies of Brazil (1945-64), Argentina (1955-66) and Turkey. It may well be an unstable regime type, because unity and differentiation are threatened by the military´s political role.

Factional Regimes. These are distinguished from the moderator type by low unity, and in consequence often by low differentiation also. This type of regime is the almost inevitable result of the personal coup by a disgruntled officer, such as Acheampong´s intervention in Ghana in 1972, or Amin´s in Uganda the previous year, still more so of an NCO´s coup such as that of Batista in Cuba. It may equally follow from the decline of unity and differentiation in an initially moderator regime. The military, and equally in the latter case groups within it, become participants in the political process in alliance with one or another set of civilian political actors or factions, with which they may be linked on grounds of ethnicity, ideology, or simply mutual tactical convenience.

This is potentially a highly unstable pattern, and such regimes, when they fall, may fall very hard indeed; most of the extreme examples of fragmentation, such as Uganda and Bangladesh, fairly clearly belong to it, while in appropriate conditions, as in Cuba or Nicaragua, it may give rise to a revolutionary situation. It is nonetheless possible for a sufficiently skilful leader with an adequate political base, such as Mobutu in Zaire or even Somoza in Nicaragua, to construct a personalist regime which may be surprisingly long-lasting.

Breakthrough Regimes. This, one of the most useful of Huntington´s categories, is nonetheless difficult to classify in terms of our initial variables. It is the classic type of radical reforming military regime, and normally requires low differentiation and (since it usually results from a junior officers´ coup) low unity. Thailand (1930), Egypt (1952), Libya (1969) and Ethiopia (1974) are among the clearest examples, all of them resulting from coups against monarchies. Breakthrough coups may also be fomented, as in Sudan (1969), Ethiopia and Portugal (1974) by the radicalising effects on the lower ranks of the military of prolonged involvement in unsuccessful counter-insurgency operations. There are few if any recent Latin American examples, perhaps the closest being Peru (1968-75), where the increased popular mobilisation promoted by a radical military regime led to growing threats to military unity, and in turn to the abandonment of the venture; the military was in a sense too differentiated to embark on a strategy of this kind. The most distinctive feature of a breakthrough regime is the peculiar form of threat which prompts intervention. Rather than seeking, as with the veto regime, to defend an existing social order with which its own interests are identified, the military seeks to attack a social order which presents a threat to the radical nationalism of a modernising army. While repression by the veto regime is defensive, and mobilisation by civilian groups is discouraged, that by the breakthrough regime is offensive, and selective mobilisation at least is positively encouraged. This leads in turn to a decline in differentiation as other groups come to share the values of the military.

While these regime types are, we believe, useful, and will be used to structure our discussion of political outcomes, they do not imply any rigid set of categories. Actual regimes are mixtures derived from specific conditions, not mere examplars of ideal types. They are affected not only by circumstances peculiar to particular countries, but also by more general variables which, because of their uneven impact, cannot easily be fitted into an outline like this one. One striking example is the role of external influence. We reject that stereotype which sees military regimes as neo-colonialist impositions, tied to some metropolitan power either by military dependence (for training and arms supply) or by economic interest. Too many regimes (Burma, Ethiopia, Ghana after 1981) not only fail to fit this stereotype, but run dramatically counter to it. At the same time, it would be foolish and biased to exclude the degree of external influence which frequently affects not only the military itself, but (in often heavily penetrated societies) other social groups and indeed the whole structure of state, society and economy as well. One of the advantages of a case study format is that it permits such variables to be admitted as and when they are needed.

Military Regime Outcomes

Our final set of variables consists of outcomes. At its crudest, the dilemma facing military regimes is whether to go or to stay: whether to demilitarise, by establishing and transferring power to some civilian political structure, or to institutionalise the regime by entrenching it at the centre of a civil-military structure of a more or less authoritarian kind. Even the choice between going and staying is not as stark as this suggests, however, since demilitarisation will almost inevitably be accompanied by some attempt by the military to guarantee its vital interests by placing restrictions on its successors, while institutionalisation will require some association of civilian groups with the regime. Equally, there are important variations within each main type. The following are the main possibilities:

Handback. This is the classic process of demilitarisation in which characteristically the military leadership supervises the drafting of a new constitution (usually devised in an often vain attempt to overcome what it sees as the deficiencies of the previous civilian regime), and holds elections in which familiar politicians, their parties sometimes slightly realigned or disguised under new names, compete for office. An alternative form appears when the military precipitately abandons power in the face of threats to its own unity and differentiation, or of overwhelming pressure from an external patron or domestic political forces. There is no more difficult military operation to manage than a retreat, and the retreat from power may be anything from a tactical withdrawal to a rout. The term handback emphasises the continuity with previous periods of civilian rule, and indicates the main problem to which the chapters by Adekanye and Karakartal draw attention: that the new civilian regime will embody many of the deficiencies of the old, and may well lead to further military intervention, and very possibly to a cycle of successive interventions and demilitarisations.

Civilian Renewal. Though ostensibly similar to the handback option, this is distinguished by the new civilian regime´s capacity to break away from previous political structures and attitudes. Almost invariably, it requires a very long period of military rule, or else a particularly sharp and very likely violent jolt to the pattern of both civilian and military politics. Otherwise entrenched political structures, the resilience of which is very easily underestimated by military regimes which place their faith in constitutional engineering, will be likely to reassert themselves. One way in which this jolt may be produced is by a failure of military rule so dramatic as to cure both civilian politicians of calling for intervention, and officers of wishing to intervene; Greece after 1974 and possibly Argentina in the wake of revelations about the ´dirty war´ following the 1983 return to civilian rule may perhaps provide examples. Spain and Portugal are cases of civilian renewal after long periods of authoritarian rule. The capacity of renewal to lead to stable liberal democratic systems should not however be taken for granted. Such systems rest on general conditions for the maintenance of democratic government which go beyond the process of demilitarisation.

Authoritarian Clientelism. The institutionalisation of a military regime depends on its capacity to acquire civilian allies who are willing to accept subordination to military leadership in exchange for some share in running the state and especially some share in the benefits which it provides. The nature of such a relationship is inherently clientelistic: it is an essentially transactional arrangement, in which the military patron offers some of the resources derived from its control over the state, notably physical protection and economic payoffs, and in return receives political support from the civilian client. The essential element in the transaction is the military's capacity to attract subordinates who are on the one hand sufficiently influential to make their support worth having, and on the other insufficiently strong and independent to threaten the military itself. This in turn requires a fairly low level of autonomous political organisation, or alternatively serious divisions among subordinated civilian groups which facilitate a strategy of 'divide and rule'. There are however different forms of clientelism, which depend on the unity of the military command structure and its differentiation from civil society, as well as on the character of the civilian clients thus recruited. By authoritarian clientelism we have in mind a united military which, despite possibly close links with the civilian bureaucracy, is well differentiated from (and consequently impermeable to) civilian political groups. This type is close to O'Donnell's conception of bureaucratic authoritarianism, and is consequently most familiar from southern Europe and the southern cone of South America.(4)

Factional Clientelism. This closely corresponds to the factional regime type already noted, and is distinguished from authoritarian clientelism by the military's lack of unity, and usually of differentiation. It may be queried to what degree this is a form of institutionalisation at all, or indeed to what degree it is a form of military regime. It is essentially a personalist regime led by an individual who, having gained power by means of a military coup, has then used his personal skills to establish himself through alliances with groups both military and civilian, and very possibly also the backing of external allies. It does not differ substantially from personalist regimes led by civilian party politicians, and often includes the establishment of a party which serves as a conduit for patronage. Like equivalent civilian regimes, it may be longer or shorter lived. It is certainly an option which is open to military leaders, however, and a popular one with many of them.

The Military Party State. This is rather a distinctive option, and involves the attempt to mobilise both the military and civilians within a single party state. It is especially associated with breakthrough regimes, and is distinguished both from handback and from the clientelist options by its conscious attempts to expand participation while destroying any previous structures through which participation has been organised. It is in this sense most closely akin to civilian renewal, but is distinguished from it both by the choice of authoritarian rather than liberal political forms, and by the continued involvement in government of a military leadership committed to programmatic goals. It may also be accompanied by a strong sense of threat. In a way, it may be seen as an attempt to create the kind of merger between army and party which results from guerilla revolutionary wars or wars of national liberation in such states as China, Cuba or Mozambique. If it succeeds, it may result, as in Mexico, in a uniquely stable and effective form of regime. As our case study of Ethiopia shows, however, it may involve considerable strains in the relationships between military, civilians, and external sources of influence.

Impasse. The preceding discussion may have given the impression that at the end of every military regime there is some more or less stable pattern of civil-military accommodation. That is far from being the case. Military regimes usually, though not always, set themselves some kind of political strategy which is intended, implicitly or explicitly, to lead to one of the outcomes noted above. Often, they do not achieve it. In particular, there may come a point at which the regime has clearly boxed itself into a corner, in which it can neither create new political institutions itself, nor do deals with existing political groupings, either by buying their support or by handing over to them. The length of time for which such a regime can struggle on will then depend very largely on the degree to which the rest of the military shares the predicament which has overtaken its leaders. Where the regime faces a threat which also confronts the military institution and civilian elite groups as a whole, the result may well be foreign intervention, invited by the beleaguered

14

authorities; something of this kind has happened recently in El Salvador. Where the threat is less drastic, the commonest fate for the impasse regime is for it to be overthrown by a group within the armed forces which instantly sets about trying to reopen the political options which its predecessor has closed. This was the fate of the Acheampong government in Ghana after the failure of its ´union government´ scheme in 1978, or of the Galtieri government in Argentina after the failure of the Malvinas adventure in 1982. The alternative may be the midnight flit: a quick and undignified abandonment of power which leaves it to an incoming government to pick up the pieces, and which leaves the military in no condition to take over political responsibilities for several years to come.

PATTERNS OF REGIME SUCCESSION

The discussion so far has suggested that, despite the varieties of national experience and inevitable blurring of conceptual categories, there are only a limited number of regime types and of outcomes to which they may lead. From these, several characteristic patterns of regime succession can be derived. The most convenient point from which to trace these patterns is from the different regime types, which may be related both back to the key civil-military variables and forward to the possible outcomes. We will take each major regime type in turn, linking the pattern of outcomes to the much more detailed case studies examined in the later chapters.

Veto Regimes

The distinguishing feature of veto regimes is that they seize power at moments of high threat, either to the military itself or to some broader interests associated with it, and resort to highly repressive measures, usually of a counter-revolutionary kind, in order to remove this threat by dramatically reducing the level of political participation. This initial period of repression or state terror, sufficiently instanced by Chile, Argentina and Indonesia, is likely to be of fairly short duration. The most important reason for this is that, over the medium and longer term, the use of terror is likely to have corrosive effects on the unity of the military command structure. The initial coup may

ALLEGHENY COLLEGE LIBRARY

well command a high level of support within the military, especially when it is clearly directed against a threatening communist revolutionary movement, whether this is in government (as in Chile) or directing its own high level of violence against an ineffective civilian regime. During the ´dirty war´ that follows, any kind of behaviour may be accepted. Once the immediate crisis is over, continued terror is likely to increase dissent between ´moderates´ and ´hard liners´ within the military, especially when repression is directed against middle-class intellectuals who may be drawn from the same social groups as the officer corps. Another threat to unity may come from the security forces themselves, which forming an elite within the military with access to its own intelligence sources and with unscrupulous operating methods, may be used for internal factional advantage. State terror also has high costs in terms of international acceptability.

The most important criterion affecting succession to veto regimes is then whether this initial period of repression succeeds in removing the main threat to the regime, and thus weakening the autonomy of civilian political organisation, while maintaining the unity of the military itself. In this (from the regime´s viewpoint) ideal situation, the way is open for the transformation of the regime into authoritarian clientelism. This involves a high degree of military/bureaucratic domination of civil society, which obliges civilian political leaders, lacking the autonomy needed to maintain any prolonged challenge to the regime, to seek accommodation with it as the best deal they can get. The result, even if legitimised by reasonably fair elections, is not genuine participation, but rather a limited show of it within constraints which the military lays down. This is essentially what is meant by the ´limited pluralism´ which Linz identifies as a feature of his authoritarian model. On the side of the military, this requires a measure of autonomy of the regime from the military itself, which permits the military to seek support from civilian groups without arousing a backlash from the barracks. This, in the aftermath of the Peronist experience, is one of the impediments to authoritarian clientelism in Argentina, while within the context of a much more factionalised military, suspicions of Zia-ur Rahman´s political links with a civilian clientele in Bangladesh helped to provoke his assassination by a rival army faction. A

ALLEGHENY COLLEGE LIBRARY

further feature of such limited participation is that it can much more easily be extended to the countryside, through the co-optation of existing clientele networks, than to the mass politics of the towns where political demands are likely to be much more inherently threatening to the regime. Authoritarian clientelist regimes are nonetheless capable, with reasonable luck and good management, of lasting as in Spain or Brazil for several decades, in the course of which thoroughgoing social and economic changes may take place which eventually open the possibility of civilian renewal. If Portugal under Salazar and Caetano is admitted as a variant of this type of regime, then an equivalent process of civilian renewal may follow from its overthrow by a short-lived junior officers' regime approximating in some respects to the breakthrough type.

The main problems for a veto regime arise if its potentially high cost bid for military domination fails to achieve its goal. The most drastic failure is that it may succumb directly to the threat which it set out to remove, and be overthrown by the revolutionary movement itself, though this is rare given the regime's high repressive capability and probable access to external support. It is more likely that, while dealing with the immediate threat, the regime will be unable to move to the authoritarian-clientelist solution because of divisions within the command hierarchy or because the continued autonomy of civilian organisations prevents the military from establishing the necessary clientelist relationship of dominance and dependence. This is most evidently the case with the military and the Peronist movement in Argentina. The first possibility may lead to a factional regime, especially if the differentiation of the military from civilian society also breaks down, while in Argentina in both 1971 and again in 1982, the second helped to lead to impasse, eventually followed by a disorderly handback. Even an apparently well-established authoritarian clientelist regime may fall victim to an urban reaction against the military-countryside alliance which maintains it, usually taking the form of strikes, riots and demonstrations which the regime is unable to contain. Pakistan in 1969, where Ayub Khan's programme of 'basic democracies' embodied just such an alliance, is perhaps the most dramatic example, but the difficulties of urban political management in Chile suggest another potential case.

Moderator Regimes

The idea of the military as an independent arbiter and guarantor of national political values is an attractive one to many military leaders, which ties in well with their identification with the state, as an institution with interests over and above the level of ordinary political conflict, and with their distaste (or incapacity) for political organisation. It presupposes a high level of unity and differentiation (even though actual intervention may soon reveal that these are inadequate) and also requires, if the army is to play its moderating role successfully, a low level of threat. Where these conditions are met, the way is open to a simple handback solution, though even then it may be aborted by such factors as the personal ambitions of the military head of state. Handback is also, as already suggested, potentially a highly unstable solution. In part, this is because the constitutionalist assumptions on which the strategy relies are inadequate to rectify a much more deep-rooted political malaise. A moderator regime only too often assumes that the trouble with the previous government (which provided the reason or excuse for its own intervention) was some readily identified and easily cured defect: an unacceptable degree of dictatorship (or anarchy) which could be solved by increasing (or removing) constitutional controls on the executive; an unworkable federal system, or merely the personal greed or incompetence of a particular set of politicians. Changing the constitution (or removing the specified set of politicians) not only fails to solve the problem; it intensifies it, by dividing the civilian political constituency into groups who see their interests as being either favoured or threatened by further intervention, encouraging the former to knock on the door of the barracks, and at the same time legitimising renewed involvement on the part of ambitious or disgruntled sections of the military. The Nigerian reintervention of December 1983 provides a classic example, and the chapter by Adekanye explores this problem in greater detail.

Reintervention is not inevitable. Much may depend on the political support, skill and luck of the head of the successor administration. If it does occur, it is likely to lead, either immediately or after a further handback and reintervention, to one of the other possible outcomes for a moderator regime. Which, depends to a large extent on the military's capacity to maintain its initially high levels of unity and differentiation. If it succeeds, then the most likely progression is, as in Turkey, towards some form of authoritarian clientelism. The second or third time round, the arny's tenure of power will be longer, and its conception of the 'corrective' measures required before returning to civilian rule will be more basic. In the process, it will tend to impose on any would-be successor conditions which imply a much more direct subordination to the military, and a strong and lasting military role in the regime, even if this is nominally civilian.

A much more likely outcome, especially in the case of armies which are weakly institutionalised to begin with, is the fragmentation of military unity, and the breakdown of differentiation as members of the military make common cause with civilian political allies. The corrosive effects of political participation on military unity are clear from a large number of case studies, especially of African and Asian militaries. These can be ascribed at the most general level to the clash between the authoritarian organisational structure of the military, and the differences of attitude and identification induced by using this structure to enforce decisions which are seen as 'political' in the sense of favouring some groups (within the military, or in the country at large) at the expense of others. The normal fate of a moderator regime is then to decline into a factional one, and the differences between armies which have and have not succumbed to this fate are interesting and important. There is however a further possibility, which is that the steadily declining competence of successive regimes, whether military or civilian, may provoke a radical military seizure of power which leads to a breakthrough regime. Ghana under Flight Lieutenant Jerry Rawlings is the nearest example, but the same possibility must be open in other states where unity, differentiation and autonomy are all low, and where national political power has come to alternate between ineffective civil and military elites whose rule is resented both by the lower ranks of the military and by a civilian mass constituency to which these can appeal. Even where unity and differentiation are not so low, as in Peru in 1968, a series of incompetent military and civilian regimes may lead to the development of the ´negative threat´ mentality conducive to military radicalism.

Factional Regimes

Factionalism is the price of military disunity. When a fragmented military (or a section of it) seizes political power, or the military breaks apart beneath the pressures of political decision-making, the regime can maintain itself only by a highly dangerous policy of intra-military repression, or else by manipulating internal factions. Disunity is the critical problem for military regimes, and several of their most distinctive features may be seen as means to overcome it. One example is the propensity for collective leadership, which acknowledges the existence of factions but seeks to limit their disintegrative effect by building them into the structure of the regime itself. Different forms of collective leadership in turn reflect different forms of factionalism. The classic military junta, characteristic of fairly highly institutionalised militaries and of veto regimes, seeks to reconcile the interests of major institutional sections of the military, usually army, navy and air force. The military council, usually larger than the junta and composed of junior or middle-level officers, seeks to contain the danger provoked by junior officers´ coups which take the dangerously fragmenting form of challenges to the existing command hierarchy. A horizontally linked collective of junior officers thus substitutes for the vertical hierarchy of normal command. Councils of this kind are also very commonly used, especially for example in West Africa, to contain ethnic differences by including representatives from each of the major ethnic or regional groups. At the extreme, the Ethiopian Derg sought to counteract the danger of fragmentation during its ´creeping revolution´ against the Haile-Selassie regime in 1974 by systematically representing both different ranks and different units within the armed forces. This cumbersome mechanism achieved its immediate purpose, but broke apart beneath the strains of government.

So long as collective leadership holds, the major dangers of factionalism can be averted, even in cases where unity and differentiation are low. It is generally easier for collective than for individual leaders to return to civilian rule, for example, both because the leadership can unite the

armed forces behind the move, and because single
individuals are more reluctant to abandon power.
Even collectives may be unable to maintain unity, as
in Nigeria in 1966-67, but the potentially most
destructive forms of factionalism arise under single
leaders who face disunity within the military. This
is likely to be compounded by equivalent divisions
within the country as a whole. What one is then
essentially talking about is a personalist regime
with a military leader, which will survive or fail
according to the skills, support and luck of its
chief. Whether this should be regarded as a
'military' regime or not may be a matter for debate.
In states such as those of black Africa where
personal rule is in any event the norm, the way in
which an individual exercises power may be more
significant than the way in which he acquires it.(5)
Certainly some of the worst excesses of personal
government, as in Uganda under Amin or the Central
African Republic (and briefly Empire) under Bokassa,
have come from military leaders; but other
factional clientelist regimes have proved remarkably
long-lived, especially when the ruler has used some
form of single party structure as a means of
associating civilian factions with his government.

A factional regime then has two principal
avenues open to it, of impasse and disintegration on
the one hand, or consolidation into factional
clientelism on the other. Impasse may lead directly
to a handback option, as in both Uganda and the
Central African Republic, as a means of picking up
the pieces and attempting to put the state together
again under the protection of an external power.
Otherwise handback is an unlikely option, simply
because a personalist leader will see no reason to
indulge in it, so long as he feels capable of
clinging on to power. Much more likely is the
nominal civilianisation of the regime through a
cosmetic transformation in which the military
leader converts himself into an elected president
(or annointed emperor). It has been demonstrated
that military regimes which form their own political
parties are likely to be significantly longer lived
than those which do not;(6) but this may be
ascribed not so much to the inherent strength of the
party itself, which is likely to be a clientelist
structure of a highly instrumental kind, as to the
fact that a leader who is able to construct such a
party will already have achieved the basic
conditions for longevity, notably a degree of
independence from the army and the subordination of

civilian factions. One of the conditions for success will be the overcoming of divisions within the armed forces, and if the leader succeeds over a period in consolidating both unity and differentiation, the regime may develop into authoritarian clientelism. Unless some such process of institutionalisation takes place, the eventual demise of the leader will be followed either by more of the same, or else by a bout of instability and fragmentation.

Breakthrough Regimes

The breakthrough regime is the most interesting of all the military regime types, not merely because of its implicitly radical ideology, but because it offers the real possibility of creating new and effective institutions through a process of social mobilisation. Before this possibility can be achieved, however, it has to surmount challenges at two levels: the immediate challenge of maintaining its radical aspirations while securing order and control, and the longer term one of reconciling political mobilisation with its commitment to the structure of the state.

While a veto regime comes to power in order to meet the threat posed by political mobilisation, a breakthrough regime creates its own threat by seeking to overthrow an established oligarchy. This is likely to lead to a traumatic period in the immediate aftermath of takeover, which may result in a wide variety of outcomes. Since a breakthrough coup will almost inevitably be directed against, among others, senior officers loyal to the old regime, it implies a fairly low (though potentially very variable) level of military unity, which provides one strain on the new government; even if unity is not shattered by the coup itself, it is likely to be threatened, as in Peru after 1968, by new policies of political mobilisation.(7) A breakthrough military may well take drastic action against leading figures of the old regime, whether because they are viewed as a danger, or as a simple gut reaction against a group which the new leaders view with disgust, as in Ethiopia in 1974 and Liberia in 1980. A further source of trauma arises when the coup has been hastened or provoked by the army´s involvement in counter-insurgency warfare, in which case the new regime will very rapidly have to decide whether to reach a political settlement with the insurgents (as in Sudan after 1969 and Portugal

after 1974) or to oppose them with renewed intensity
(as in Ethiopia after 1974). Either course will
probably intensify stresses within the regime. It
helps if, as in the Peruvian case, the insurgents
have already been decisively defeated. If
autonomous civilian political organisation is fairly
strong, and the differentiation of the military from
civil society fairly low, as perhaps in Portugal,
the military may lose control over events to
civilian actors, leading to a process of civilian
renewal. Alternatively, the military may recoil
from the consequences of its own actions, and
stabilise itself into a moderator or clientelist
regime, in response to internal or external threats
which it lacks confidence in its ability to deal
with. In Peru after 1975, this reaction sprang from
the fear of a well-differentiated military of
autonomous popular participation; in Sudan after
1971, from the defection of the regime's principal
ally, the Communist Party, which attempted an
internal coup wih Soviet support; in Liberia after
1980, from the regime's recognition of its economic
fragility and need for external aid.

Where the immediate trauma of establishing
control is overcome without impairing the regime's
radical aspirations, a critical problem then arises
as to how these can be stabilised in some settled
institutional form. The basic difficulty is that
unlike any other form of military regime, a
breakthrough regime may implicitly run counter,
through its policy of social mobilisation, to the
two structural constraints which characterise the
military as an institution: its commitment to the
state as an instrument of the central bureaucracy,
and its extremely limited capacity to absorb
political organisation. While in a sense the
'natural' outcome of a breakthrough coup is the
military party state, in practice this is very
difficult to achieve, since the military will
already have established interests which the party,
unlike the clientelist parties of factional or
authoritarian regimes, will tend to threaten.
Mexico is one example of a successful transition
from military to party rule, faciliated in part
through the diffusion of military power to state
governors, the creation of an accepted set of
organisational procedures, and the establishment of
local level institutions such as the peasant
leagues. The transition may also be achieved if the
army can combine high internal unity with an
ideology (most obviously one of a Marxist kind)

which denies the validity of a purely military
viewpoint. The process works more effectively in
reverse, when the party predates the military, which
is created as the armed wing of the party during a
process of armed decolonisation or revolutionary
insurrection. Even this does not entirely resolve
the problem, since the capture of central state
power creates the same tension between the interests
derived from social mobilisation on the one hand and
central control on the other, and these may result
in coups such as those in Algeria (1965) or
Guinea-Bissau (1979). It is nonetheless more likely
to result in a union of military and political
institutions which may eventually lead back, by way
of the creation of a new governing elite, to a new
form of authoritarian clientelism.

CONCLUSION

Patterns of military regime succession are rather
like paths through the jungle: there are various
trails, all pretty rough going (though some much
rougher than others), and most of them not leading
where you want to go anyhow, unless by a long and
circuitous route. But any of them can be tried, and
there is nothing to stop you leaving the path
altogether and trying to hack your way up the
hillside, even though one may conclude that you are
unlikely to get through. On the whole, from lack of
foresight or lack of energy, or from the simple
force of circumstances, you are likely to follow the
path of least resistance and come out where it
leads.
        The following chapters track some of the paths
which actual regimes have taken, many of them
starting at different points and ending at different
points, but nonetheless illustrating, along the way,
similarities in the dilemmas which they have had to
face and in their responses to them. They include a
veto regime in Greece which collapsed beneath the
weight of military disaster and was obliged to give
way to the process of civilian renewal which it had
sought to obstruct; and a similar regime in
Argentina, smitten by military adventurism in just
the same way, where the eventual outcome following
demilitarisation remains much more uncertain.
Argentina in turn provides one case in a comparison
of the veto regimes of southern South America which
shows how apparently rather similar authoritarian
militaries, reacting to different crises with

different patterns of social mobilisation, have achieved varying degrees of success at a varying cost in blood. While the South American cases demonstrate, on the whole, the autonomy of the military within the state and of the state within the society and international system, none of these are true of Central America, where the inability of the military to achieve any of the outcomes discussed above has resulted in the severest conditions of impasse, and in their wake domestic revolution and external intervention. The South and South-East Asian cases demonstrate the need for the military to maintain sufficient unity and differentiation, and to be able to overcome the autonomy of civilian political organisation, if it is to have any success either as a moderator or, if that fails, as an authoritarian clientelist regime. Indonesia is in this respect, from the military regime's viewpoint, a comparative success; the military in both Pakistan and Bangladesh, intervening in a nominally moderator role, found itself unable to sustain it, and having alienated the principal civilian political organisation, found itself having to resort to various clientelist devices, which in Bangladesh especially were further weakened by the fragility of the military itself. Our two more authentic sets of moderator regimes, in West Africa and Turkey, pursued rather similar handback strategies under very different circumstances both of military unity and differentiation, and of civil autonomy. While the difficulties and frequent failures of handback regimes in both cases reinforce our general view of the hazards of this solution, the reaction to failure is different, leading to authoritarian clientelism in the united and differentiated Turkish military, towards breakthrough at least in the fragmented and poorly differentiated Ghanaian one. Finally, the two breakthrough regimes considered in some detail, Ethiopia and Sudan, demonstrate two contrasting outcomes to which this distinctive form of military intervention may lead: in Ethiopia along the difficult and still incomplete path towards a military party state, in Sudan back to factional clientelism. Under other circumstances, breakthrough may lead, as in Portugal, towards an apparently successful civilian renewal.

NOTES
   1.   See   R.D.McKinlay   and   A.S.Cohan,   "A
comparative   analysis   of   the Political and Economic
Peformance   of   Military   and   Civilian   Regimes",
Comparative Politics, Vol.8 No.1, 1975, pp.1-30.
   2.   The   classic   demolition   of   military
attitudes as a guide to military regime behaviour is
that by B.J.O.Dudley on the Nigerian military, in J.
van Doorn, The Military Profession and Military
Regimes (Mouton, 1969).
   3.   S.P.Huntington, Political Order in Changing
Societies (Yale, 1968).
   4.   See   J.J.Linz,   "An   Authoritarian Regime:
Spain", in   E.Allardt   and   S.Rokkan, Mass   Politics
(Free Press, 1970).
   5.   See R.H.Jackson and C.G.Rosberg, Personal
Rule in Black Africa (California, 1982).
   6.   T.Dunmore, "Determinants of the Political
Stability of Military Regimes", Workshop on Military
Regimes, ECPR Joint Sessions, Freiburg-im-Breisgau,
1983.
   7. G. Philip, The Rise and Fall of the
Peruvian Military Radicals, 1968-76 (Athlone Press,
1980).

Chapter Two

GREECE: VETO AND IMPASSE, 1967-74

Thanos Veremis

THE GREEK MILITARY IN POLITICS

Historical Origins of Military Involvement

The phenomenon of military intervention in politics is a latecomer in modern Greek history. Military coups acquired a disquietening frequency after the end of Greece's irredentist wars in 1922, and coincided with the waning of parliamentary practices elsewhere in Europe.(1) Civilian supremacy was never really challenged, however, and coups that aspired to a lasting impact on politics merely sought to replace one civilian order with another, rather than (in Finer's words) permanently hand over the government to the army.(2) In this sense, military intervention before 1967 was restricted to an essentially moderator pattern. Even the Metaxas dictatorship of 1936-41, which enjoyed the approval of a compliant army, was blessed by the King and run by civilians. The same regime, with its emphasis on nationalism and anti-communism, its concern for re-education, social discipline and a synthesis of ancient and Christian values, and its distaste for parliamentary and democratic procedures, also anticipated themes which would be appropriated after 1967 by the Colonels, many of whom entered the Military Academy when General Metaxas was already firmly entrenched in power.

Greece's entry into the Second World War and the subsequent developments of occupation, resistance and civil strife, generated profound transformations in society and politics which could not fail to affect the military. The most fundamental break with the past was the result of a settling of old scores between republican and royalist officers. When the Axis forces occupied Greece, the remnants of the Greek army were

27

reconstituted in the Middle East under British supervision. The regular officer corps, which was mostly loyal to the King of the Hellenes, was joined in 1941 by republicans who had been cashiered in 1935, and were readmitted to active service when Crete fell to the Germans. Divergent loyalties and rivalries for scarce commissions soon revived the former antagonisms, which were sharpened by the introduction of an altogether new factor. In Greece the legitimacy and representative nature of the government in exile came to be seriously challenged by the broadly based but Communist-led resistance movement of EAM-ELAS. King George II´s support for the Metaxas dictatorship had made him the target of liberals and communists alike.(3) During the war, the rapid growth of anti-monarchist sentiment affected not only Greece but also the forces in the Middle East. The resulting mutinies of 1943 and 1944 were suppressed by the British, and the Greek forces were purged of all but the loyalist officers. Although the Army and Navy were no longer in a position to play a serious role in the liberation of Greece, they were now ideologically homogeneous and would henceforth display an unquestioning loyalty to the nationalist and anti-communist cause.

Post-War Developments in the Officer Corps

Since the Military Academy, with its free tuition and board, provided young peasants with the quickest escape route from rural hardship, the post-war army came to be dominated by officers of peasant background who embraced middle class values with enthusiasm. The expansion and diversity of career opportunities after the war caused a further decline in the prestige of the military profession. A sense of inferiority among officers vis-a-vis civilian elites was compounded by their frustration at missing out on the development bonanza. Their role in the Greek civil wars between Nationalist and Communist forces became their chief claim to prominence, and they strove to perpetuate the memory of the confrontation long after its culmination in 1949. Because the effects of this war persisted well into the sixties, the military were able to retain their posture as guardians of the nationalist regime. Furthermore the state encouraged and rewarded the anti-communist fervour of its employees, so that the more keen would scale the hierarchy while moderates would be forced to resign for lack of prospects.

The circumstances of civil strife also account for the penetration of Greek military institutions by American missions whose main concern was to maximise the operational capabilities of their proteges, often at the expense of their respect for democratic institutions.(4) Skills in ideological warfare and intelligence were carefully disseminated among officers who would later use them to promote their corporate interests. Meanwhile the NATO alliance helped to strengthen the nationalist cause in Greece, while providing the rationale for the retention and modernisation of a large standing army after the conclusion of the civil war. Some demobilisation was however inevitable, and gave rise to a promotion bottleneck in the middle ranks. Those most vulnerable were the officers without social connections and political contacts, who were at a clear disadvantage in the contest for assignments and promotions. The fear of early retirement was compounded by the absence of a regular family income. In this context, conspiracy and plotting were not just a pastime for officers stranded with idle frontier assignments, but were seen as the ultimate remedy for their career problems. Champions of nationalist doctrine, whose ardour was often inversely proportional to their professional merit, formed associations to protect and promote their corporate interests. Such barracks politicos would not only lobby for the appointment of their own kind to important posts, but would seek to undermine other officers under the pretext of safeguarding the armed forces from leftist influence. Hence the antagonism between the more prominent royalists and the conservative but less well-connected officers of a secret organisation known as IDEA (Holy Bond of Greek Officers), which began to simmer in the early fifties, and culminated in 1967 with the victory of the latter.

Royal patronage was the coveted prize for eager military clients, but this was usually reserved for a restricted number of officers. The less secure and the more ambitious rallied round IDEA, whose abortive attempt in May 1951 to prevent the resignation of Field Marshal Alexander Papagos constituted an early act of defiance against the royal monopoly of influence in the armed forces.(5) As commander of the victorious government forces in the civil war and leader of the successful campaign against the Italians in 1940, Papagos enjoyed a popularity among officers that caused discomfort to the royal family, and provoked displeasure against his followers. Although the 1951 coup failed, mainly because Papagos himself denounced it and called on the insurgents to lay down their arms, its impact on Greek politics was far-reaching. The rebellious protagonists, who were cashiered and imprisoned, were all restored to their positions after their mentor won a resounding victory at the polls in 1952. Although IDEA officers never enjoyed a monopoly of influence in the army, which until 1967 was controlled by the royalists, they did manage to occupy vital posts and to pass on their positions to younger proteges. Membership in this secret society, which expounded nationalist orthodoxy but also promoted the corporate interests of its followers, became a guarantee of survival and indeed success for the least prominent elements in the army. IDEA was moreover a symptom of the factionalism now to be found in the ideologically monolithic officer corps that had emerged from the civil war. Since the raison d´etre for such a corps (i.e. the communist challenge) had ceased to exist, the various factions began to assert their rival professional claims and to voice their separate grievances.

The Coup of 1967

The members of the 1967 junta missed no opportunity for contrasting the singleminded unity of the officer corps with the ´divisive opportunism´ of the politicians. However, it was the factionalism of the officer corps that had much to do with their involvement in politics and their eagerness to intervene, just as it would later contribute to their downfall. They were further politicised by the change of government that followed the 1963 elections, in which the former conservative Prime Minister, Constantine Karamanlis, in power since 1955, was defeated by the Centre Union led by Georgios Papandreou, assisted by his son Andreas. Rather than depend on communist support for his parliamentary majority, Papandreou called for new elections in 1964, when the Centre Union secured 53% of the vote - the largest recorded for any one party. This leftward shift by the electorate reflected a widespread desire for political change and for social reform, as well as a mounting unease at the tight security measures and press censorship still enforced some fourteen years after the end of the civil war.

The new Prime Minister, given his commitment to

a programme of liberalisation, particularly in the
area of internal security, was anxious to assure
himself of the loyalty of the armed forces. At the
same time there were allegations that Andreas
Papandreou, who may have expected before long to
succeed his father as party leader, was in contact
with a group of officers politically more
sympathetic to the government than the majority of
their military colleagues. In the ensuing
controversy the Prime Minister sought, in 1965, to
remove his defence minister and to occupy the post
himself. But the Throne was not prepared to
relinquish its control over the army and the King
withheld his consent, precipitating the resignation
of an undoubtedly popular Prime Minister, and
unleashing a constitutional crisis at a time of
mounting economic problems at home and renewed
difficulties in Cyprus. Rather than risk new
elections the King preferred to temporise, looking
for a possible successor to Papandreou within his
own party, and meanwhile appointing a series of weak
and unstable governments. Parliament was finally
dissolved on 14 April 1967, and elections were
announced for 28 May. As Papandreou was still
expected to return to power, perhaps with an even
larger majority than before, there were rumours that
the King and a number of generals might attempt a
pre-emptive coup. But when military intervention
came, on 21 April, it was masterminded by a group of
colonels with a common IDEA background, in defiance
of the King and to the surprise of the junta of
senior officers that had itself planned to take
power.(6)
     The factors that prompted the military to
intervene were varied: the conflict between Throne
and Prime Minister; the fear of liberalising
measures to be initiated by the Centre Union party
which would destroy the institutional framework of
right-wing dominance within the state; and finally
the professional grievances of the officers
involved, accompanied by the usual rationalisations
of an internal communist threat and claims that the
coup had the approval of Washington. While the
allegation of American support was never
substantiated, the initial silence and eventual
approval of US officials provided the colonels with
the imprimatur of a powerful ally and the legitimacy
that it can confer.(7) The role of foreign
influence in Greek politics is a variable that
should neither be underestimated nor exaggerated.
The psychological attachment of Greek officers to

the United States, forged during their
apprenticeship under American tutelage, was no less
significant than the army's dependence on US
military aid and technical assistance.

Equally important in provoking the colonels to
action was the fear, especially among the more
intransigent officers, that a victory of the Centre
Union at the polls would mean a purge of extreme
rightist elements from the armed forces. The coup
may thus be seen to have been prompted by a sense of
threat, if not to the structure of society, then at
least to the career prospects of officers who felt
their position endangered by the consequences of
popular participation. Colonel George Papadopoulos,
leader of the successful intervention, was himself
the prime suspect of a 1965 sabotage in a frontier
division which was designed to remind public opinion
and the government of the communist danger. The
operation backfired and the future dictator
(although he escaped prosecution) was probably
earmarked for retirement.

The success of the April coup was due not only
to the speed and timing of its execution, but also
to the initial incredulity of the Greek populace.
Although warnings of military intervention had been
voiced repeatedly by the press, the actual takeover
by a group of hitherto unknown and undistinguished
colonels took everyone by surprise. Only
left-wingers, whose fate under a right-wing military
regime was all too obvious, retained a clear view of
what was transpiring. Conservatives and even a few
liberals were relieved at not having to face the
impending elections, which promised to be the most
explosive in the post civil war period. Their sense
of relief was short-lived, but helped the colonels
to consolidate their power without having to
confront any substantial opposition.

THE COLONELS IN POWER

The Establishment of the Regime
During its first year in power the collective
leadership of the junta strove to justify its
position by claiming to have averted a communist
conspiracy, although no evidence of any such threat
was ever produced. Indeed, the colonels would seem
to have come to power with no clear policies, no
coherent ideology of their own, and no very
consistent views about the shape of the regime or
the nature of its future options. Having first

secured his own personal rule, Papadopoulos did
however embark on a more ambitious programme - that
of rejuvenating Greece. His plan provided for
nothing less than a total purge of the decadent
western influences which he held responsible for the
spread of anarchy in Greek society, and which he saw
as threatening the very foundations of the
"Hellenic-Christian civilisation".(8) In the
dictator´s improvised utopia, social classes would
be prohibited and general consensus on vital issues
would be arrived at via systematic training in
whatever was deemed expedient for the nation. But
the realisation of this nebulous scheme, under the
supervision of the military, was soon found to
require more time than had initially been foreseen,
so that promises of a speedy return to parliamentary
politics were postponed indefinitely.

The pretensions of the junta were initially
limited to putting society in order, rather than
coping with the complex problems of development. No
one, including the colonels themselves, believed
that they were equipped for such an ambitious task.
Yet they eventually decided that running a state was
not so difficult after all, and they were also aware
that if they failed to diversify their activities
they would soon run out of excuses for retaining
power. Such terms as ´growth´ and ´development´
began to feature prominently in their discourse, and
became part of an effort to modernise the image of
the military. The new posture was also encouraged by
a timely proliferation of works on military
sociology, which argued that the organisational
strength and monopoly of force wielded by the
officer corps qualified it for resolving problems of
development.(9) These ideas were adopted by a small
circle of advisers to the junta, and provided a
theoretical mantle for Papadopoulos´ budding
aspirations. Having patronised works which
emphasised the role of the military as modernisers,
the dictator was in turn convinced by his own
rationalisations and propaganda that his was the
task not merely of policing the state but of
modernising it as well.(10) The reality of military
rule in Greece, however, more closely approximated
to the role ascribed by Huntington to the "guardian"
soldier,(11) while Stepan´s refutation of theories
that viewed the military as agents of development in
Brazil could equally be applied to the polity of the
Greek colonels: "The Brazilian experience indicates
that ... the pattern of civil-military relations
which the military attempted to impose after 1964

has left the military internally divided, increasingly isolated from civilians, reliant upon torture as a mechanism of political control, and without a creative programme of social development."(12)

The actual exercise of power by the Greek junta was to a large extent based on clientelistic networks and kinship, restricted for the most part to reliable army officers, their relatives and associates. Apart from the decision to relieve farmers of their bank debts, announced in advance of the 1968 constitutional referendum, the regime made little effort to attract civilian support, still less to create a viable political base. Their anti-communism may have tempered any aspirations to a programme of social reform, while the colonels were never widely popular outside the army, and seem to have had an infinite capacity for alienating even those party leaders who might otherwise have been expected to show sympathy for at least some of their aims. Not long after the coup the former conservative prime minister, Karamanlis, denounced the regime as "tyrannical", calling on the army itself to remove it, while his later intervention, in April 1973, was an unequivocal demand for the military to quit government altogether. Much of the old middle class remained implacably hostile to military rule right to the end. And within the civil service the extensive purge of unreliable or opposition elements, their replacement by soldiers and their kin, and the introduction into each ministry or bureau of a military "watchdog", all led to increasing friction between the military and the civil service.

From the outset the real and effective base of the junta was in the army, whose cadres gained disproportionately, both socially and materially, from the 1967 coup and subsequent military rule, and could be said in that sense to constitute a new and privileged establishment. Officers who were not forcibly retired benefitted from higher salaries, loans for cars and houses, improved promotion prospects, and discounts in the shops. They therefore had little incentive to return power to the civilians. Meanwhile the purge of senior officers, which soon extended downwards, offered accelerated promotion to those at the bottom of the hierarchy, while with the military in government there were ample opportunities for patronage. In time, however, rapid promotion would bring new blockages and renewed frustrations, compounded by the declining reputation of the military and mounting criticism of its administration. Even within the army, the regime betrayed its origins in the factional struggles of the previous decade, as the more dependable units, commanded by those close to the junta, were favoured with arms and other equipment and came increasingly to be deployed in the Athens region. The navy and air force, traditionally the aristocracy of the services, had no part in the 1967 coup and played no very significant role in the ensuing government, and naval officers were implicated in an unsuccessful coup discovered in May 1973.

The purge in the armed forces and the civil service of enemies of the regime, and those suspected or accused of left-wing sympathies or background, availed ample opportunities for the regime´s political payoffs. In the autumn of 1967 King Constantine was presented with a list of officers - originally estimated at some 400, but later said to have been reduced to 144 - earmarked for early retirement. Since most of them were friends of the Throne, Constantine, who had failed to make his stand against the colonels in April, was belatedly faced with the dilemma of either playing his hand or losing what influence he still had within the army. The colonels´ inept handling of a crisis in Cyprus not only threatened the island with a Turkish invasion that year, but also provided the King with an excellent opportunity for stepping in to oust the junta. As it turned out, it was he who had to abandon his high office and flee the country. His abortive coup proved that his loyal senior officers, although professionally the more competent, were no match for the colonels in conspiratorial skills. After the King´s flight to Italy, the officer corps was purged of all royalist elements to a degree that adversely affected the operational capabilities of the armed forces. Between 1967 and 1968, one sixth of the officer corps was cashiered or retired. Some three thousand officers in all were retired or dismissed between 1967 and 1972, while congestion in the middle ranks reached a high level. By 1973, officers between the ranks of lieutenant and captain formed 43% of the entire corps, while those in the ranks of major and colonel amounted to no less than 54%.(13)

Institutional Changes

We have already suggested that the regime of the

21st of April was gradually shaped after Papadopoulos´ own vision. When the royal threat was out of the way, the dictator assumed at different times a variety of combinations of offices which included those of Prime Minister, as well as Minister of Foreign Affairs, National Defence, and Education. In March 1972 he became Regent, before proclaiming the Republic and assuming the presidency the following year. Although his prototypes were those furnished him by the right-wing parliamentary governments of the fifties and early sixties, he also sought to establish the army as the guarantor of future regimes. The constitution of 1968 bears evidence of Papadopoulos´ idea of the political regime best suited for Greece. A committee of jurists that toiled between May and December 1967 presented the government with a draft constitution that was ultimately ignored by the regime. Instead, the officers produced their own draft between March and August 1968, and had it ratified by plebiscite in a country still under a state of emergency. According to the new constitution, which was approved by 92% of the voters, the system of "Crowned Democracy" was retained, but royal prerogatives were somewhat curtailed, and a "Council of the Nation" was set up to act as the King´s adviser in times of crisis.

Provision was also made for a parliament which would be elected by universal and secret ballot, and would be divided into two sections. "Most of the key articles of the constitution however were to remain inoperative for an indefinite period of time."(14) The new constitution provided the army with an institutional foothold in politics. Much of the authority of the Defence Minister was transferred to the leadership of the armed forces, and promotions, retirements and commissions became the exclusive preserve of the military. Furthermore, there was explicit reference in the document to the army´s right to safeguard the integrity of the existing political and social order, while politically motivated strikes were outlawed.(15) Papadopoulos nevertheless attempted to consolidate his own position, basing his authority increasingly on the constitution and at the same time trying to ease the army out of the government. He presented the regime not as a dictatorship but as a "parenthesis" that was "necessary to put things straight". The revolutionary committee that had acted as the conscience of the regime and met regularly during the first year seems to have been disbanded once the constitution was approved. By May 1970 Papadopoulos had emerged as the most powerful personality in the junta and its undisputed leader. In 1971 the governmental structure was radically revised. The country was divided into seven administrative districts, each to be supervised by a governor with the rank of deputy minister. Far from attempting to decentralise the administration, as the government claimed, the new system in fact tightened the grip of central authority on the periphery.(16) Such measures, like the fifteen year Development Plan announced in 1972, had long-term implications for the flow of authority while indicating Papadopoulos' own plans for a protracted term in power. The decision to dig in for a more permanent stay in office presupposed a substantial investment in the means of mass repression. Thus the budget of the Ministry of Public Order increased from 1,798 million drachmas in 1966 to 2,520 million in 1968, an increase of 40%. Simultaneously, the military expanded their range of activities by assuming a greater share of internal security. The notorious military police, a ubiquitous unit under Colonel Dimitrios Ioannides, became a veritable state within a state.(17) By 1969 the Defence Ministry absorbed 49.8% of all government expenditure, while the budget for education fell from 15% in 1966 to 13.1% in 1969.(18) Greek military expenditure averaged 4.8% of the GNP between 1967 and 1970, a high percentage compared with 3.5% which was the average of NATO members' military expenditure for the same period.(19)

In spite of the prodigious growth in military expenses, few arms purchases were effected during the junta's period in power, and the large 1974 order was not delivered until after the fall of the military regime. Most of the extra funds were apparently allocated to propaganda or used for internal security purposes. The deplorable condition of discipline and morale among the conscripts during the Cyprus crisis of 1974 betrayed the dictatorship's neglect of the army's preparedness for battle. Such neglect could have stemmed from adoption by the colonels of a dogma concerning Greece's defence posture which originated in the late forties. According to an American National Security Report of 1949, Greece ought to have "a military establishment capable of maintaining internal security in order to avoid communist domination", while Turkey was designated with military capabilities "of sufficient size and effectiveness to insure Turkey´s continued resistance to Soviet pressures."(20) The splinter group within the junta that engineered the attempt against Makarios´ life in the summer of 1974 did not for a moment doubt that the United States would avert any Turkish reaction that might result in war with Greece.(21)

Reactions to the Papadopoulos Regime

In May 1973 a group of naval officers loyal to the King launched their coup against Papadopoulos. The spectacular mutiny of the destroyer ´Velos´ indicated to the rest of Europe that the regime had failed to secure the passivity of the entire officer corps. Since the King had traditionally commanded the loyalty of the Navy, the dictator accused Constantine of instigating the coup from his self-imposed exile in Rome. On 1 June, he declared the monarch deposed and proclaimed the creation of a "Presidential Parliamentary Republic", subject to popular approval. Papadopoulos now appeared to be completely in control, with nothing to prevent his assumption of the presidency. According to the new regime, the President would be elected by direct popular vote for an eight-year term, and would have wide legislative and executive authority, with control over foreign affairs, public order, and matters of national security. The plebiscite of July 1973 was held while martial law was still in force, and served a double purpose: a) the ratification of the amendments to the constitution of 1968, and b) the election of Papadopoulos as President of the Republic. The dictator assumed the presidential office with a 78% ´yes´ vote, 3,843,000 being in favour and 1,050,000 against.(22)

Since the plebiscite was conducted under repressive conditions, an analysis of its outcome and voting patterns can only be the subject of speculation. Unlike the previous plebiscite of 1968, however, this one provoked vociferous criticism from various quarters. Political leaders began to regroup and voice their anger after several years of muffled opposition and underground activities. Politicians of the right, centre and left, who had been bitter opponents before 1967, met again in prison cells, police headquarters, and the islands to which they had been exiled. Their hatred of the junta became a point of consensus which led to a reappraisal of past errors, some modification of political passions, and an outright dismissal of the civil war legacy of polarisation. Thus the ground was laid for a post-regime process of civilian renewal.

Impasse

It was precisely Papadopoulos´ realisation that he could no longer appeal to virulent anti-communism for support that had led him to seek a wider mandate by transforming his rule eventually into a sort of parliamentary system or "directed democracy". While the President alone was responsible for foreign policy, defence and internal security, and remained until a parliament was elected the sole source of power under the constitution, he did appear ready for the first time to delegate some of his responsibilities to the Prime Minister and an all civilian government. His choice for Prime Minister in October 1973 was Spyros Markezinis, a one-time Minister for Coordination under Alexander Papagos, and a leader of the small Progressive Party in parliament. Markezinis was almost alone among former politicians in having kept silent about the regime in public, while privately offering himself as a possible ´bridge´ between the present dictatorship and some more democratic system of rule.

At the same time Papadopoulos acted to remove his remaining military colleagues from the government, notwithstanding their support for and participation in the coup of 1967 and their undoubtedly ´revolutionary´ credentials. While there was a display of disaffection from some of those involved, a far more serious threat to the government was the growing discontent within the army itself, arising from a combination of corporate and other grievances. Officers were sensitive not only to the problem of promotional blockages, but also to the charges of ineptitude and corruption levelled against the regime, which also served to discredit the military as a whole. Complaints of one-man rule and electoral manipulation were coupled with acute resentment by some senior officers of the President´s recent overtures to old-time politicians to participate in the parliamentary elections promised before the end of 1974. Not only had the regime lost contact with its original ideals, but it was becoming increasingly divorced from its military constituency, which was also its only political base.

The President could not move in the direction

of the politicians and parties without risking the
loss of military backing, notably from the military
police under Brigadier Ioannides who controlled the
security apparatus that kept Papadopoulos in power.
Ioannides had not only refused all offers of a
government job, but had successfully resisted
attempts to dismantle the security apparatus
following the July plebiscite, the lifting of
martial law and the amnesty for political prisoners
- all intended to signal a relaxation of the
repression. Paradoxically, as Papadopoulos ascended
the hierarchy of state offices, he became
increasingly dependent on Ioannides to ensure the
continuing loyalty of the army, and in particular
that of the seven crack units stationed in and
around Athens. Ioannides was not among those
officers who may have shared the President´s
conviction that the future of the military regime
was best assured by an accommodation with the
political forces.

Nor were the party leaders in a mood to
cooperate with the government, or convinced that the
´half democracy´ offered by the President was better
than none. Their threat to boycott elections in 1974
was, in the circumstances, as serious a challenge to
the President as the hard line being taken by an
important section of the army. Moreover, one result
of the attempt to ´unfreeze´ the authoritarian
regime was an increase in the level of criticism
that managed to find its way to the public, leading
in turn to a revolt of university students - that
most sensitive barometer of political change. The
reimposition of martial law and the brutal
suppression of the Athens Polytechnic uprising in
November 1973 made the cause of the students popular
across the nation. On November 25, a bloodless coup
under Ioannides overthrew Papadopoulos for having
adulterated the principles of 21 April 1967. General
Phaedon Gizikis was installed as President, and a
civilian puppet government set up. While some of the
newly promoted commanders may earlier have favoured
the return of Karamanlis from self-imposed exile as
the best remaining option for the military, that
does not seem to have been the view of Ioannides,
who wanted no truck with the former politicians. The
more puritanical faction of the junta not only
attempted to put the lid on the boiling cauldron of
internal dissent, but also blundered into a
disastrous course in its foreign policy. The
attempted assassination of President Makarios of
Cyprus at Ioannides´ behest on 15 July 1974

precipitated the Turkish invasion of the island and the collapse of the military regime in Greece. The move had been intended, at least partly, to improve the prestige of the regime and to restore the reputation of the military in Greece itself. The Turkish reaction meant, however, that the junta had either to declare war and risk the consequences, or back down and face public humiliation. Unable or unwilling to choose the former, they preferred to stand down in favour of the politicians. Faced with an ultimatum by the Third Army Corps in northern Greece, and by the hostility of troops caught up in a chaotic general mobilisation, the junta transferred its authority to the very political leaders against whom it had risen in 1967 - and faded quickly into the background.

With the return of Karamanlis from Paris, there remained the problem of reconstructing a democratic system from the rubble of the discredited and now deposed dictatorship. Here Greece, unlike Portugal, had the advantage of politicians who had fairly recently operated a viable and democratic political system. Moreover, a condition of Karamanlis' acceptance of office was a pledge that the armed forces should return to their former military duties, and desist from further interference with government. His temporary authority was reinforced by the crisis and the threat of war, coupled with general mobilisation at home which placed the youth of the country under military discipline and enabled the government to transfer units to the north, thereby breaking up the powerful military apparatus in the Athens region. Despite some military resistance, a constitutional amendment was adopted that again made the defence minister responsible for appointments to the key military commands. All the army leaders closely associated with the military regime were quickly removed, while the others were placed under the command of General Dionysios Arbouzis, one of the respected generals purged after the 1967 coup. The civil servants dismissed by the military were likewise reintegrated into the administration. Because of the continuing crisis, Karamanlis was able to prolong martial law on the one hand while expounding the merits of political democracy on the other, and promising elections to a new parliament within a few months.

CONCLUSIONS

The dictatorship of 21 April 1967 shares with other military regimes certain features that invite generalisation. As is often the case with actual regimes, the Greek experience is a "mixture derived from specific conditions", which fails to conform entirely to the requirements of any ideal type. While in the past, even during the inter-war era, the Greek military had always been subordinate to civilian governments, the 1967-74 regime most closely resembles the Veto type. At the same time, it lacked the degree of military unity usually associated with this type, and from its origins in a factional coup directed against royalist senior officers as well as against democratic politicians, it degenerated in many respects to the level of a factional regime. The Revolutionary Council of twelve colonels who launched the coup was eventually superceded by George Papadopoulos´ personalised rule and his aspiration to achieve the crowning glory of civilian legitimacy. Papadopoulos´s effort to transfer limited authority to a government of makeshift politicians provoked the wrath of Ioannides, the strongman of the military police, who sought to prevent the ´Revolution´ from straying into political corruption. The regime thus possessed neither the military unity nor the civilian clientele necessary for the transformation into authoritarian clientelism.

The high level of autonomy enjoyed by the military and the perceived threats from civil society would also rank the Greek case with other veto regimes. Whether real or imaginary, the perceived threat to the social order which prompted the colonels to act was of a high level. Perceptions are subjective matters, and it is difficult to draw the line between self-deception and deliberate misrepresentation. The Greek officers chose to intervene however at a time when international detente threatened to render redundant their position as guardians of the nationalist order. In structural terms, the officers upheld middle class interests, a choice which was highlighted by their role in the civil war of 1946-49. Yet the colonels viewed their power as unrelated to the outcome of economic class conflict, and insisted that theirs was a system that favoured the least privileged.(23) This alleged detachment from narrow class interests served to protect them from accusations of self-seeking behaviour, while

42

providing them with a justification for extending their term in power. In fact the values of Greek officers do not differ from the stereotype military virtues of discipline, efficiency and valour, and their esprit de corps thinly veiled their awareness that the opportunities to improve their social status within the confines of their profession were indeed limited.

Although the military regime sought to elevate the officer corps to the position of guarantor of the social order, the members of the junta basically aspired to acquire the legitimacy that was inseparable from civilian authority. The protagonists of military intervention therefore tried to shed their corporate identity and assume the more respected civilian garb, thus confirming the fragility of their professional self-image. It is this absence of a strong corporate identity that, more than anything else, differentiates the Greek military from their colleagues in some emerging states.(24) The vital task of modernisation which constitutes a major source of pride for the military in certain developing societies, is not one for which the Greek military is well suited. Greek officers have more often been identified with political turmoil than with orderly change and social innovation, while their declining position on the social ladder generated a sense of isolation which before 1967 contributed to their hostility against the ruling political elite, and reinforced their desire for social acceptance. While charging civilian governments with offences against the nation, the Colonels thus aspired to establish themselves in positions of civilian eminence, duly legitimised by the prevailing civilian norms and values. It was an aspiration which they lacked the ability to achieve.

NOTES

1. For an analysis of inter-war coups in Greece, see T. Veremis, "Some Observations on the Greek Military in the Inter-War Period, 1918-35", Armed Forces and Society, 4, May 1978, pp.527-38.
2. S.E. Finer, The Man on Horseback (London: Pall Mall, 1962), p.118.
3. The most balanced and well-documented account of the Middle East mutinies can be found in Hagen Fleischer, "The ´Anomalies´ in the Greek

Middle East Forces, 1941-44", Journal of the Hellenic Diaspora, 5, Fall 1978, pp.5-36.

4. Michael Mark Amen, "American Institutional Penetration into Greek Military and Political Policymaking Structures: June 1947 - October 1949", Journal of the Hellenic Diaspora, 5, Fall 1978, pp.94-113.

5. Information about IDEA and its offshoot the "National Union of Young Officers", founded in 1958 and headed by the future dictator George Papadopoulos, can be found in N. Stavrou, Allied Policy and Military Interventions: The Political Role of the Greek Military (Athens: Papazissis, 1976); see also G. Karayannis, The Drama of Greece: Glories and Miseries, IDEA 1940-1952 (To Drama tis Ellados: Epi kai Athliotites, IDEA, 1940-1952), Athens, published by the author, no date; Karayannis was a protagonist of IDEA, and his book was withdrawn from circulation.

6. G. Karayorgas, From the IDEA to the Junta (in Greek, Papazissis, 1975); a journalistic account which includes interesting insights and inside information on the Greek officer corps, pp.7-43.

7. American relief with the junta was no doubt caused by a widespread impression in the US that the Papandreou family was dangerously left wing in its inclinations; see Richard Stebbins, The United States in World Affairs 1967 (Council on Foreign Relations, Simon & Schuster, New York, 1968), p.215.

8. Richard Clogg & George Yannopoulos, eds, Greece under Military Rule (Papazissis, 1976), pp.19-21, 81-93.

9. A. Stepan, The Military in Politics: Changing Patterns in Brazil (Princeton, 1971), p.5.

10. Issue No.7-8 (Jan-June 1971) of the state supervised Review of Social Research was dedicated to the proceedings of a conference on military sociology which stressed the contribution of the military to development. Jean Siotis´ article "Some Notes on the Military in Greek Politics" was the exception in pointing out that the Greek officers have been agents of political turmoil rather than champions of development; the article appeared with the others, although the author had refused to grant permission for publication.

11. In a society possessing a developed civilian culture, the military view themselves neither as the modernisers of society nor as the creators of a new political order, but rather as "the guardians and perhaps the purifiers of the

existing order", Samuel Huntington, The Soldier and the State (Harvard, 1957), pp.222, 225-26.
12. Stepan, op.cit., p.5.
13. N. Pantelakis, L'Armee dans la Societe Grecque contemporaine, unpublished Ph.D. dissertation, Universite Rene Descartes (Paris V), 1980, pp.74-75.
14. G. Kousoulas, Modern Greece: Profile of a Nation (Charles Scribner's Sons, 1974), p.283.
15. R. Clogg, "The Dictatorship of the 21st of April", in Greece: History and Civilisation, Vol.6 (Thessaloniki, Malliaris, 1982), p.249.
16. Clogg & Yannopoulos, op.cit., p.16.
17. ibid., p.17.
18. ibid.
19. John Pesmazoglou, "The Greek Economy after 1967", in Clogg & Yannopoulos, op.cit., p.181.
20. Y. Roybatis, "The United States and the Operational Responsibilities of the Greek Armed Forces, 1947-1987", Journal of the Hellenic Diaspora, 6, Spring 1979, p.46.
21. The evening of Karamanlis' return to Greece (24 July 1974), the author of this chapter struck up a street conversation with a group of what proved to be ESA soldiers. These Junta diehards did not hesitate to express their conviction that the United States had deliberately misled Ioannides into believing that the Turks would remain passive in the event of an attempt against Makarios' life.
22. Clogg, loc.cit., p.253.
23. According to Stepan, the military is a situational and not a class elite, which will take action "against those aspects of middle- and upper-class life which threaten their institutional position". Stepan, op.cit., pp.269-270.
24. Theodore Couloumbis has rightly criticised theories which group together a variety of military interventions under the heading of 'modernisation'; see his Problems of Greek-American Relations (in Greek, Athens, Kollaros, 1978), pp.95-96.

Chapter Three

TURKEY : THE ARMY AS GUARDIAN OF THE POLITICAL ORDER

Bener Karakartal

THE TURKISH ARMY IN POLITICS

There is no such thing as a typical army. Military
institutions vary so much that we must start by
abandoning the idea of ´the army´ as a concrete
reality existing in a similar form across states.
Instead, we would do better to treat the ´military´
as a political variable, equivalent to other
comparative concepts which we have long been used
to, such as ´political party´ or ´trade union´. It
is only by starting from such comparative concepts,
capable of encompassing a considerable range of
cases across time and space, that we will be able to
develop hypotheses which enable us to organise
research and extend our knowledge of military
intervention. The variables outlined by Clapham and
Philip in the introductory chapter to this volume
provide in this respect an appropriate starting
point. At the same time, such comparative schema
need to be supplemented by empirical data drawn from
a wide variety of cases, and an indispensable
contribution to the comparative study of the
military is thus made by detailed national case
studies. Rustow´s work on Turkey may be cited as a
case in point.(1) Such studies, designed to
illuminate the distinctive features produced by
national cultural characteristics and historical
experience, can help to make up the deficiencies of
comparative approaches inevitably based on an
inadequate amount of local information. This chapter
on the different Turkish military interventions
indicates that not only do these fail to square
entirely with any universal theoretical schema, but
also that there are considerable variations between
one Turkish example and another.(2) It suggests that
our search for theoretical understanding,

indispensable though this is, must return to studies at the national level, and distinguish even there between structural factors which evolve very slowly, and situational variables which give their specific character to each particular case.

Structural Constants

At the most basic structural level, a historical approach is essential to examine the complex interrelations between national culture and institutions, and to illuminate the role of military institutions in particular within the local historical tradition. In the case of Turkey, such an approach indicates that from the start political institutions have been, so to speak, encased in the coat of armour provided by the military, and that this structure has been carried over from one to another of the various states which the Turks have established. After the Seljuk Empire, the Turks founded the Ottoman Empire which lasted from 1299 until 1918. During the Ottoman period the Sultan, whose territories spread over three continents, was backed by a Janissary army of an extremely distinctive kind. It was composed of Christian children, fostered at a very early age in Turkish families which brought them up according to Moslem customs, who were subsequently sent to a state school before being admitted to the army. Very little was required of a Janissary beyond a knowledge of the customs of the Ottoman army, obedience to the Sultan, and belief in Islam. Possessing no social roots outside the patrimonial state, the all-powerful army had no rights and almost limitless duties. In an empire in which all land belonged to the Sultan, the accumulation of capital was prohibited, and neither an aristocratic nor a bourgeois class was permitted to develop. Instead, all state functions were carried out by the army: it made war, collected taxes, administered the provinces, supervised agricultural production, and looked after state enterprises. Being in the army certainly allowed upward social mobility, since a Janissary could become Grand Vizier, the second person in the state after the Sultan. But this Grand Vizier possessed absolutely no autonomy. It was the custom in the Ottoman Empire, in order to prevent the formation of an aristocracy, for the Sultan to order the execution of the Grand Vizier. Following this customary practice, which no Sultan hesitated to invoke, the Grand Vizier was decapitated and his goods confiscated.(3) This army, whose duty it was to maintain the empire, was thus entirely dependent on the Sultan. Being itself, like the whole empire, the property of the Sultan, it was fundamentally subordinated to the authority of the state. Serif Mardin sees in this military bureaucracy dedicated to the Sultan an instrument which acted with ´machine-like fidelity´. Certainly this period of ´military society´ is also rich in revolts. But once these were crushed, the supremacy of the civil power was always established as the norm in this empire maintained by the army.

This tradition did not change with the proclamation of the constitutional monarchy, which came about in 1908 following a military coup d´etat fomented by the clandestine Union and Progress party. After overthrowing the autocratic Sultan Abdulhamid II, the victorious Unionist officers started to govern the country through the medium of a civilian cabinet. Union and Progress remained in semi-clandestinity even after the seizure of power, and its officers, even while manipulating the government, still remained within the army. The army was nonetheless effectively in power, and this soon gave rise to internal military cleavages, factions and clienteles. Aware of the dangers which this presented, both for the army and for the country, Mustafa Kemal criticised the situation during the Union and Progress congress held at Salonika in 1909. He failed to pesuade his colleagues to avoid a confusion of functions by choosing either a political career or a military one, and made his own choice by leaving the Union and thus political life. He then devoted himself entirely to his military duties, until after the total defeat and flight abroad of the Unionist officers at the end of the First World War in 1918.

Following the occupation of the Ottoman Empire by the allies in 1919, Mustafa Kemal united the resistance movement and became its unchallenged leader. But even while conducting the war of national independence, he applied the political principles which he had held for the previous decade. Following his belief in the separation of the military from politics, and in the supremacy of the civil power, he left the army and convened a parliament composed of elected deputies. This commitment to civil political supremacy thus followed the national cultural tradition. Following the war of national independence, he took a further step by creating the People's Republican Party. Any army officer who joined the party was obliged to resign his commission. The army stayed out of politics and in its barracks.

In order to understand Kemal's political thought, however, it is also necessary to take account of his speech at Konya: this apolitical army, totally subordinated to the civil power, is at the same time entrusted with the mission of securing the unconditional defence of the political institutions of the state against both external and internal attack. The system is placed beneath its protection, and the internal regulation of the army recognises its right to intervene in case of danger. The three military interventions of 1960, 1971 and 1980 were, according to their leaders, carried out in accordance with this provision. It is therefore necessary to analyse the political situations which were regarded by the leaders of the Turkish army at the time as triggering the application of the Konya speech as an 'order of the day'.(4)

The 'threshold' which seems to constitute the critical point in activating an eventual military intervention was in these three cases the same: the proclamation by the politicians currently in power, legally and by parliamentary vote, of a state of siege. Menderes, the Democratic Party Prime Minister in 1960, decreed the state of siege essentially in order to curb the opposition in the face of a movement of voters towards the rival Republican Party. One month later, he was overthrown by the army, arrested, and eventually hanged. Ten years later, it was the Liberal Prime Minister Demirel who decreed the state of siege in order to contain extreme left-wing trade union opposition. He was ousted by the army on 12 March 1971. In 1978 it was a Social Democrat Prime Minister, Bulent Ecevit, who decreed the state of siege in the face of his government's inability to contain violence from both left-wing and right-wing extremists. The army took power on 12 September 1980, and arrested all the main political leaders including both Ecevit and Demirel. In all three cases, the army was officially invited to associate itself with the civil power, in order to maintain order in the face of that power's evident incapacity to do so on its own. The military thus fulfilled its role as protector of the political order, while formally indicating its lack of confidence, and warning that the system was entering a danger zone. In each case official letters, signed by the Chief of Staff and the other principal commanding officers of the armed forces, were sent to the responsible civilian leaders: the President of the Republic, the Prime Minister, party leaders, and so forth. These letters, best described as warning notices, called on the political leaders to re-establish civil peace. A few weeks later, the army took over. In a country such as Turkey, whose army is the second largest in NATO after that of the United States, intervention generally takes the form of a simple declaration to the mass media, without the need to fire a single shot.

A military intervention in Turkey is thus not only highly predictable, but one can also detect in the military a certain reluctance to intervene. In almost every interview, military leaders insist that they have been forced into power against their own wishes. A military intervention in Turkey is perceived by its authors as a serious and dramatic act in a political situation close to total collapse, when the sole alternative seems to be civil war. During the two years which immediately preceded the most recent intervention, terrorism had resulted in some five thousand political killings. On some days, the number of deaths rose to more than a hundred, with a daily average of thirty in the period immediately before the takeover. There was no equivalent degree of violence before the 1960 and 1971 interventions, but no objective observer was in any doubt that the country was sliding towards a division into hostile camps which could unleash a civil war. A military takeover in Turkey is therefore seen by public opinion more as an accomplishment than as an affront to democracy. It helps to overcome a major crisis, and at the moment of takeover, the army thus appears in the public eye in a doubly favourable light: it has fulfilled its historic mission, and at the same time saved the country from a serious threat of which citizens were immediately aware.

These preconditions help to explain why some interventions succeed and are welcomed by the public, whereas others fail. The two coup attempts made by Colonel Aydemir in 1962 and 1963 provide an example of failure. None of the necessary structural conditions for a successful intervention were present. The democratic institutions were working normally, the country was in no danger, and political life was calm. The leader in power, Inonu, held a deep respect for democratic principles and the rights of the opposition. When Aydemir came out on the streets of Ankara with his cadets and his armoured cars, no one in an army of six hundred thousand men could be found to support him. Knowing that public opinion would be entirely opposed to an intervention, Turkish officers did not follow Aydemir, but on the contrary arrested and sentenced him. The first time, he was pardoned; when he tried again the following year, he was hanged.

At a structural level, the Turkish case certainly provides one example of the political role of the military. Historically, Turkey has always had a large army, whether justified by the urge for conquest or by the need for self-defence against an external foe. This army has always been subordinated to the civil power. Changing political ideas have no doubt penetrated the army along with the rest of society, and have left soldiers with very varied individual political opinions: during periods of pluralist democracy, one can see quite a number of officers resigning in order to stand for election on the most diverse political platforms. But the intervention in politics of the army as an institution takes place at a very different level, as a dramatic response to a perceived public need. Were it not for this, military coups would not gain the level of support which they evidently receive. They take place only when this need is felt both by public opinion and by most of the officer corps. In summary, the Turkish army acts according to an entrenched set of norms. This army established two constitutional monarchies, fought a war of national independence, created the modern secular Turkish state, presided over the transition to pluralist democracy, and supervised the preparation of the three constitutions of 1924, 1961 and 1982. It is nonetheless in normal times an apolitical force. Only the post of President of the Republic is traditionally held by soldiers, the sole civilian President, Bayar, having been ousted in the coup of 27 May 1960. Politics in normal times is the domain of civilian politicians. Even though the army is the guardian of the system, it has never sought in any way to influence the results of elections. Military intervention takes place at a different level, as a check on the pluralist system itself. Once the army is in power, it seeks to correct the system and pull out as rapidly as possible. The period of military rule is felt to be exceptional and anomalous. It would however be a mistake to take this as a starting point for conclusions applicable to all countries or interventions. The Turkish case must be understood and explained in terms of its own specific cultural and historic characteristics.

Situational Variables

In addition to the historical and structural characteristics of particular countries, it is also essential to take account of the extremely complex factors in effect at the moment of each intervention, since these must in turn be integrated with the structural constants just outlined.

Environmental Differences. One of the first factors which contributes to the specific nature of each intervention is simply its date. Passing time dramatically changes the environment in which intervention takes place. In 1908, when the army overthrew the autocratic Sultan Abdulhamid II after a reign of thirty-three years, they found an institutional void. They convened a parliament, and authorised the publication of political newspapers and the creation of parties and trade unions. Within weeks an institutional explosion had taken place, and within months their lack of experience in managing a pluralist political system had led to a revivalist Moslem reaction, socialist strikes and occupations, the paralysis of public services in the cities, violent demonstrations, attempted coups, and political assassinations. It should be added that the semi-clandestine ruling Union and Progress party itself resorted to the same methods, and assassinated its own opponents. Even though the Unionist leaders were doubtless patriotic soldiers who believed in the democratic virtues for the sake of which they had seized power, after the assassination of the Prime Minister in 1913, they did not hesitate to arrest all their opponents, and to establish a dictatorship which lasted until the end of the empire and their flight abroad in 1918.

After the fall of the empire, the allied powers occupied Turkey in 1919, and Mustafa Kemal, a former Unionist opposed to the combination of military and political powers, united the national resistance. His problem was how to fill the new institutional void. He too convened a parliament, composed of elected deputies, and in accordance with his belief in civilian supremacy he created a party, the People´s Republican Party (PRP). The army returned to barracks, and the PRP became a tutelary party, the founding party of the state. To the society which it supervised, it propounded a secular, modernist and European ideology, with the support especially of youth, women, and the Houses of the People, cultural centres which had been established to encourage the process of secular modernisation.

The interventions of 1960, 1971 and 1980 fell within the pluralist democratic era introduced by the PRP in 1946, but within a political structure marked by an increasing level of differentiation. Before the first of these interventions, the political scene was dominated by two parties: the PRP, the former single party now led by Inonu, and the new Democatic Party (DP) formed by four PRP dissidents and led by the Prime Minister, Menderes. A political upheaval resulted from the Democrats´ intention to outlaw the Republicans, and the Republicans´ struggle to overthrow the Democrats. By 1971, the political structure was still more diversified, since the party system was supplemented by a Marxist party, the Turkish Workers Party, by two trade union organisations, Turk-Is and DISK, and by hundreds of pressure groups containing some hundreds of thousands of members and militants. The liberal Prime Minister, Demirel, was leader of the Justice Party, which had inherited the mantle of the old Democratic Party dissolved by the previous military regime. He and the JP were assaulted by political strikes and violent demonstrations organised by the extreme left in conditions of rapidly escalating political terrorism. The period before the 1980 intervention was marked by a process of political polarisation, leading to a multiplication of groups on the left and extreme left (where forty-nine different organisations have been identified), and on the Islamic and ultranationalist right. This led to an escalation of violence resulting in more than five thousand deaths, among politicians (including a former prime minister), journalists, academics, leading trade unionists, industrialists and others. The two main parties, the PRP and JP, were caught up in this process, in the course of which each side established its respective zones of occupation in a situation rapidly escalating towards civil war. After the intervention, the army seized some 900,000 firearms, including a number of heavy weapons.

In all five cases, the army claimed to have acted in order to ´save´, ´protect´, ´renew´, ´purge´ or ´cure´ the political system, but in each case within a fundamentally different political context. The level of institutionalisation, the nature of the problems facing the system, and the kind of crisis which prompted intervention varied substantially. These situational variables must thus be related to the permanent political culture of the military.

Leadership Variables. The temperament, character and behaviour of leaders vary from one intervention to another, quite apart from the considerable changes induced by the tenure of power itself. The main problem which they face concerns the length and outcome of the intervention. Should they stay in power or leave it? If the latter, when and how? Military rulers are likewise divided by the type and scope of the institutions which they seek to establish, and the thoroughness of the reforms which they try to put into effect. In a sense, they are transformed into ´politicians´ whether they like it or not: they need to manage their relations with the press, appear on television, and manipulate essential contacts with interest groups and even with the politicians whom they have overthrown. Frequently they look for allies at the opposite end of the political spectrum from that which they have purged, and the political coalitions which they construct may therefore differ sharply from one intervention to another, even if some of the soldiers involved are the same in either case. In 1960, when the Democrats were deprived of power, the military regime sought allies on the left, among the Republicans, the youth associations, and the trade unions. In 1971, when the soldiers struck at the left (including both trade unions and youth associations), they co-operated with liberal politicians. In 1980, they imprisoned extremists of both left and right, while at the same time purging centrist groups; as a result, they had no natural political allies, and instead built up clientelist networks of a new kind at many levels, including for example both the trade unions and the universities. Proclaiming a general scepticism towards the entire political class, they sought an institutional and organisational reconstruction, and the creation of a new political leadership.(5)

The leadership variable thus affects the character of each military regime. In 1960, power was exercised by the thirty-seven officers who formed the Committee of National Union. There were two main factions within the Committee: the moderates led by General Gursel who wanted to hand over power to the politicians, and the radicals led

54

by Colonel Turkes who sought to institute a lasting and authoritarian military regime. The moderates eventually arrested the fourteen radicals, and expelled the Turkes group from the Committee; as a result, power was restored to civilians. In 1971, the army operated virtually in a vacuum; having induced the resignation of the Demirel government, it did not formally assume power, but allowed civilian groups to form administrations which on each occasion were legally invested after a vote of confidence passed by the National Assembly which had been elected before the takeover. In 1973, two and a half years later, Demirel and Ecevit got together in order to block the election of the army chief of staff to the presidency of the Republic, and the army returned to barracks. 1980 was different again: the Demirel government was once more overthrown by a communique issued by the general staff, but this time the intervention threw up an unchallenged leader, General Kenan Evren. It was always he alone, surrounded by the commanding officers of the three services and the gendarmerie, who spoke in the name of the government, and he was elected President at the same time as the referendum which approved the new constitution in 1982.

A further variable which helps to distinguish one intervention from another is the nature of the political elite in office when the intervention takes place. There is rarely a complete break between the soldiers who launch the coup and the professional politicians whom they displace. These are almost always people who have known one another for a long time, and who come into contact on numerous occasions. The semi-conflictual relations established between them after the takeover are determined by the personalities of the individuals in each camp. There are plenty of examples which could be used to establish a typology of forms of behaviour. Inonu, an experienced statesman concerned with the survival of civilian government more than with his own short term political interests, established relations with the military immediately after the 1960 and 1971 interventions in order to speed a return to democratic pluralism. Ecevit in both 1971 and 1980 went to the opposite extreme, and issued radical manifestoes against the military rulers. The silent and cautious Demirel opted for a war of attrition, abandoning direct political discourse in favour of hints and manoeuvres conducted behind the scenes.

POLITICS AND THE MILITARY

The combination of this great variety of structural, cultural, historic, situational and psychological variables makes it possible to establish models and typologies of a genuinely comparative kind. These should permit us to develop a whole series of hypotheses related to military involvement in politics, and even to make predictions of a limited kind. The particular questions with which we are concerned here are the quantity and type of political participation allowed by the military after the intervention, the choice faced by the regime between institutionalisation and demilitarisation, and the political structure, especially the party structure, which characterises the normalisation of the political process.

Political Participation after the Intervention
No general conclusions can be drawn as to the attitude of military regimes towards the level of participation which they wish to promote after their seizure of power. Each intervention appears to have its own particular character, derived from a mixture of structural and situational variables. Among the most important of the latter are the nature and scale of the crisis immediately preceding the intervention, the degree of authoritarianism within the military leadership, the scope and target of any purges, the political alliances sought by the regime, and the degree of conflict or co-operation among civilian politicians. Turkey provides examples drawn from across the entire spectrum. In 1908, the political system passed rapidly from virtually zero participation under the autocracy to an almost unlimited degree of participation which tolerated subversive organisation by both the religious sects on the extreme right and the socialists on the extreme left. After an abortive Moslem counter-coup and the unleashing of violent strikes, zero participation was once more imposed. Opponents of all kinds were arrested and imprisoned, and the triumvirate which assumed power did not even deign to consult a parliament composed of its own partisans before deciding to take the Ottoman Empire into the First World War on the German side. During the Kemalist period after 1919, and especially after the war of independence in 1922, the scope for

56

participation was entirely different. A single party, the PRP, enjoined participation within the strict limits of a secular, modernist and pro-western ideology. Both the extreme left and the fundamentalist extreme right were banned during this period of tutelary modernisation.

The three interventions since the transition to pluralism evidence sharp contrasts in the level, direction and type of participation allowed by the military authorities. After the 1960 intervention, the Democratic Party was dissolved, its members arrested, and its Prime Minister hanged along with his ministers of finance and foreign affairs. The military then sought a coalition with the other end of the political spectrum. Not only the Republicans, but also the youth associations and trade unions were encouraged to participate. The right to strike, previously denied by the civilian government, was thus enshrined in the new constitution drafted by a constituent assembly which had been drawn by the military from the ranks of its allies. The 1971 intervention, directed against a set of left-wing groups including those same former allies, purged all of these and strictly prohibited their participation in politics. The chiefs of staff then looked for help to the liberal politicians, in whose hands was left the task of forming governments and enacting restrictive amendments to the 1961 constitution. In 1980, the military restricted participation not only from both extremes, but even from the whole political elite which they blamed for the crisis which had led to the intervention. The military rulers then drew up a timetable for a gradual transition back to pluralism, by way of a referendum, new laws on political parties, and the creation of a new political elite.

Institutionalisation or Demilitarisation

The duration of a military intervention likewise depends on a multiplicity of structural and situational variables. In the case of a regime which seeks to institutionalise itself, the most important factor is the breakdown of communications with the previous governing elite. This is accompanied by a continual changing or renewal of goals by the regime. Institutionalisation is a process which takes place over time: in order to maintain the support needed for survival, it is necessary to create constantly renewed sources of legitimacy. The 'enemy' in the rulers' vocabulary changes its identity. At the start, it is the disorder which led to intervention which justifies the military´s presence; later, this may be replaced by the need to overcome underdevelopment. The replacement of limited political goals by longer term cultural and economic ones is, just as in the Greek example cited in the previous chapter, one indicator of the regime´s desire to break with the existing political elite and establish itself on a semi-permanent basis. There may in this way be a regular series of stages through which a regime goes as it seeks to institutionalise itself.

Demilitarisation, on the other hand, takes a great variety of forms. Following the 1908 intervention, there was no demilitarisation since the regime collapsed along with the Ottoman Empire itself in the wake of military defeat. The regime of 1923 turned itself into a democratic pluralist political system in 1946, after which the opposition party gained power peacefully and legally in the 1950 elections. The 1960 military regime demilitarised at the price of an internal coup in which the moderates eliminated the authoritarian radicals and returned power to the civilian politicians after holding free elections. In 1971, the army had to retreat from power following its failure to get the chief of staff elected to the presidency, when the two principal political leaders, Ecevit and Demirel, joined forces to block the election in parliament. The 1980 regime organised its demilitarisation by stages in the manner just described, while leaving its leader behind as the new President.

Politics and Parties after Normalisation

In a political system such as Turkey´s, which oscillates between elections on the one hand and military interventions on the other, professional politicians must manage their tactics in such a way as to take account of these various eventualities. When a military regime seeks to demilitarise, while at the same time laying down the . party structure which will succeed it, these tactics may upset the best laid plans, and lead to results quite the opposite of what the military intended. As a whole, Turkish politicians adopt a stance of total hostility to the army during the period leading to civilian rule; a dialogue with the incumbent regime, while leading to a smoother return to democratic pluralism and strengthening the position of moderates over radicals within the armed forces, may well prove costly in electoral terms. A stance of opposition to the military authorities has conversely been shown to pay off. This certainly does not facilitate an easy transition, but may well lead to eventual electoral victory even though it delays it. Inonu provides a good example of the kind of politician, anxious for the preservation of democracy, who has been prepared to compromise with the military in order to hasten the return to civilian rule; but this cost him victory at the polls in 1961 and the leadership of the PRP in 1971. Ecevit, who went to the opposite extreme, both succeeded in gaining the PRP leadership after the 1971 intervention, and established the party at subsequent elections as the dominant national political organisation. The policy of distancing himself from the military regime which Demirel adopted after 1960 likewise enabled him to establish the electoral supremacy of his party in the period after 1961, and to become Prime Minister in 1965.

The return to pluralism following the 1980 intervention is particularly interesting, since the level of polarisation before the takeover had led the military regime to ban all existing political parties. The framework for the transition was established by he 1982 referendum, in which the new constitution was adopted with 91.5% of the votes, General Evren being in the process elected to a seven year term as President of the Republic. The military subsequently authorised the formation of new political parties, and after a period of uncertainty during which several prospective parties were banned, five main contestants eventually emerged. Two of these were linear descendants of the two dominant parties of the post-1946 era: the Social Democratic Party (SODEP) was led by Erdal Inonu, son of the former President Inonu, whose PRP had become the Social Democratic Party under Ecevit; the Right Road Party (Dogru Yol Partisi) was widely regarded as the successor to the Liberal Party of former Prime Minister Demirel. General Evren´s National Security Council allowed these two parties to form, but nonetheless refused to let them contest the first legislative elections held on 6 November 1983. The three remaining parties which contested the elections were all new ones: the National Democratic Party (NDP), which presented itself as the party of continuity with the intervention of 12 September 1980; the Populist Party (HP), which took a social democratic stance; and the Motherland Party

(Anavatan Partisi, or AP), which in contrast to the other two presented an ultra-liberal platform opposed to all forms of state intervention in the economy. Following the pattern of previous post-military elections, it was the party most clearly disapproved by the regime, Turgut Ozal´s AP, which won with 211 seats in the new parliament, followed by the HP with 117 seats, and leaving the NDP, the party most favoured by the military, in third place with only 71. The result may be seen as confirming the longstanding separation in Turkish political culture between the military and civilian politics.

CONCLUSION

In situating the Turkish case within the typology of military regimes and their outcomes suggested in the introduction to this volume, the most important structural variables are the high internal unity of the military command structure, and its high level of differentiation from civil society. Both of these are not only evident in the modern Turkish army, but are strongly derived from a military tradition going back into the Ottoman period. During the exceptional period between 1908 and 1918, when power was exercised by officers through the Union and Progress party, this unity was badly damaged, and the criticisms which Mustafa Kemal had made of this system in 1909 proved to be justified. The officer corps was split between he factions supporting and opposing Union and Progress, and the Ottoman Empire subsequently lost the First Balkan War of 1911-12. This example of the effects of the direct politicisation of the army was taken to heart by the Turkish officer corps, and subsequently enabled Mustafa Kemal to put his ideas into effect. Following the war of national independence, military unity was maintained through the dominance of Mustafa Kemal himself, while the Ottoman legacy of differentiation, threatened by the merging of military and political functions during the 1908-18 period, was reasserted and combined with a new system of party government. The most evident threat to unity during the post-1946 period surfaced in the split between moderates and radicals in the 1960-61 military regime, and in so far as the radicals sought a prolonged period of military government, this carried with it a threat to differentiation also. The victory of the moderate group re-established both the principle of differentiation and the supremacy of the command hierarchy. Since that time, unity and differentiation have not been seriously threatened. The Aydemir incidents of 1962 and 1963 demonstrated the army's capacity to deal with attempted coups launched from outside the central command hierarchy, while the supremacy of General Evren and the National Security Council within the 1980-83 regime provides a further indication of unity.

While unity and differentiation have been fairly constant, the autonomy of civilian political organisations and level of threat which these presented to the political order protected by the military have been more variable. Not that the threat to the military itself has ever been particularly great. Its size, unity and differentiation have always enabled it to take control when it wished to do so, with very little difficulty even in the near civil war conditions of 1980. A sense of threat has been created, not by the breakdown of relations between the civilian political structures and the military, but by breakdowns within the civilian structures themselves. After 1908, initially unrestricted political participation led to a rapid retreat to autocracy before any autonomous political structure had had much chance to establish itself. After 1923, autonomy was restricted by the close control which Mustafa Kemal and the PRP maintained over the expansion of political participation. Autonomy has become an issue largely since 1946, expressed in the development of a two-party system and accompanied by the escalation of political violence on both left and right. Further indicators of a growing level of autonomy are provided by the Ecevit-Demirel pact which resulted in the army's return to barracks in 1973, and by the clear electoral advantage to civilian politicians of avoiding too close a dependence on the military. Following the intervention of 1980-83, autonomy has been re-established in phases. While participation in the legislative elections of November 1983 was restricted to new political parties, the military's desire to restructure the party system has not been fully realised, since the old parties have been allowed to contest the municipal elections due in March 1984.

The Turkish military regime types themselves must sharply differentiate between those in power before and after the transition to pluralism. Those before the transition were clearly Breakthrough regimes, whose intervention took place in response either to classic monarchical autocracy or to the need for national liberation from foreign occupation. Both regimes were of a self-confidently modernising kind, and promoted (though in very different ways) an increase in political participation. The interventions since the transition to pluralism have by contrast combined elements of the Veto and Moderator types, with a preponderance of the latter. In 1960, 1971 and 1980, the army intervened in order to save Turkish democracy from ´impasse´, and it was this which made the army acceptable to public opinion, which regarded it as performing a moderator role. The moderator role is likewise indicated by the rapidity with which the military has been prepared to return to barracks, following a tenure of power of at most little more than three years, and by the comparative openness of the elections which (despite the restrictions imposed in 1983) have taken place under military tutelage. On the first two occasions, following the interventions of 1960 and 1971, the demilitarisation took the form of ´handback´ to existing political organisations, with results in the form of renewed political violence and reintervention which confirm the gloomy view of this option suggested in the introductory chapter. However the shock to the Turkish political class was greater at the time of the 1980 intervention, doubtless due to the level of violence which was substantially greater than that preceding any previous takeover. It remains to be seen whether the military government´s desire to create a new political elite will press the existing political class, which does not after all want to see itself totally removed from power, towards a process of civilian renewal.

NOTES

1. D. Rustow, <u>Ataturk as a Founder of a State</u> (Ankara, SBF, 1969); "The Army and the founding of the Turkish Republic", <u>World Politics</u>, 11, 1958-59.
2. See also B. Karakartal, "Les processus politiques dans les partis militaires: essai de determination des variables dans le cas turc", in L. Hamon, ed, <u>Mort des Dictatures</u> (Paris, Economica, 1981).

3. See N. Berkes, Turkiyede Cagdaslasma (Ankara, Bilgiyay, 1973); S. Mardin, Historical Determinants of Social Stratification, Social Class and Class Consciousness in Turkey (Ankara, SBF, 1967).

4. Ataturk'un Soylev ve Demecleri (Ankara, TITE, 1952).

5. Turkiye Cumhuriyeti devlet baskani Orgeneral Kenan Evren'in Soylev ve Demecleri, 12 Eylul 1980 - 12 Eylul 1982 (Ankara, Basbakanlit basimevi, 1982).

Chapter Four

THE POLITICS OF THE POST-MILITARY STATE IN AFRICA

J. 'Bayo Adekanye

INTRODUCTION

It is rare for the process of demilitarisation to
lead to any stable pattern of civilian rule. Much
more often, the military's return to barracks is the
prelude to a period of weak civilian government
which sooner or later ends in reintervention. The
inadequacy of the 'handback' option has been
illustrated in several of the studies in this
volume, including those on Turkey and Argentina.
This chapter takes a more general and comparative
look at the problems of handback in Africa,
concentrating not on the process by which the
military itself determines on this as the optimum
strategy, but on the difficulties that then confront
the civilian successor regime.
    By 'post-military states', I mean those that
have become reconstitutionalised, and where
executive power and the direction of government has
been handed back to civilian authorities after a
period of military rule. Twenty-four African states
have at one time or another fallen victim to
military coups, and in eight of these executive
power has at some time been returned to civilians,
excluding states such as Egypt or Zaire in which the
original military regime has given way to a
quasi-civilian form of government directly descended
from it. Yet in all but one of those eight states
the military has later returned to power, and all
but two had military regimes at the start of 1984.
The most recent example of return by the military
was the overthrow of President Shehu Shagari in
Nigeria in December 1983.(1)
    The longest post-military experience,
uninterrupted as yet by further intervention, has
been that of Sierra Leone. There the All People's

64

Congress (APC) party of Prime Minister (later President) Siaka Stevens won a parliamentary majority for the first time at the 1967 elections, but was unable to take office because of military intervention. Stevens was eventually installed in power in April 1968, but only after two further coups, one by more junior officers and the other by privates and NCOs.(2) The other surviving post-military regime is that in Uganda, which dates only from April 1979 and the overthrow of General Amin, following an invasion by Tanzanian troops and Ugandan emigres. Yusuf Lule became the first civilian president of the new provisional government, to be followed by Godfrey Binaisa, and after further military intervention on 11 May 1980 by the former civilian president, Dr. Milton Obote. His return to the presidency was then legitimised by means of national elections held in December 1980.(3)

Although the experience of Sierra Leone, and that of the short-lived post-military governments of Ghana and Nigeria are the central concern of this chapter, it is important to remember that these, along with Uganda, are not the only African countries to have had post-military regimes. Others include Togo under President Grunitsky, 1963-67; Sudan, the subject of another chapter in this volume, between 1964 and 1969; Central African Republic, following the overthrow of ´Emperor´ Jean Bokassa in September 1979 and his replacement by the former civilian president David Dacko, who was removed in yet another coup two years later; and the vicious oscillation between military regimes and civilian administrations that characterised the politics of Dahomey (now Benin) until 1972.(4) Although I have chosen to concentrate on three West African examples of post-military restoration government, the experience of other African states has nevertheless helped me to pose, and hopefully to answer, some of the more pertinent questions. What is there about the post-military state that makes it so vulnerable to political re-entry by the military? And is the return of the military in any sense inevitable? Before beginning to answer such questions, however, it will be necessary to examine in more detail the nature of the post-military state, the contending groups and social forces therein, and the dominant pattern of civil-military relations.

CONTENDING SOCIAL GROUPS AND THEIR INTERESTS

The return of the military to barracks invariably finds society divided roughly into two opposing political camps, the ´pro-military´ and ´anti-military´ groups, each based on divergent interests with a related network of external linkages. The ´pro-military´ groups are those most favourably disposed to military re-entry into government - and perhaps already working towards that end - while the ´anti-military´ elements are those most anxious to prevent such an outcome or delay it for as long as possible. It is my contention that these rival coalitions, together with their constituent groups, are the main factor shaping politics in the typical post-military state, and that this new pattern of conflict is superimposed on, and may even help to redefine, existing lines of cleavage in such societies, whether regional, ethnic, religious or linguistic.(5)

Pro-Military Groups

The Military Establishment. The military is far from being a homogeneous group. While more senior officers may already have derived sufficient benefit from their association with the previous regime, and thus have little to gain from further intervention, for officers in the middle ranks and below another coup may offer a promising avenue for self-advancement. Indeed for most members of the military, coups have proved both an important and a rapid means for achieving ´inter-rank mobility´.(6) In any post-military state, therefore, ambitious military elements are likely to feature prominently among the pro-coup groups, and their attitude to the regime is all the more critical since (together with the police) they already control much of the coercive apparatus of the state.

The Bureaucratic Elite. Comprising the civil service and public sector employees, this is the second major potential pro-military group with an active interest in the politics of the post-military state. Where the military in many African countries has lacked the requisite technical skills and administrative resources for government, these deficiencies have often been remedied by means of an

66

alliance with the civil service, which shares with the military a common bureaucratic ethos, informed by similar corporate ideals of discipline, hierarchy and top-down authority.(7) Under military rule the civil servants have been able to expand their influence and enhance their status and prestige, and have come to enjoy considerable discretion regarding the economic and financial aspects of government: planning, the allocation of contracts and licences, state purchases, and all the privileges - some say kick-backs - which go with these. With the return to civilian rule, however, the bureaucratic elite loses much of its power and status to the incoming civilian politicians bent on taking over control, relegating civil servants once again to the back seat, and usually provoking considerable resentment in the process.

Certain Business Interests. Closely linked with the last group are those business interests that are pro-military, usually comprising the nouveaux riches who prospered under the previous military regime. In additon there are the ´comprador´ merchants and petty traders in the import and export business, a few small-scale domestic manufacturers attached to multi-national corporations, various ´emergency´ contractors and retired military officers now in private business having links of all sorts with the military establishment. In Nigeria these interests have combined to form what a former chief of army staff, Lt.-General T.Y. Danjumah, once referred to as an emergent ´military-business complex´.(8) The process derives from what Ali Mazrui has described as the embourgeoisement of a significant section of the African military and society.(9)

Under military rule the process was greatly assisted by programmes of economic ´indigenisation´, providing for statutory levels of African participation in the ownership and control of certain types of enterprise.(10) In Uganda under Amin, this resulted in military expropriation of middle-class Indian property;(11) in Ghana under Acheampong, there was a strengthening of the bureaucratic bourgeoisie as well as the comprador merchant class;(12) and in Nigeria under the successive regimes of Gowon, Murtala and Obasanjo, there were opportunities for indigenous businessmen to purchase various foreign undertakings, assisted by public loans.(13) It is probable that with the end of military rule, the incoming politicians will want to create their own new economic clientele, if they do not attempt to revive pre-military patterns of support. However, any attempt to reverse the economic status quo is likely to encounter opposition from the existing military-business complex - as Milton Obote discovered in connection with the proposed return of Indian property. Offended business interests may then be tempted to suborn sections of the military into staging another coup. A rich Nigerian businessman from Borno state, a civilian and card-carrying member of the then ruling National Party, Alhaji Mandara, was convicted in 1982 for precisely this kind of move.

<u>Opposition Political Groups.</u> Then there are those groups, based on party, or on regional, ethnic, religious or other interests, which having lost out in the contest to succeed the military, tend to be irreparably against the present incumbents. They may even, like some of the opposition parties in Nigeria after 1979, be prepared to condone another coup, in anticipation of a more favourable outcome to the next succession tussle. No doubt such behaviour betrays a streak of opportunism, but the explanation lies mainly in the zero-sum structure of politics in most African states, where one party´s win (feast) is another´s complete loss (famine). Such conditions are not conducive to a belief in <u>civilianism</u> per se, or to any deep-felt respect for constitutional norms and procedures.

<u>The Urban Unemployed.</u> Among the other main social categories usually to be found in the ´pro-military´ camp are the urban unemployed, comprising the young and unskilled, primary and secondary school leavers, and drop-outs, as well as discharged soldiers without pension benefits, beggars, wanderers, gangsters, ex-prisoners and slum-dwellers. All live on the fringes of the cities and towns, to which of late they have been attracted in growing numbers, usually by the prospect of non-existent jobs. Such volatile and easily-mobilised elements are highly susceptible to the appeals of Bonapartism.(14) They tend to prefer the reign of force to the luxury of constitutionalism, although they may not expect to see much improvement in their lot under either kind of regime.(15)

<u>Anti-Military Groups</u>

Arrayed against the above are the social forces

comprising the ´anti-military´ camp, which include:
The Restoration Government. The most obvious group
on this second list is the restoration government
itself, and those of the political class who
identify with the post-military regime, not
necessarily for any ideological reason, but simply
because the return of the military would mean the
end of their rule and termination of the benefits
and perquisites of office.(16) Because they have so
much to lose in material terms by further
intervention, they may try to buy off the military,
perhaps through cooptation of the commanders. They
may also rely ʷ to some extent on those few but
usually important military elements (the cincinnati
of classic memory) genuinely committed to remaining
in barracks and to the pursuit of the ideals of
military professionalism and political neutrality.

The Old Aristocracy. Next come the old members of
the aristocracy, whether of birth, land or wealth,
who include the old propertied classes, long
established families, and the chiefly estates who
have been eclipsed under the rule of the military
and, for that reason among others, are opposed to
their return. Members of the group will tend to
spurn the pretensions of the nouveaux riches,
created by the military, which they see as
contributing to their own decline. They are also
inclined to welcome the return of politics, hoping
by that means to recover much of their former power
and authority. Here they count on being able to
influence the choice of representatives at all
levels by employing traditional forms of patronage
and by sponsoring the creation of supportive
electoral networks.

The Intelligentsia. These comprise a third,
highly-diversified group, whose members may find
themselves ranged in the anti-military camp for
rather different reasons. There are the
intellectuals proper, including senior staff and
students of universities and other civilian
institutes of higher learning, whose relationship to
the military establishment is informed by the
´brain´ versus ´brawn´ dialectic.(17) It is true
that in the pre-military era many intellectuals did
manifest views and attitudes closer to ´civilian
militarism´.(18) They may even have contributed to
the arrival in power of the military. However, any
hopes they may have entertained at the time about
the distinctive nature of military rule and its

capacity to solve purely technico-administrative problems bearing on the country´s development, were soon disappointed.

Whatever accommodation was reached under military rule, between soldiers and intellectuals, was short-lived and could not conceal the basic difference in their background and approach to government, and the enormous disparity in their organisational resources. Resentful of the ´supercilious´ intellectuals and their patronising manner, the military were always eager for a show of force to demonstrate that it was ´soldierly qualities´ that mattered most in the conduct of public affairs and the running of military governments. Confrontation almost invariably followed, with the universities playing an active role in the opposition to such regimes and, occasionally, in precipitating their downfall. There was the role played by the University of Khartoum in the ´October Revolution´ that brought down the Abboud government in Sudan (1964). Universities were again prominent in the agitation that led to the removal of General Gowon in Nigeria (1975). There was also a strong element of academic as well as professional protest in the organised civilian resistance to military rule in Ghana during 1976-78, which led to the termination of General Acheampong´s ´Union Government´ project and his overthrow.

This Ghanaian case also underlines the important role played by one section of the intelligentsia, the lawyers´ associations, together with the judiciary. While a part of the legal fraternity may in the past have collaborated with military regimes, seeking at the same time to defend the rule of law and extend the range of its application, this also furnished the basis for their potential anti-military stance and their resistance to the introduction by the military of unorthodox ´legal´ tribunals and summary ´judicial´ procedures. Like the lawyers and judges, members of the press are also likely to cherish the return of politics, particularly where journalism remains virile and its practitioners retain some degree of independence. They welcome the post-military regime as affording them much greater opportunity to write and publish without the constraints familiar under military rule. Much, however, will depend on the manner in which the press is financed and the amount of control exercised either by the incoming civilian government, by opposition groups, or even by external interests. Its stand on the pro- or anti-military issue may merely reflect the views and interests of its current patrons.

Organised labour. The trade unions are another of the anti-military forces that tend to dominate the politics of the post-military state. Organised labour, like the intelligentsia but for slightly different reasons, has often achieved a temporary accommodation with military regimes. But the discrepancy between their interests and those of the soldiers is even more marked than in the case of the intellectuals. The military are oriented towards the maintenance of a given socio-political ´order´, while the trade unions, in pursuance of their objectives, are more or less committed to agitate against it. Moreover, the army has frequently been used by governments everywhere, whether civilian or military, to suppress strikes, especially when they threaten the stability or survival of the government. Again, strikes are usually banned under the ´state of emergency´ that accompanies military rule. Finally, military regimes are notorious for the imposition of wage freezes under the guise of economic stabilisation.

For these reasons, relations between military governments and the trade unions are usually uneasy at best and conflictual at worst, especially where such regimes are seen or held to favour private (business) interests. Conversely, union leaders will favour the return of competitive party politics, hoping to regain their right to strike for higher pay. In Nigeria, scarcely had the Obasanjo regime handed over than the Nigerian Labour Congress presented the new civilian rulers with demands for a national minimum wage. These demands were backed by a country-wide strike and were fuelled by news of the generous salaries and allowances which the new rulers voted themselves upon assuming office. Yet another general strike was threatened when the military unexpectedly returned to power at the end of 1983.

To summarise, the typical post-military state has contending within it two broad amalgams of social interests, which divide roughly into pro- and anti-military groups. That division then forms the principal line of domestic political cleavage, in many ways analogous to the split between government and opposition in a pre-military multi-party state. The categories are not, however, meant to be rigid and the 'fit' may not be perfect in every case. Relations will continue between groups, both within and across the two main tendencies, e.g., between the military establishment and the old aristocracy, and the urban unemployed and urban labour. The picture is further complicated by the fact that the attitude of civilian groups will vary, among other things, with the character and complexion of the military itself. Thus in Nigeria there have been different responses to military government depending on leadership style and performance, and on the strength of its commitment to hand over power to civilians.

The brief but energetic administration of General Murtala Mohammed, in 1975-76, was widely popular, in particular with groups like the intelligentsia and students, not otherwise noted for their military leanings. The same regime also purged some 10,000 civil servants and public employees, reversing the familiar partnership between military and bureaucracy. Murtala's military successor effected an uneasy reconciliation with the civil service but, with the change of administration, the students soon returned to their more traditional adversary stance, while union leaders were only prevailed on to moderate their demands by the threat of reprisals and the argument that widespread industrial action would prolong military rule beyond 1979. In Ghana, too, the first administration of Flight-Lieutenant Rawlings, after June 1979, represented a clear break with the personnel, style and, to some extent, the policies of previous military regimes - and it did succeed, like Murtala's government, in attracting civilian support from unaccustomed quarters. In the end, however, the more familiar patterns tend to re-assert themselves.

Finally, the categories themselves do not exhaust all the possibilities. There is, for example, the betwixt and between stand of the growing population of young retired military officers, swollen by the high rate of mobility and rapid circulation of ranks that has followed the repeated crises of civil-military relations in Africa since independence.(19) Their attitude to the post-military state will largely depend on the extent and success of their re-integration into civilian society, which in turn depends on the kind of employment, if any, that they secure. Meanwhile, their experience, their military and administrative contacts, and their perhaps frustrated ambitions, all mark them out as a significant force in most African countries.

Despite these qualifications regarding our two categories and the groups assigned to each, our study clearly reveals the extent to which the format of government in a typical post-military state has become fractured as a result of military intervention and rule. During the pre-military era, it was axiomatic that practically all the units comprising the government, including the executive and legislature, the party organisations, judiciary, public bureaucracy, and even the military and police force, were one with the rulers in their defence of civilian rule. What our analysis has shown is that no such consensus now exists. Previous coups have so unhinged things that the governmental structure no longer holds. This is a central problem for the post-military state, particularly in the area of civil-military relations.

POLITICS OF THE POST-MILITARY STATE

The Military and Elections
At no time is the problem more manifest than during competitive elections, when much is at stake, the outcome is uncertain, the military factor looms large in political calculations, and the conflict between pro- and anti-military tendencies becomes more explicit. This has happened in Sudan (1965), Dahomey (now Benin, in December 1965 and May 1970), Sierra Leone (with elections in 1973, 1977 and 1982), Central African Republic (in the March 1980 presidential elections which had to be postponed because of violence), and lastly in Nigeria during the post-military elections in the third quarter of 1983.

The immediate conflict is between such opposition parties as are permitted to run and the restoration government, and it centres on which group will secure control of the government apparatus so essential for the distribution of scarce economic resources, political spoils and pay-offs. But the prospect of renewed military intervention can never be discounted. Popular participation, accompanied by growing polarisation and in the context of the recent praetorian experience, all make the intrusion of the military factor more or less inevitable. Other considerations are also working towards the same

end. There is the intensity of the inter-party
competition, which often results in violence because
of the high stakes involved and the absence of
entrenched constitutional mores. There is the
governing party's de jure monopoly of operational
control of the military with the risk of their being
deployed in a partisan way. And, in the course of
the campaign, one or other of the parties may
deliberately invoke the name of the military either
to blackmail its rivals or to show just who are the
'friends' and who the 'foes' of the military.

In Africa therefore elections are a time of
acute stress and uncertainty for the post-military
regime. This is then reflected in the odd reversal
of roles, between governing and opposition parties,
that one encounters in the run-up to the contest.
The restoration government may try to improve its
chances of re-election by elaborating on the
possible consequences of a defeat: the ensuing
anarchy would be likely to provoke another military
intervention. It is a case of "either we are in
power or all of us lose out to the military".
Earlier, the same government would quickly have
discounted any hint of a coup. The risk of
precipitating military intervention certainly did
not deter the ruling National Party of Nigeria (NPN)
from using its legislative majority in Kaduna State
in 1981 to impeach and remove the elected governor,
who happened to belong to the opposing People's
Redemption Party (PRP). The same threat was,
however, freely invoked in the approach to the 1983
national elections as NPN propaganda underlined the
probability of a military coup following any victory
by the so-called 'progressives' led by Chief Obafemi
Awolowo's Unity Party of Nigeria (UPN). Ironically,
it was the electoral victory of the incumbents that
was followed, within a few months, by another
military coup.

Even the attitude of the opposition parties to
the military is contingent on such factors as the
proximity of elections and the chances of its coming
to power by peaceful, constitutional means. There
was a shift in the UPN position in Nigeria, away
from the panegyric to coups, familiar to readers of
its mouthpiece the Nigerian Tribune in the first
three years of civilian rule, to strong opposition,
in 1982, to any proposal to involve the Nigerian
army in the conduct of the elections due in 1983.
The same party also condemned President Shehu
Shagari's takeover of the defence portfolio in
October 1982, calling it an expedient move aimed at

involving the military in politics.(20) In the heat of the contest it is likely that similar permutations are taking place in the attitudes of other social groups regarding the military factor, particularly among the intelligentsia and organised labour.

The process serves only to confirm the shallow nature of the civilianist outlook in Nigeria, as well as the zero-sum structure and concept of politics common to most African societies. This is why few post-military governments make it through elections into a second term of constitutional rule, without in the process provoking a military return to power. Given the environment we have described, governments are lucky to reach the first post-military election; luckier still if they survive it; and luckiest of all if they succeed in keeping the military from further intervention for a long time thereafter.(21)

Keeping the Military in Check

The fact is that for much of their formative years, and until their experiment in political reconstitutionalisation has taken root, governments of post-military states are haunted by the spectre of a military return to power. Finer´s explanation of this is that "in most cases, the military that have intervened in politics...can neither stay nor go", and that "those armed forces that have tried to disengage from politics have had to hasten back as soon as their quondam political enemies come within sight of regaining power".(22) On this view much seems to depend on the nature of the threat from civilian society as it is perceived by the military as a whole or by a section of it. Such a threat is most likely to surface during general elections which therefore provide a useful test of Finer´s thesis.

The thesis may well have been valid in some of the larger South American states, where the military soon came to distrust and even fear the mass-based, populist-inclined parties with their nationalist appeal and their demagogic leadership. At the other extreme it may help explain the vulnerability of post-military governments in several of the smaller African states, where civilian authority was concentrated in the person of the leader, where administration was centralised and government was conducted on the basis of a one-party, or precarious two-party system. There military intervention has in the past been directed at a particular party or regime and I have in mind such examples as pre-1966 Ghana under the Convention People's Party (CPP), or pre-1967 Sierra Leone under the Sierra Leone People' Party (SLPP).

The Finer thesis does not, however, explain either intervention or the spectre of re-intervention in a large, sprawling country like Nigeria, with a widely dispersed heterogeneous population, which in pre-military days operated under a federal constitution and with a multi-party system. Here there was no obvious threat to the military from any readily indentifiable civilian source, political or otherwise. The same can be said of Nigeria under the post-military regime (1979-83). Nor should one conclude that since the military are basically conservative, they will have for 'quondam political enemies' parties with a socialist ideology. In Africa the socialist left has on the whole had rather more success with the military than with the electorate - although much, of course, depends on the country and the context. It is true that a regime such as General Obasanjo's in Nigeria was hostile to such parties, as was clear in 1978 from his purge of the 'radical left' from the universities. But it is also probable that Flight Lieutenant Jerry Rawlings in Ghana would have handed over to a party of this kind in September 1979 had there been one at hand.(23)

The Finer hypothesis seems to provide an incomplete and therefore inadequate explanation for the vulnerability of post-military states to further takeovers. It is not only that there are other variables that may help account for first-generation coups,(24) and may also be relevant to the special case of re-entry, but that military intervention, to be effective, depends above all on the acquiescence and a degree of civilian support and collaboration. In other words it cannot profitably be discussed, still less understood, without reference to the kind of social forces described in the previous section. And that applies even more directly to the question of re-entry. In particular, a prior intervention breaks down the former boundaries between 'civil' and 'military', and tends to recruit into the pro-military camp many groups which, but for that, would have stayed civil. An earlier coup tilts the parallelogram of social forces further to the military side, making subsequent interventions increasingly difficult to resist. Re-entry takes place because there is no longer anything to prevent it.

Restoration governments are acutely aware of the problem and tend to give it priority over other issues of public policy. In the circumstances their behaviour in office becomes more comprehensible. If correct, our observations would seem to cast doubt on the commonly held view that the antidote to coups is ´good government´: that to exorcise the spectre of military return a government need only ´stay good´, ´maintain probity´ ´be just´, ´work hard´, and ´rule effectively´. The problem with such injunctions is that, although indispensible to the stability of any rule in the long run, both civil and military, they can also be (and are) invoked by intervening soldiers to rationalise even the most blatant and egotistical of coups. Unfortunately for most post-military states, the structural impermanence of power and the fear of this entertained by the political class, induces a behaviour pattern which, in a rather self-fulfilling way, plays into the hand of such military rationalisers.

STRATAGEMS AND SPOILS OF SURVIVAL POLITICS

Preoccupied with the military spectre, and aware of their uncertain popular support, restoration governments frequently re-direct their energies and the country´s resources away from the more urgent and pressing economic priorities, towards what they perceive - albeit imperfectly and often inaccurately - as the threat from the military. Meanwhile their behaviour while in office betrays an exaggerated concern for self-enrichment, stemming from the ´winner takes all´ approach and recognition of their own uncertain future. The almost inevitable result is to precipitate the very outcome the restoration government is most anxious to avoid.

Because of the constant fear of losing out again to the military, public policy in the post-military state becomes largely reduced to the question of survival. So much of the rulers´ time is devoted to experimenting with and perfecting various survival stratagems, admixed with spoils(25), that before long everything else is subordinated to that one over-riding consideration. Thus there is concern about the problems of employment, inflation or recession, not because of their deleterious effects on a country´s standard of

living, but because the government sees them as
threatening its continued rule. The external debt
problem and relations with international lending
agencies tend to be viewed from the same narrow
perspective. The national budget becomes a useful
instrument not for purposes of national economic
planning, but for juggling domestic social groups
and trying to satisfy the most critical ones,
notably the military. In short, the crux of the
rulers´ occupations in the immediate aftermath of
any post-military restoration is about "how to
control the military" and prevent it from coming
back. The case studies of Ghana, Sierra Leone and
Nigeria, among others, provide considerable evidence
to support that contention.

Ghana, 1969-72 and 1979-81

The Busia administration would, on the face of it,
seem to have pursued policies completely unmindful
of the problem of military re-entry. For example,
there were cuts in both the recurrent and capital
allocations to the defence ministry in the first
national budget to be passed by the administration
(1970); plans were mooted to put the military to
work on constructive tasks; while a number of fringe
benefits hitherto enjoyed by the military as well as
by other public servants, such as car, telephone and
rent allowances, were to be abolished.(26) So that
when Busia was subsequently overthrown by a military
coup, in January 1972, he was to describe it as an
"officers´ amenities coup" arising from the
government´s efforts to save money.(27)

    This is not to say that when Busia took over,
in September 1969, the spectre of possible military
re-entry had been exorcised in Ghana. As early as
June 1968, while the National Liberation Council
(NLC) was still in power, a regular correspondent to
The Legon Observer had expressed concern "that there
is not a too immediate re-return by the
military".(28) In somewhat lighter vein he proposed
a number of remedies which were no doubt influenced
by military accounts of the 1966 coup and its
origins.(29) They included improved accommodation
for all ranks and expecially officers, more than
adequate remuneration for retired military
administrators and outgoing members of the NLC, and
compulsory re-orientation courses for all serving
officers, preferably abroad and at Sandhurst.

The fear of military re-entry was sufficient to have induced both the Constitutional Commission and the Constituent Assembly to comtemplate military co-optation as a formula for stabilising the post-1969 government. The result was the establishment of a three-man army-cum-police Presidential Commission that would permit the three leading NLC members, the chairman, his deputy, and the chief of defence staff, to continue in office as part of the new civilian government for the first three years of post-military rule.(30) Some Constituent Assemblymen had earlier called for "control over the armed forces" to be written as a specific clause into the Constitution,(31) very much like their Nigerian counterparts ten years later; in debating the transitional provisions of the draft Constitution, the Ghanaian assembly had also approved proposals that NLC members might retire from the army and police on full salary at any time before or after the coming into force of the Constitution.(32)

Busia´s supporters in the Progress Party were largely responsible for the Constituent Assembly adopting the proposed Presidential Commission,(33) apparently for reasons of self-interest. Firstly, the Busia group were under some obligation to leading NLC members who had spared no effort to groom them for the civilian succession. Secondly, they would have seen the Commission as providing much-needed insurance against any possible military re-entry in the earlier phase of post military rule.

Nevertheless these measures were subject to critical comment from other Ghanaians, including the well-known historian, Professor Adu Boahen. In September 1969 he advised the incoming government that the prevention of coups lay in honest and constitutional government, sensible and successful economic policies, and above all in the ballot box, but not in any unnecessary concessions to the military. This warning was prompted by the realisation that "one of the urgent concerns of the new crop of politicians on the eve of the return from military to civilian rule is the fear of the re-entry of the military into politics." Unless this fear was dispelled the politicians "will be compelled, blackmailed or bullied into making certain concessions or compromises which may not be in the best interest of the country."(34)

By September 1970, the Ghanaian National Assembly had voted to terminate the Presidential Commission, leaving the Busia government again to worry about the military and the related problem of a successful comeback by ex-President Nkrumah. Here Busia´s task was made easier by the fact that the NLC had not only disqualified top Nkrumah supporters from holding political office, but had also retired senior military officers associated with the deposed President. This did not stop Busia, in August 1971, from rushing through the National Assembly - under a "certificate of urgency" - a bill making the sale of portraits of the former President, and the advocacy of his return, a criminal offence.(35) At the same time the government began to plant Akan-speaking officers, particularly Ashanti elements, in military and police high commands, while excluding most of the Ewe who were suspected of opposition sympathies.(36) It was naive, however, to assume that fellow clansmen would necessarily go along with any government measures, however unpalatable. Busia had forgotten, or misread, one of the lessons of the 1966 coup and it is ironic that the leader of the coup that toppled him, in January 1972, was Lt.-Col. I.K. Acheampong, himself an Ashanti.

The second round of military rule in Ghana, lasting until September 1979, was interspersed by two succesful countercoups, the first of a ´palace´ kind, resulting in the replacement of Acheampong by General Akuffo in July 1978, and the second of a ´populist´ nature, marking the ´first coming´ of Flight-Lt Rawlings and his Armed Forces Revolutionary Council in May 1979.(37) Ghana´s third republican government, under Dr. Hilla Limann´s People´s National Party (PNP), lasted for only twenty-seven months, from September 1979 to December 1981. But the fear of yet another military return proved even more crippling under Limann than under Busia. Throughout Limann´s short-lived presidency, the political atmosphere was filled with alarms, provoking streams of official statements and frequent panic measures to counteract such varied threats as rumoured conspiracies, coup plots, intramilitary clique formations, suspicious troop movements, and especially the return of Rawlings. Limann spent the whole of his first twelve months in office preoccupied with this ´problem of Rawlings´ among the many other problems then facing Ghana.(38) The retired military personalities whose names were repeatedly mentioned in these post-1979 coup alarms were Rawlings himself, Brig. Arnold Quainoo, Brig. Nunoo-Mensah, ex-capt. Kojo Tsikata, and ex-Corporal Alex Dautey. Tsikata and his lawyer brother,Mr. Tsatsu Tsikata, dominated the news as much as Rawlings. But how genuine were these threats of impending military re-entry which so preoccupied the Limann administration? Were they a machiavellian device aimed at rallying behind Limann those Ghanaian social groups, especially the professionals, academics and students, known for their anti-military stance from the Union Government days? Whatever the answer the threats, real or imagined, nevertheless prompted Limann to retire the suspect soldiers, who included not only Rawlings, but also senior officers and lower-ranking elements, as well as dozens of NCOs.(39) As a solution to the perceived problem of military return, his action was predicated on the naive assumption that only regular officers could effect coups, while retired personnel could not. Only a little reflection on the experience not only of neighbouring Togo in 1964, but of Ghana itself under Nkrumah in 1965-66,(40) would have persuaded the Limann administration of the dubiousness of this as a coup-preventing technique.

It is in Ghana, more than any other country in Africa, that the typical post-military government faces its most challenging economic problems, with a stagnating economy since the mid-1960s, deteriorating foreign exchange earnings, chronic shortages of essential commodities, combined with an ever-expanding bureaucracy and mass incidence of rising frustrations. No government can give these problems the attention they require while it is obsessed, as was Limann´s and to a lesser extent Busia´s, with the question of a military return. At the same time, only an effective long-term economic programme can provide some at least of the conditions for post-military stability.

Sierra Leone, 1968-84

As previously remarked, Sierra Leone has had the longest, most continuous experience of post-military rule in contemporary Africa. The experiment began only a year after the March 1967 coup which necessitated it in the first place.(41) That coup had been staged by the top brass of the Sierra Leonean army to prevent Siaka Stevens´ opposition party, the All People´s Congress (APC), from constitutionally replacing the ruling Sierra Leone People´s Party (SLPP) of Sir Albert Margai. The SLPP had been defeated in general elections, but it required two counter-coups in quick succession before Stevens and the APC were installed in government in April 1968.

It is now sixteen years since the post-military state of Sierra Leone came into existence and, as it continues to the present, it might be thought that the military spectre has, at least in this case, considerably receded. However, in the years immediately following the restoration of civilian rule, Sierra Leone had to deal with the problem like any other post-military state. In fact Stevens was nearly toppled by a coup attempt on 23 March 1971, which was followed by yet another abortive coup in July 1974. Indeed, as Thomas Cox has detailed in his excellent account of civil-military relations in Sierra Leone in this period, many of the initial measures taken by Prime Minister (later President) Stevens in his first four years of government were aimed at tackling this very problem.

These measures included: (1) the trial and detention for treason of the key principals involved in the 1967 round of coups; (2) the trial and execution by firing squad of the four officers, Brig. Bangura, Major S. E. Momoh, Major F. Jawara, and Lt. J. B. Kolugbonda, linked to the subsequent coup attempt against the Stevens government in March 1971; (3) release from jail and reinstatement at their former ranks of all the pro-Stevens military elements imprisoned in the 1967-68 upheavals; (4) weeding from the army of those officers and men who, because of ethnic affiliations, especially the Mende elements, were suspected of doubtful loyalty to the APC government; (5) formation of an officer corps that was ethnically and in political orientation considered to be sympathetic to the Siaka Stevens government; (6) initial increases in personal emoluments and appropriations for the military; (7) building up more units for the regular army, as well as a new paramilitary force, the Internal Security Unit, to perform a countervailing role vis-a-vis the army; and last, but by no means least, (8) the use of a defence pact with neighbouring Sekou Toure´s Guinea.

Of these measures, perhaps the most efficacious were the last two, especially the last. Cox observed that Siaka Stevens and his APC government had, since taking over in April 1968, "been forced to rely increasingly upon the threat of intervention by the Guinean armed forces and the build-up of his own security guards".(42) The use or even threat of this ´Guinean factor´ has had such a persistent effect on the conduct of Sierra Leonean civil-military relations that it can be considered the single most important variable that has kept the experiment going for so long. But for this it is almost certain the experiment would have foundered in any one of the many periods of civil-military crisis encountered by Sierra Leone after 1968. Such crises were not confined to the abortive coup attempts of March 1971 and July 1974 already alluded to, but have also coincided with the various general elections that have been held to date (1973, 1977 and 1982), each of which was accompanied by acute political violence, not to mention strikes, food riots, and student protests.

Hence the explanation for Sierra Leone's experience as the longest surviving post-military experiment does not lie in any special character of her civil-military relations, nor is it to be found in any unique quality of the government, which has since its 'restoration' gone the way of most African governments, imposing one-party rule, suppressing opposition and dissidence, and imprisoning without trial. President Siaka Stevens and the APC have survived so long as a post-military government largely because of the continuous military involvement, both actual and threatened, from neighbouring Guinea.

Nigeria, 1979-83

Finally, there is the case of Shagari's Nigeria, and the experiment in post-military rule that was begun in October 1979 and terminated by a further coup in December 1983.(43) As in the Ghanaian case, the spectre of a return to power by the military was worrying Nigeria's emergent politicians even before the military had left office. Elsewhere the author has detailed how the Constituent Assemblymen spent much time and a good deal of effort searching for a magic constitutional formula which would prevent future coups.(44) The result was Section 1 (2) of the final Constitution of the Federal Republic of Nigeria (1979), which stipulated rather naively that "the Federal Republic of Nigeria shall not be governed, nor shall any person or group of persons take control of the government of Nigeria or any part thereof, except in accordance with the provisions of this Constitution".(45)

The circumstances of Alhaji Shagari's rise to the presidency and the "truncated legitimacy" with which his government began,(46) necessitated immediate measures to stabilise the civil-military environment. These included the prompt restructuring of the officer corps with the compulsory retirement of senior officers who had been too prominent in the previous military regime. We are not just talking of Obasanjo, Danjuma, Yar´Adua, Shuwa, Oluleye, Olutoye, among other army generals who voluntarily retired with the handover of power in 1979, and were followed shortly after by other service heads such as Adelanwa and Yissa-Doko. Rather we have in mind the three charismatic military personalities, Olu Bajowa, Joseph Garba, and George Innih, who were retired early in 1980 while on courses abroad. Almost simultaneously came the news of promotions to fill the vacancies created.

The Shagari government also made use of the "federal character" provisions of the new Nigerian Constitution, namely Articles 14 (3), 197 (29), and 199, to build up a reliable political base within the military. Interpreted to mean quota representation through state and/or ethnic balancing, according to the make-up of the federation, these provisions were invoked in the military domain to effect a reduction in the number of representatives of some states and ethnic groups, including the Yoruba from the western part of the country, thought to predominate especially at the officer command level, and to increase the representation of others, including the Hausa-Fulani elements from far northern states. President Shagari´s prerogative, as the commander-in-chief of the armed forces of the Federal Republic under the 1979 Constitution, also permitted him to decide, politically, which among the officers, from colonels and upwards, were qualified to fill what senior posts. In making such decisions, Shagari paid particular attention to considerations of state balancing, some ethnic arithmeticking, and suspected party loyalty.

These techniques of control should be familiar to anyone conversant with civil-military relations in Nigeria in the period before 1966. In the political sphere, the transactional exchanges among parties, which aimed at control over men and resources and involved stratagems of bargaining, co-optation, coalition-building and ´spoils´ distribution, were not unlike those of the pre-1966 period so admirably treated by the late Professor Billy J. Dudley.(47) In the military sphere, the use of the "federal character" principle as a device for re-shaping the officer corps recalls the old quota form of military recruitment,(48) merely writ large and within a political context that was only slightly modified. Also familiar was the practice of appointing two or more officers from different ethnic and/or state backgrounds to positions of overlapping responsibility within key military units. Again not unlike the past, Shagari sought to maximise some of the structural constraints in the political set-up, particularly those that make coup execution - though not coup planning - relatively difficult in Nigeria compared with other African countries. These include the country´s enormous population, dispersed over a large geographical area and having as many governmental power centres as there are composite federal units, with a similar spread of military garrisons under a heterogenous command structure.

On the positive side, there were the salary increases introduced by the Shagari government on taking office, resulting in an across-the-board increase of N300 per annum for all categories of military officers, as well as considerable pay increases (the so-called ´Shagari awards´) for the other ranks. The former was the officers´ own share of new pay increases wrung from the Shagari government by public employees, including university lecturers, civil servants, and police personnel; the latter was ostensibly intended as the equivalent of, or rather as a counterbalance to, the minimum wage demands of the Nigerian labour Congress. There was also the increasing trend of budgetary allocations to defence continued under the Shagari administration, despite decreasing levels of oil-derived federal revenues over its last three years. These and similar policies were largely reactive and were necessitated by the government´s perception of the civil-military environment as far from certain and in need of stabilisation. The Nigerian military were kept well-supplied, were even better equipped than before and would, hopefully, stay content and in barracks.

In foreign affairs, President Shagari´s attitudes to coups and related events in West Africa during his term of office can be similarly interpreted. We have particularly in mind his reaction to Sergeant Doe´s coup in Liberia (April 1980), resulting in strained diplomatic relations between Nigeria and that country; and to the ´second coming´ of Flight-Lt. Rawlings in Ghana (December 1981), when President Shagari not only

stopped Nigerian oil supplies to Ghana, but refused
even to confer with the new Ghanaian head of
state.(49) Such a show of displeasure at the return
of Rawlings, and also at the Doe coup in Liberia,
may have stemmed from personal considerations, as
well as from an understandable fear of the
demonstration effects that they would have on
Nigeria´s own experiment with post-military
government. Some of Shagari´s misgivings about
Rawlings were undoubtedly shared by senior military
officers in Nigeria whose main concern, however, was
with the discipline and cohesion of the military and
the preservation of its hierarchy. Indeed, fear of
a junior officers´ coup, following rumours of an
earlier planned attempt, may well have motivated the
military intervention on December 31, 1983 - two
years to the day after Rawlings´ own return. But
before acting against a civilian regime, and one for
which they themselves were in some sense
responsible, the Major-Generals and Brigadiers had
first to consider likely civilian reactions and here
elections again played a crucial role in the success
or failure of a post-military regime.

As the 1983 Nigerian elections approached,
inter-political competition began to assume a more
violent character that reminded practitioners and
observers alike of the 1964/65 experience which had
culminated in the coup of 1966. At the same time, a
mutation of social forces was fast taking place with
the result that groups like the intelligentsia and
organised labour, usually to be found in the
anti-military camp, were reported as fast losing
confidence in civil rule and as being once more
susceptible to the allure of military
adventurism.(50) Any explanation must, of course,
take into account the generally volatile atmosphere
surrounding the elections, and the nervousness that
this engendered in everyone, both leaders and led.
Then there was the catastrophic fall in the
country´s oil-derived revenues, leading to economic
recession, austerity, disappointed aspirations, and
a growing sense of frustration against the
government. Finally there was the alarming growth
of corruption in public places, which President
Shagari was himself forced to acknowledge in calling
for an "ethical revolution". So blatant had this
become that one may wonder whether the incoming
politicians of post-military Nigeria, like the
Bourbons of post-revolutionary France, had indeed
learnt anything from the country´s recent past - or
whether they, too, had not forgotten everything.

CONCLUSION

Corruption is not new to African politics, but there
is a sense in which it assumes a different dimension
in a typical post-military state such as those we
have examined in this study. It can be argued that
the new corruption is directly linked to the
structural impermanence of power, and to the
politicians´ awareness of this induced by previous
military rule. The fear that power may not last
encourages the incoming politicians to grab what is
grabbable in case the military should return to
clear the deck. Conversely, this kind of corruption
may be expected to decrease with time, as
governmental instability diminishes, or as the
spectre of military return recedes: in short, as
tenure of power under a post-military state becomes
´institutionalised´ in the Huntingtonian sense. In
the Nigerian Second Republic, as in most of the
post-military regimes which we have considered,
this stage was never reached.

Such have been the central problems of the
post-military state in Africa. In this study, we
have sought to define the nature of the problem, to
explain why there is such a preoccupation with the
military factor, and to describe the ´survival
politics´ that this induces and the various
stratagems and spoils associated with it. Our
central thesis is that prior intervention breaks
down the previous boundaries between the ´civil´ and
´military´, tilts the parallelogram of social forces
towards the military side, and makes subsequent
interventions more and more difficult to resist.
But it is also argued that long-term planning, to
tackle the development problems of a more
socio-economic nature, becomes more difficult when
rulers are preoccupied with political survival and
short-run calculations, which is the dilemma of the
post-military state. We conclude that not until
tenure of power is institutionalised, and succession
to government is regularised through some
acceptable constitutional mechanism, can the
post-military state be freed of survival problems
and allowed to concentrate, instead, on more
developmental issues. Yet neglecting the latter to
concentrate on the former is itself destabilising.
There is a vicious circle here that only time,
perhaps, can break.

This chapter has been concerned primarily with

87

the problems of the post-military state, and we have given little attention to what is usually the central dilemma confronting military regimes. This is the necessity, sooner or later, to choose from a limited range of outcomes, each of which has very evident shortcomings from a military point of view. Besides the ´option´ of promoting revolution or ´breakthrough´, for which African militaries are not, as a rule, particularly well qualified, the only alternatives are ´handover´, with the risks and uncertainties it entails, or ´institutionalisation´, usually involving the acquisition of civilian support and their participation in the regime often at the expense of the original military constituency. Impasse, although experienced frequently in Africa and elsewhere in the Third World, scarcely qualifies as an option and, in any. case, is not confined to military regimes.

However, both ´impasse´ and ´handover´ are, in their separate ways, evidence of the failure of all but a few military regimes to impose and maintain themselves in government for more than a very limited time. It remains to be seen whether the military, now back in power in Ghana and Nigeria, will be any more successful either in remaining there, or in managing the transition to some more durable kind of post-military regime.

The most stable military regimes in the continent to date have been those in the North African states (Egypt, Libya, Algeria), where the military is relatively cohesive and ´professional´ in orientation; where society is more disposed to accept and cooperate with the military on a long-term basis; where economic development is far enough advanced, or economic resources are sufficiently abundant, to provide additional means of securing the necessary civilian backing; and where the military can usually invoke a credible external threat to legitimise its rule. The situation is very different in Africa south of the Sahara, where most militaries exhibit fairly low levels of discipline and corporate unity; the boundaries between civil and military are poorly defined and highly permeable; large populations and chronic under-development generate relatively little or no surplus with which to purchase military (let alone civilian) support; where any regime is likely to be judged on its performance, mainly in the economic area; and where there are few plausible external threats to counter or offset the real ones emanating from inside the country.

The Post-Military State in Africa

In these difficult circumstances, the chances
of the military, or a faction of it, remaining in
office for any considerable length of time are far
from good. The most stable military regimes in
sub-Saharan Africa have been those organised along
clientist lines with a pragmatic orientation capable
of accommodating the most diverse and often opposed
groups. Such governments are now to be found
seemingly entrenched in Zaire and Somalia.
Following intervention by the army, a leading
military figure has in each case consolidated his
personal rule, progressively ´civilianising´ the
government by incorporating strategically placed
groups into a loosely integrated network of tribal,
clan and communal support, and by cementing the
resulting coalition with a judicious distribution of
patronage and economic largesse. This is not to say
that the military does not remain the chief prop of
the regime, but rather that the leader has also been
able to tap significant sources of support outside
the military. In Zaire, Sudan and Somalia he has,
moreover, been adept at manipulating real or
imagined external threats to secure international
backing and overcome or minimise the risk of
internal dissidence. Significantly, the army in
such states was neither united nor assertive enough
to be able to stop the gradual usurpation of power
by the dominant military personality.

In Nigeria and Ghana, however, the military has
in the past shown itself unwilling to be relegated
for long to a subordinate role and, in Nigeria at
least, was able to intervene in July 1975 to defend
its privileged status against civilian encroachment
and to maintain the principle of collective military
decision-taking. In that way it avoided impasse
but had, nevertheless, to concede a return to
civilian rule by 1979. In Ghana, on the other hand,
the result of protracted military rule and a dismal
economic performance in the seventies was
constitutional deadlock, with the failure of the
Union Government proposals, followed by a palace
coup, the removal of Acheampong, and the reluctant
acceptance by the military of the handover option.
But it was too late to prevent a revolt by the other
ranks and the emergence in 1979 of Flight-Lieutenant
Jerry Rawlings at the head of a Revolutionary
Council of junior officers, NCOs and privates.
Despite his return to power in December 1981, after
the brief and unsatisfactory Limann interlude,
Rawlings has had little success to date in
confirming his revolutionary credentials or

establishing a 'breakthrough' regime, despite the promise of mass popular participation to be channelled through a network of People's Defence Committees. Indeed, in the past two years he has been as preoccupied with threats to his personal security and his regime's survival as was the preceding government of Hilla Limann.

The last Nigerian military administration, confronting a serious domestic and internal crisis in 1975, was able to maintain itself in power only by forcing a change of leadership and conceding the principle of civilian government from 1979. The middle ranking officers who initiated that change in July 1975 were again prominent in the intervention against President Shagari in December 1983, although the former Lieutenant-Colonels are now Major-Generals and Brigadiers. But the handover option seems no longer available or even relevant - certainly not in its old form. Although the 1983 coup was extremely popular in Nigeria, the prospects of securing civilian support and collaboration in the country's present economic difficulties appear much more doubtful. Meanwhile the opportunities for satisfying key military constituencies are limited, given that the new rulers are themselves at the top of the military hierarchy, that no new states are to be created inside Nigeria, and that retrenchment is the order of the day in the administration as in the public sector as a whole.

NOTES

1. The current (March 1984) military-ruled states of Africa are: Benin (formerly Dahomey), Burundi, Central African Republic, Chad, Congo, Egypt, Equatorial Guinea, Ethiopia, Ghana, Liberia, Libya, Mali, Madagascar, Mauritania, Niger, Nigeria, Rwanda, Somalia, Sudan, Togo, Upper Volta, and Zaire.

2. See the section on Sierra Leone below.

3. Milton Obote's comeback in Uganda (1980) in the wake of Amin's overthrow is the second successful attempt by a former civilian president to regain office from a military leader who had toppled him, the first being in Central African Republic (September 1979) when David Dacko regained power from 'Emperor' Bokassa. Both cases were made possible largely through external military assistance.

4. For details of the Dahomean (or Beninois) experience, see Samuel Decalo, Coups and Army Rule in Africa (Yale, 1976).

5. These dimensions of the problem have been treated by the author in previous essays, especially "Towards Explaining Civil-Military Instability in Contemporary Sub-Saharan Africa : A Comparative Political Model", Current Research on Peace and Violence, 8, 1978, pp.192-94; "Ethnicity and Army Recruitment in Colonial Plural Societies", Ethnic and Racial Studies, 2, 1979, pp.151-65; "Army in a Multi-Ethnic Society : The Case of Nkrumah´s Ghana, 1957-1966", Armed Forces and Society, 2, 1976, pp.251-72; "Ethnicity, the Military, and Domination : The Case of Obote´s Uganda, 1962-1971", Plural Societies, 9, 1978, pp.85-110; and "Military Organisation in Multi-Ethnically Segmented Societies", in Cora B. Marrett & Cheryl Leggon, eds, Research in Race and Ethnic Relations (Greenwich, Conn.: JAI Press, 1979).

6. As I have argued in "Towards Explaining Civil-Military Instability ...", loc.cit.

7. See J. ´Bayo Adekanye (Adekson), "On the Theory of a Modernising Soldier : A Critique", Current Research on Peace and Violence, 8, 1978, p.35.

8. Quoted in New Nigerian, 3 January 1978, pp.1-5.

9. Ali A. Mazrui, "The Lumpen Proletariat and the Lumpen Militariat : African Soldiers as a New Political Class", Political Studies, 21, 1973, pp.1-12.

10. The theme is discussed, though not necessarily with reference to the military, in Adebayo Adedeji, ed, Indigenization of African Economies (London: Hutchinson, 1981).

11. Ali A. Mazrui, Soldiers and Kinsmen in Uganda, Ch.12, "Economic Transformation under a Military Ethnocracy" (London: Sage, 1975).

12. Eboe Hutchful, "A Tale of Two Regimes : Imperialism, Military Intervention, and Class in Ghana", Review of African Political Economy, 14, 1979.

13. J.F.E. Ohiorhenuan, "Nigerian Economic Policy Under the Military", in Nigerian Economic Society, The Nigerian Economy under the Military (University of Ibadan, 1980), pp.79-83.

14. See Karl Marx, The Eighteenth Brumaire of Louis Bonaparte.

15. Yet experience under the Nkrumah government in Ghana suggests that it is possible to wean this

class of persons - the so-called "verandah boys" - from militarism, through a vigorous public works programme promising jobs to most, though in the process they cease to be "urban unemployed" and become part of "organised labour".

16. This assumes of course that the restoration government is drawn from other than radical parties, which has to date been the case in all African post-military regimes.

17. See J. ´Bayo Adekanye (Adekson), "The ´Brawn´ versus ´Brain´ Conflict in Contemporary African Civil-Military History and Thought", Plural Societies, 10, 1979, pp.7-10.

18. A phrase borrowed from Alfred Vagts, A History of Militarism (revised edition, New York: Free Press, 1959).

19. Vagts, op.cit., pp.355-59, writing admittedly from a different milieu, would consider these as a straightforwardly ´pro-military´ group in any political context.

20. West Africa, 18 October 1982, p.2747.

21. Sierra Leone is the only exception here, having since 1968 held as many as three general elections (1973, 1977, 1982) and one national referendum, all characterised by intense political violence; see below for factors explaining Sierra Leone´s uniqueness as a post-military state.

22. S.E. Finer, The Man on Horseback (second edition, London: Penguin, 1975) p.221.

23. Emmanuel Hansen & Paul Collins, "The Army, the State and the ´Rawlings Revolution´ in Ghana", African Affairs, 79, 1980, pp.3-23.

24. See my "Towards Explaining Civil-Military Instability ...", loc.cit.

25. To adapt the title of F.G. Bailey, Stratagems and Spoils (Oxford: Blackwell, 1969).

26. Dennis Austin & Robin Luckham, eds, Politics and Soldiers in Ghana (London: Cass, 1975) pp.300-02.

27. ibid.

28. Writing under the pseudonym of Kontopiaat, "Return to the Barracks", The Legon Observer, 3, 7-20 June 1968.

29. See A.A. Afrifa, The Ghana Coup (London: Cass, 1967), and A.K. Ocran, A Myth is Broken (London: Longmans, 1968).

30. Austin & Luckham, op.cit., p.115.

31. ibid., p.102.

32. ibid., p.115.

33. ibid., p.116.

34. Adu Boahen, "The New Crop of Politicians

and the Military", <u>The Legon Observer</u>, 4, 1-5 September 1969, pp.6, 20.

35. Austin & Luckham, <u>op.cit.</u>, p.304.

36. <u>ibid.</u>

37. For a detailed, if slightly jaundiced, account of this period of Ghana´s military rule, see Mike Oquaye, <u>Politics in Ghana 1972-1979</u> (Accra: Tornado Publications, 1980).

38. <u>West Africa</u>, 25 February 1980, pp.370-71; 10 March 1980, p.455; 19 May 1980, p.898.

39. Other options believed to have been toyed with, but never implemented, included sending Rawlings on a course abroad, palming him off with a foreign ambassadorial posting, or offering him a seat in the new Council of State in an advisory capacity to the Limann government; he apparently showed no interest in any of these offers.

40. Nkrumah had tried a similar technique, by retiring Generals Ankrah and Otu.

41. See Thomas S. Cox, <u>Civil-Military Relations in Sierra Leone : A Case Study of African Soldiers in Politics</u> (Harvard, 1976) for the best study of Sierra Leone´s civil-military relations during this period; other complementary materials bearing on the problem can be obtained from Christopher Clapham, <u>Liberia and Sierra Leone : An Essay in Comparative Politics</u> (Cambridge, 1976).

42. Cox, <u>op.cit.</u>, p.206.

43. For useful background materials, see the two works edited by Oye Oyediran, <u>Nigerian Government and Politics under Military Rule 1966-79</u> (London: Macmillan, 1979), and <u>The Nigerian 1979 Elections</u> (Macmillan, 1981). See also the concluding section of J.´B. Adekanye, <u>Nigeria in Search of a Stable Civil-Military System</u> (Aldershot: Gower, 1981), pp.140-42.

44. Adekanye, <u>op.cit.</u>, pp.121-29.

45. <u>ibid.</u>, p.44.

46. <u>ibid.</u>, pp.134-36.

47. Billy J. Dudley, <u>Instability and Political Order : Politics and Crisis in Nigeria</u> (Ibadan University Press, 1973).

48. See Robin Luckham, <u>The Nigerian Military</u> (Cambridge, 1971), and N.J. Miners <u>The Nigerian Army 1958-66</u> (London: Methuen, 1971).

49. General Obasanjo´ had reacted similarly to Rawlings´ first coup of May 1979, but even in this case one could not rule out an element of self-interest. The Rawlings coup, like the subsequent Doe one, being an action organised by lower-ranking military elements, carried

considerable potential for a revolutionary attack on the military hierarchy, to which no ruling general would take kindly. In other words, for General Obasanjo as for President Shagari, one detects an understandable fear of the domino effect of this kind of action sweeping across West Africa.

50. This was the message of student demonstrations and continuous threats of labour unrest in Nigeria during 1983.

Chapter Five

INDONESIA : SLOW MARCH INTO AN UNCERTAIN FUTURE

Ulf Sundhaussen and Barry R. Green

INTRODUCTION

The army under General Soeharto assumed power in
Indonesia in 1966/67.(1) Since then Soeharto has
continuously held the office of President of the
Republic of Indonesia, and in all likelihood will
continue to do so for some time to come, having been
re-elected to another five-year term early in 1983.
Soeharto is thus one of the longest serving military
men in the office of head of state. Yet his rule
cannot continue indefinitely. By Indonesian life
expectancy standards he is becoming an old man.(2)
There are, moreover, other indications for change.
One is that the military, the primary pillar on
which his rule rests, is undergoing drastic
personnel change: only a tiny handful of officers
of his generation still hold military and
governmental positions, with basically all senior
military positions passing into the hands of a
distinctly different generation of military leaders
who did not share his military and political
experiences, have different training backgrounds and
educational standards, and can therefore be expected
to have different attitudes and values. Second, the
so-called 'New Order' of General Soeharto is not,
appearances to the contrary, a static society. In
fact, as will be argued in this essay, Indonesia is
undergoing dramatic change, the dynamics of which
will require adjustments to the present distribution
and wielding of power.
    The key issue, then, to which this chapter is
addressed, is in what direction the political system
in Indonesia is developing. But before we can enter
into speculations and guesstimates about the future
of Indonesia, we have first to establish what kind
of military regime the New Order is, and what are

its options for change.

THE BASIC CHARACTERISTICS OF THE NEW ORDER

Problems in the Classification of the New Order

Indonesia is rarely included in comparative studies. One reason for this omission is that comparativists have great difficulties in coming to grips with the multitude of essential factors which have to be taken into account to make sense of Indonesian politics.(3) On the other hand, specialists on Indonesia have been, in the main, extremely parochial in their approaches, and have therefore kept well clear of finding the right slots for Indonesia in comparative typologies. Instead of integrating Indonesia into Third World studies, they have more often that not concentrated on two internal issues: first, they have disputed whether Indonesian politics is best to be explained within the terms of Indonesia's cultural traditions, or within the framework of a neo-Marxist economic determinism; and second, a lot of academic energy has been wasted on partisan declarations regarding the legitimacy of particular regimes, in which non-indigenous norms and values usually determine the final moral pronouncements. With respect to the present regime, the bloody massacres of hundreds of thousands of communists by the army in collusion with the youth organisations of the non-communist parties in late 1965 have added considerably to the bitterness of these debates, which have retarded rather than advanced our understanding of Indonesia. This essay will attempt to circumvent these pitfalls, in order to integrate Indonesia into this comparative study. Thus the mass killings of 1965 will figure here only as a factor in the civil-military relationship, rather than as a moral determinant, and greater emphasis will be placed on the normalcy of New Order politics since, say, 1970. To determine the character of the New Order of General Soeharto, we will have to establish a theoretical construct within which it can be analysed. This construct is based on the assumption that military regimes do not exist in a political vacuum, no matter how willing and capable they are to apply oppressive means to control the polity. This, then, means that military regimes and their policy options have to be evaluated within the framework of their relationship with the civilian environment.

Variables in the Civil-Military Relationship in Indonesia

The Level of Perceived Threat from Civil Society.

The perception in the military of threat from civil society has largely been determined by the internal wars fought by the army almost from its inception in 1945. These civil wars arose out of the highly divided societal system of mutually antagonistic forces that make up post-colonial Indonesia, and which politicians were unable to reconcile. Briefly, two-thirds of the population are concentrated on the comparatively small island of Java. Thus political power rests on Java, while economic prouction, especially in the export industries, is highest on Sumatra, Sulawesi and Kalimantan, a situation which has always lent itself to charges of Java exploiting the so-called ´Outer Islands´. Ethnically, linguistically and culturally, Indonesia is divided into more than three hundred groups, of which the ethnic Javanese of East and Central Java (almost 50% of the total population) and the Sundanese of West Java (about 17%) are numerically by far the most important. Among the officially recognised religions of Indonesia are Islam, Hinduism, Buddhism, and Catholic and Protestant Christianity. Often made claims that 90% of the population are Moslem are grossly misleading. A substantial percentage, especially of the ethnic Javanese (the so-called abangans) distinguishes itself from orthodox Moslems (santris) by adhering to the agama Java, the ´Javanese religion´, a syncretic mixture of animism, Hinduism and Buddhism, with Islam being only the last layer. But even within the santri community there is a deep division between traditional and modernising strands in Islam. Socially, the society was divided into nobility (priyayi), the normally wealthier santris, and the poorer abangans.(4) These traditional status and income categories are gradually changing with the emergence of modern elite groups, an industrial urban prolatariat, and increasing landlessness among the rural poor.(5) Along these ethnic, social and religious lines the Indonesian political elites created political parties. The Nationalist Party (PNI) was largely the party of the priyayis, the Communists (PKI) recruited primarily among the abangans, while the Party of Islamic Scholars (NU) represented the

traditional _santris_.   These   three   parties   were
mainly backed by the ethnic Javanese, while   the
Masyumi,   the   party   of   the   modernising   Moslems,
enjoyed most of its support in West Java and   the
Outer Islands.

The   army   officer corps has always been mainly
recruited from among the ethnic Javanese, and   in
religious and cultural terms adhered overwhelmingly
to the _agama Java_.   At   the   outbreak   of   the
anti-colonial   revolution, the army accepted the PKI
as just   another   force   backing   the   struggle   for
independence.   But   by 1946 the clashes between the
regular army and the Communists began with an armed
confrontation in the city of Cirebon. In 1948 the
PKI started a large scale uprising in Madium, East
Java,   which   the   army   crushed on   the   orders of
President Sukarno. In the latter half of the era of
Guided Democracy (1959-65), the PKI emerged as   the
most serious challenger to the army´s position of
junior partner   in   the   government   coalition.   To
undermine   the   army´s   position,   the   Communists
demanded the creation of   a network of political
commissars in   the   military, and the creation of a
militia of workers and peasants. They also spread
the   rumour   that the army leadership, with the help
of the CIA, planned to overthrow Sukarno.   They
maintained   close   contact with elements of   the
Presidential Guard Regiment, the Jakarta garrison,
and the air force, who with the help of Communist
and Nationalist youths kidnapped and murdered the
army commander, General Yani, and five of his
colleagues on 1 October 1965. When Sukarno refused
the army´s request that Communist leaders be tried
for their involvement in these events, the army and
its civilian allies eliminated the PKI in an orgy of
mass killings.

While   the   clash   with   the   PKI   has to be
explained mainly in ideological and, in   the   later
stage, in class terms, rather than in terms of
religious and cultural cleavages, the confrontation
with Islamic fundamentalists lends itself more to
the latter kind of explanation. Although the army
always contained _santri_ officers like A.H. Nasution,
the officer corps including its devout Moslems were
never willing to tolerate Moslem radicals striving
for an Islamic state. Clashes with an Islamic Army
of Indonesia began in late 1948 in West Java, and
spread to other parts of Indonesia. It took fifteen
years of prolonged fighting before the _Darul Islam_
was finally crushed in 1963.

The third major force with which the   army   did

battle comprised a motley of separatists and groups opposed to a unitary state. When the Dutch after the failure of their second attack on the Republic agreed to transfer sovereignty to the Indonesians in 1949, they did so with the proviso that the nationalists accept a federal structure for the post-colonial state. But within half a year of this treaty, the federal order had been dismantled. Most of the federal states voluntarily or under political pressure agreed to merge into a unitary state, but in West Java and Sulawesi federalist forces had to be put down by the army. Thereupon the Ambonese of the South Moluccas seceded and fought a guerilla war until 1962. Moreover, the forceful integration of the federalist inclined minorities in West Java and the Outer Islands during 1950 had not eliminated the fears of Javanese domination. By 1956 most of the Outer Islands were in rebellion against Jakarta, and this two years later led to open warfare.

The army regards itself not only as the defender of the state against outside forces but also as the guarantor of internal security, and for the first two decades of its existence found itself in constant struggle against either the Communists, regionalists supported by the Masyumi and the Socialist Party (a party of Western democratically inclined intellectuals), or Islamic fundamentalists. Although armed rebellion has never succeeded, and except for some token activities by Communists in West Kalimantan, Papuan resistance in West New Guinea, and Fretilin's struggle in newly-acquired East Timor, has basically stopped since General Soeharto assumed government, the military not only feels hostile towards, but even threatened by, Communism, religious fanaticism, and regionalism. These forces are denied their own political organisations and representation, and this, for fear of revenge, will remain unchanged at least as long as the military can maintain itself as the supreme political force in Indonesia.

The Unity of the Military. To confront these various forces in the past and present has required a relatively high degree of military unity. It may well be argued that such unity has not always existed: after all, most rebellions have involved, or even been led by, military personnel.(6) On the other hand, every uprising involving military officers led to purges of the armed forces, making it increasingly an ideologically more cohesive force.(7) After the events of 1 October 1965 and their aftermath, which led to the most extensive purges in all services of leftists, Sukarnoists and, by 1969, of radically democratic officers in sympathy with the underground Socialist Party, the military has become even more monolithic.

Before Soeharto's presidency, service commanders used to maintain a degree of cohesiveness by keeping close control over promotions and assignments. This method of control has been perfected since 1969. Moreover, a distinct ethos regarding the duties of the soldier not only as a military professional but as a socio-political actor responsible for safeguarding the integrity of the state, has been fostered from that moment in late 1948 when the civilian cabinet surrendered to advancing Dutch troops while the army decided to keep fighting. This ethos has taken even deeper root in the military ever since an army seminar on the role of the army in the New Order had somewhat presumptuously concluded that "all the people's hopes for well-being are focussed on the Armed Forces in general and the Army in particular".(8)

The practical consequences of these policies are that the military has become a united force providing firm support for the regime. In fact, they are the most important pillar of the regime, strong but silent, confined to carrying out orders without being allowed to influence the process of decision-making. Practically all decision-making power, inside and outside the military, rests with one man, the President, regardless of the fact that Soeharto has officially retired from military service. There are senior officers who have influence, in that they have the ear of the President and may be able to affect policies, but they can neither pressurise him nor make decisions independently of the President or against his will.(9) Those who come to be suspected of stepping out of line are fired, as happened to General Nasution who headed the MPR until 1972, or General Soemitro, the chief of the all-powerful internal security agency, KOPKAMTIB, when he seemed to have become too friendly with student protesters in 1974.

Conversely, the President picks his chief executives inside and outside the military singlehandedly and without much consultation, as is evidenced in his choice of the last two armed forces commanders (nether of whom, by the prevailing standards guiding military promotions and assignments, had been eligible for the post), or in the surprise elevation of a retired general without

great standing in either the military or political
life, Umar Wirahadikusumah, as his running mate in
the 1983 presidential election. All these decisions
were, without so much as a murmur, accepted by the
officer corps on active duty.

Yet there are cracks in the unity of the
military, some visible and some not. The most
visible, or vocal, criticism of the regime emanating
from military circles comes from retired senior
officers, like Generals Nasution, Dharsono, and Ali
Sadikin, who have formed associations with the more
or less explicit purpose of reforming the regime and
altering at least some of its policies.(10) These
groups have the so far passive sympathy of civilian
activists, and more importantly some placid support
among serving officers as well. The so far
invisible crack in the unity of the military
concerns the changing of generations in the officer
corps. The 'generation of 1945', the officers who
joined the 'revolution' against the Dutch with
little formal military training, and who developed
the particular ethos referred to above as a result
of their experience in the politically stormy years
of the Republic, has faded from active service.
They are being replaced by a new brand of officers,
men who joined the military from 1958 onwards after
an almost complete suspension of recruitment for
eight years. (The handful of officers recruited
between 1950 and 1958 now hold the most senior
positions.) This young generation (generasi muda)
not only has a very different military education and
training, but also lacks the specific revolutionary
political experiences of its superiors. The
differences in training and experience are likely to
have political repercussions,(11) but in the absence
of political pronouncements by the generasi muda it
is not clear what political attitudes have developed
among the young officers. On the surface, at least,
it looks as if military politics will remain much as
it is now. But the Indonesian authorities were
aware of the differences between the generations and
the possibility of a change in politics once the
generasi muda had taken over the government. They
therefore took measures as early as 1972 to secure
the transfer of the values of the older generation
to the younger officers. A seminar in that year
laid down the guidelines for this transfer of
values.(12)

The Differentiation of the Military from Civil
Society. While it may be argued that unity had

101

initially been quite low, and then increased, the opposite may be said for the differentiation of the military from civil society. It would be incorrect to suggest that the army had ever been completely non-political. But with a few exceptions it could be generalised that for the first decade or so civilian politicians intruded into the military sphere rather than vice versa. The army fought civilian encroachment, and especially the efforts by civilian parties and cabinets to indoctrinate it with the particular ideology of the government of the day, by declaring the 1945 Constitution and the Pancasila, proclaimed by Sukarno in early 1945 to be the state ideology of the Republic to come, as its sole ideological foundation. The Pancasila, or Five Pillars, consist of the Belief in One God, Nationalism, International Cooperation, Democracy, and Social Justice. In defence of the Pancasila and the values they stand for, the army has fought anti-nationalist separatists, atheist Communists, and intolerant religious fundamentalists, or so its leaders claim. They saw themselves above ´divisive´ party politics, and despised the party politicians who until 1957 seemed to have been primarily occupied with pursuing their own interests and toppling cabinets.

When, in 1957, parliamentary democracy folded up in Indonesia as in so many other developing countries, the army leaders came to believe that they could no longer stand aside. They would no longer be the "dead tool of the government of the day", but nor would they assume control of the government. According to the then army commander, Major General Nasution, the army would follow a ´Middle Way´, offering its services to the nation and insisting on being involved in all state activities and represented in all state agencies, but not as the dominant force; as the upholders of national integrity, the principal defenders of the Pancasila, and "shareholders of the revolution", they had historic rights to participate in charting the course of the nation.(13) In essence, the army became the junior partner in a coalition with the President to create a new political system, a more stable, and more authoritarian, Guided Democracy. The concept of the Double Function, dwi-fungsi, was born: the armed forces had not only military functions to perform, but had to shoulder civilian tasks as well.

Under the New Order, dwi-fungsi has expanded to such an extent that it no longer bears any

Indonesia: Slow March into an Uncertain Future

resemblance to the Middle Way concept which originally gave birth to it. The army is no longer the junior partner in government but, through General Soeharto, the only independent force in the government. The army is not merely represented in all state agencies, but controls them.(14) The military holds the power in Indonesia, and despite earlier assurances that "Indonesia would not practice militarism and dictatorship",(15), appears to be intent on hanging on to it at all costs. Military spokesmen have never given any indication that the concept of dwi-fungsi may be abandoned or at least scaled down.

On the other hand, the Pancasila which the army claim is the ideological foundation of the New Order, clearly stipulates democracy. Accordingly, the New Order has allowed political parties to exist provided they adhere to the Pancasila, and has held regular general elections. In order that these elections should not endanger the government, Soeharto created his own party, GOLKAR, out of a loose federation of so-called ´functional groups´ (occupational, women´s and youth organisations), which in the election campaigns enjoys all the advantages that a government can provide.(16) So far, in all three elections held since Soeharto came to power, GOLKAR has consistently outpolled all other parties together, securing over 60% of the votes. Moreover, a deal struck with the parties in the discussions over a new election law during 1967-69 stipulates that the President appoints 100 out of 460 parliamentarians. Furthermore, the MPR which consists of all parliamentarians plus an equal number of appointees from the regions, the military and other functional groups, and the political parties, and which elects the President, is packed to such an extent with loyal supporters that running a candidate against Soeharto has appeared to be an exercise in futility. To top it all, in Soeharto´s Pancasila democracy parliamentary votes are rarely counted. Since the introduction of Guided Democracy, ´Indonesian Democracy´ has been defined as a process in which decisions are made on the basis of consensus (mufakat) to be arrived at by deliberation (musyawarah), not by parliamentary majorities outvoting minorities. This makes it impossible to outvote the government, even if a majority could be mustered willing to censure Soeharto.

But musyawarah works both ways, and essentially in favour of minorities: parliamentary minorities, in this case the traditional political parties, can - if they put their minds to it - withhold their consensus and thereby block legislation without ´having the numbers´. In fact, this has been practiced several times, but by no means excessively or even extensively. This, of course, raises the question to what extent parties provide effective opposition and political alternatives, or more fundamentally, whether there still exists a degree of autonomous political organisation in <u>Pancasila</u> democracy worth speaking of.

<u>The Level of Autonomous Political Organisation</u>. The literature on current Indonesia will invariably describe civil-military relations in terms of government oppression of civilian groups and parties, interference in party congresses and the preselection of parliamentary candidates, rigging elections and intimidating voters, press censorship, the continuous holding without trial of communists arrested for their alleged involvement in the October 1965 ´coup attempt´, and the general depoliticisation of society. All of the instances recorded may be assumed to be correct. The inferences drawn from them, however, may reflect something less than the full truth.

The PKI was banned by the New Order; the Socialist Party (PSI) and the Masyumi, banned by Sukarno, have remained so for their involvement in the regional rebellion in the late 1950s, though a new party, the PMI or Parmusi, was allowed to form to cater for the former Masyumi constituency, provided that it revitalised neither the old Masyumi leaders involved in the rebellion, nor the Masyumi´s old links with radical Islamic ideas. Politicians have been edged out of ministries and government offices which they had milked in the past for either personal gain or party coffers, but at the same time parties have been given subsidies for regular as well as special (party congresses) purposes. The evolution of the party system is a particularly contentious issue. Given the inefficiency of a multi-party system which until 1957 had consistently produced unstable coalition government, the MPR(S) in its 1966 session concluded that it would serve democracy to reduce even further the number of existing parties. This ´simplification´ started in earnest after the enforced experiments with a two-party system by New Order hawks in West Java had come to a halt due to party objections and government intervention. By March 1970, following the age-old cleavages in Indonesian society, the non-Moslem parties (PNI, the protestant party Parkindo, the Catholic Party, the small nationalist IP-KI, and the Trotskyist Murba Party) had formed a 'Nationalist Alliance', and were seen as having thereby gained the upper hand over the Moslems.(17) The Moslem parties (NU, PMI, Perti, and PSII) followed suit and formed a similar alliance. After the elections of 1971, it became obvious that these loose alliances had to be transformed into united party organisations if parties did not wish to fade away completely. However, it soon became apparent that the party politicians in the new super-parties were, just as in their pre-1957 days, unable and unwilling to present a reasonably united front. Both the non-Moslem Indonesian Democratic Party (PDI) and the Moslem Unity Development Party (PPP) were, and have remained, riven by selfish cliques which have put personal interests above those of the party. And despite the initial enthusiasm which at least some of the politicians had shown for the new party system(18) - the advantages of larger alliances, after all, are all too obvious - the government and its 'bullyboy tactics' came to be blamed for a disaster which in the first place was the making of the civilian politicians.(17) Most foreign observers have followed this line of argument and, inexplicably, absolved the politicians from all blame.

The results of the three elections held under the New Order show a consistently low electoral support for all parties except the NU, no matter whether they federated into larger parties or not, as Table I indicates.(19) (For comparative purposes, the Table also shows the results of the only other election ever held, that of 1955.)

Certainly, the poor showing is partly to be attributed to voters' intimidation by the government and the army. But this is not the full story. The support for the NU shows that it has been possible to vote for the opposition. The question is, what is to be gained by casting one's vote for a religious party (whether Moslem or Christian) which is not in government, and is not going to be the government? As has been pointed out,(20) the Moslem community has become aware that, despite assumptions to the contrary, it does not constitute a majority. It was not a betrayal of principles, but rather an increasingly sophisticated pragmatism in the electorate, that led a prominent Moslem student leader to bemoan "that men no longer feel themselves drawn to the Islamic parties and organisations, and that as a result their attitude can be described with the slogan: ´Islam Yes, Islamic Party No´."(21)

TABLE I

Indonesian General Election Results, 1955-1982
(Percentage of Votes Cast by Party)

	1955	1971	1977	1982
Moslem Parties				
Masyumi/Parmusi	20.9	5.4		
Nahdatul Ulama (NU)	18.4	18.7		
PSII	2.9	2.4		
Perti	1.3	0.7		
PPP			29.3	28.0
Non-Moslem Parties				
PNI	22.3	6.9		
Parkindo	2.6	1.3		
P. Katolik	2.0	1.1		
IP-KI	1.4	0.6		
Murba	0.5	0.1		
PDI			8.6	7.9
PKI	16.3			
Functional Groups/GOLKAR		62.8	62.1	64.1

Not only do parties offer no prospects for the less principled, they also do not offer consistent programmes for the principled. In fact the only thing they offer to public view is the rather shameful bickering among themselves. Probably the best example of a party lacking a consistent ideological platform and programmatic cohesiveness, and thereby alienating the electorate, is the PNI. Originally the party of the _priyayi_ who controlled particularly the regional civil service, it emerged as the strongest party in the 1955 general elections. But the PKI provided a better appeal to the mass following of the PNI, the _abangans_. In the 1957 regional elections the PKI overtook the PNI. By the beginning of Guided Democracy, the younger and more dynamic elements in the PNI split away to form _Partindo_. The internal ideological contradictions increased when the national leadership embraced a policy of land reform, which clearly was not in the interests of the _priyayis_ in the regions. By 1966 the PNI came out in defence of President Sukarno who was clearly on the way out. Suffering the repercussions of this partisan stand from New Order hawks in the army, the PNI was only rescued from total oblivion by the intervention of Soeharto, who dreaded a political polarisation between Moslems and his secular GOLKAR: the PNI, later the PDI, at least had a function as a buffer between organised Islam and the regime. Obviously a party with such a track record is unlikely to attract mass support, nor will it earn the confidence of politically aware elites(22) or of the government.

The Dynamics of the New Order

After a period of defining goals and hesitantly setting up institutions,(23) the New Order has proceeded to provide a degree of order and stability hitherto unknown in Indonesian history. Order is not just a value in itself. For the New Order leadership, political stability is the absolutely necessary prerequisite for economic development. Military men are often greatly concerned about economic issues, and economic mismanagement, as occurred to an extravagant extent in Sukarno´s Indonesia, easily leads to military takeovers.(24) In fact, in the last analysis it was the question of the economy which led to the decision to oust Sukarno,(25) several months after the army´s arch-enemy, the PKI, had been eliminated and ceased to be an acute threat.

The rehabilitation of the economy has priority over any other issue including, or particularly, political development. One of Soeharto´s closest confidants, Major General Ali Moertopo, stated the government´s attitudes rather bluntly when he asserted that "Democracy which gives the right to vote to its citizens but does not guarantee the achievement of material objectives, the protection of health and security, is useless".(26) Although Soeharto and the army never tire to assure society that the true implementation of the <u>Pancasila</u>, including the <u>sila</u> on democracy, is their ultimate goal in the long or middle term, they would rather be measured by their economic achievements. Indeed, the regime sees itself as deriving its legitimacy primarily from the realisation of its claim that it can manage the economy much better than any previous leadership group.

This is not the place to discuss in detail the

economic policies of the New Order. Briefly then, the Soeharto regime inherited a shattered economy and an inflation rate in excess of 600% per annum, export earnings did not cover the servicing of external debts, and a Sukarno-sponsored population explosion increased the pressure on the already highly fragmented, inexpandable land resources on Java. Soeharto on the advice of his mainly Western-trained economic technocrats, the ´Berkeley mafia´, arrested the inflation and reduced it to less than 10%, rescheduled external debts, obtained foreign aid, and increased internal revenues. Expenditures were redirected from defence to the improvement of the infrastructure and developmental tasks, mainly by discontinuing the confrontation against Malaysia. For the longer term strategy, plans for a series of Five Year Development Plans were drawn up, starting in April 1969.

Harsh criticism by foreign observers of Soeharto´s economic policies started even before the first Five Year Plan had run its course,(27) and was later taken up by Indonesian critics advocating a somewhat nebulous ´Pancasila Economy´.(28) The main criticism centres on three issues: that the New Order leaders have taken Indonesia back into the world capitalist system and thereby opened her to exploitation by multinational corporations; that the economy is (therefore ?) not really improving; and, somewhat contradictorily, that if there has been economic growth it has been unevenly distributed due to the corruption of the new ´comprador class´ in the government and the army. The first charge would be readily accepted by the regime: after all, socialist economies or Third World countries practicing economic self-reliance simply do not produce the growth rates required to pull Indonesia out of the quagmire. The second charge can be simply repudiated by pointing out that the New Order had an average annual growth rate of 7%, which by 1982 had put Indonesia, once one of the most impoverished countries, into the category of the so-called middle income countries. The charge of uneven income distribution and ´scandalous corruption´ is more readily accepted;(29) clearly, there are now incredibly rich and extremely poor people in Indonesia. But on a comparative basis, Indonesia is not doing too badly; according to the 1981 World Development Report by the World Bank, the poorest 20% of Indonesian households earned 6.6% of the national income; this is exactly the same figure as Australia, Sweden and Yugoslavia, and

better than ´egalitarian´ Tanzania (5.8%), and
neighbouring countries such as the Philippines
(5.2%) and Malaysia (3.3%).(30) In any case,
Soeharto assures his people, more equality should be
achieved within the next one or two Five Year
Plans.(31)
     But probably the most significant impact of the
New Order on society is the social change it has
brought about. The excessive order and stability
may often have given the impression that present-day
Indonesia may best be compared to the dull politics
of the colonial era. But it would be more correct
to see the New Order as a socially highly dynamic
system. It provides "the political basis for a
capitalist revolution in the rural areas",(32) and
has given rise to new societal groups (classes) in
urban environments as well. The increasing
importance of technocrats and entrepreneurial groups
under the New Order has strengthened existing
professional associations or led to the formation of
new ones. These organisations are either co-opted
into the political system(33) or, where they are
not, are likely to turn antagonistic to the
military.(34) Similarly, an industrial proletariat
is emerging which is willing to flex its muscles;
thus strikes are sharply on the increase.(35)

The New Order as a Veto Regime

While it would be difficult to deny that the New
Order is a polity with a strong emphasis on (a
particular kind of) economic development, no one
would seriously contest that the regime is lagging
in terms of political modernisation. To be sure,
the Soeharto regime offers more political rights to
most of its people (provided they are neither
communists, Islamic fundamentalists, nor
separatists) than most developing countries, but
many critics inside and outside Indonesia will
regard this as irrelevant. Basically, the New Order
is a Veto regime which formed to ward off the
political threat posed by the PKI, and the economic
threat in the form of Sukarno´s gross mismanagement
of the economy and his unwillingness to make amends.
The 1965 massacres provide a convincing example of
this type of regime´s tendency to resort to
short-term measures of extreme political repression,
and its continuing perception of high threat from
civil society, and fear of what might happen if the
PKI were ever allowed to re-emerge, is a powerful,
yet not the only, motive to hang on to power at

almost any cost. It has developed an astonishing degree of unity which has so far enabled it to keep control over state and society; and it has, in the form of GOLKAR, developed political institutions which provide a modicum of democratic decorum and legitimacy for their control. Very importantly, the civilian politicians and parties whose existence is guaranteed by the continuous commitment of the regime to the <u>Pancasila</u>, a very important legitimising ritual, have assisted in the consolidation of power in the hands of Soeharto by endless bickering among themselves, rather than providing a loyal, yet credible, opposition or policy alternatives.

POLICY OPTIONS AND POLICY SELECTION

<u>The Four Basic Options</u>
As the introductory chapter suggests, the policy options facing veto regimes of the Indonesian kind are limited, and it should therefore be possible, having established what type of regime is involved and what constraints are operating on it, to predict its future evolution with reasonable accuracy. In the Indonesian case, two of the possible regime outcomes discussed in the introduction may confidently be excluded. First, the military party state, dependent as it is on a low level of differentiation between the military and civil society, and more importantly on the upsurge in participation which follows a breakthrough coup, is quite inappropriate. Second, the Indonesian military has retained during its seventeen years in power a level of unity which must render it proof against factional clientelism. The four possible policy choices which we need to consider in more detail, not quite coinciding with those given in the introductory chapter, therefore seem to us to be the following:
1. a continued veto regime;
2. authoritarian clientelism;
3. limited handback;
4. full handback/civilian renewal
These roughly correspond to Huntington´s four-fold choice for military regime leaders:(36) retain power and restrict participation; retain power and exand participation; return power to civilians and restrict participation; or return power and expand participation. In addition to these four options, there remains a fifth possibility, that of

´impasse´. If the regime leaders fail to act rationally by selecting the most appropriate policy option, they may find themselves aimlessly muddling through until they are overthrown in a counter-coup, or are otherwise forced to evacuate power in a less than dignified manner.

Policy Selection

The problem of which policy to select is not simply dependent on the regime leaders. As has been pointed out at the beginning of this essay, the military does not operate in a political vacuum. Just as military intervention depends on factors internal (disposition and capacity) as well as external (opportunity) to the military,(37) so does the decision to withdraw. Secondly, the aims of the regime in question have to be considered. A military may intervene for a very limited purpose only. Such a ´Moderator´ regime may therefore be willing to withdraw after only a short period in office. Other kinds of regime, like the essentially reactionary Veto regime, or the radical Breakthrough regime, usually assume power with the intention of staying there for a considerable time to come. By using our essentially functional variables of civil military relations, and adding other factors such as value orientations, we may be able to construct sets of reasons and preconditions(38) which will determine which of the above four policy outcomes are likely to be adopted. Various kinds of regime will weight these reasons and preconditions differently, but they will nevertheless determine the choices to be made.

The list of three sets each of reasons and preconditions is suggestive rather than exhaustive. The first set of reasons focusses on various kinds and degrees of internal opposition to the regime, ranging from armed resistance to political persuasion. In such a case the level of autonomous political organisation may have become so high that the perceived threat from civil society turns into an acute one. The choice, then, may be to increase oppression - to which there are limits - or withdraw. There may be, secondly, external opposition, in the form of external patron states withdrawing vital support, or even invasion leading to the involuntary collapse of the regime. Thirdly, officers may conclude that, in essence, military rule is not legitimate, or that holding political office endangers the ideological and functional cohesiveness of the military, and that the only way of avoiding disintegration is to pull out of government responsibility.

Of equal importance is that certain preconditions for a withdrawal from power are met. Certainly, all military units capable of unilateral actions will have to agree that leaving political office is the right course to take: otherwise, counter-coups or early reintervention may occur. second, for the military to agree to leave politics to civilian politicians requires that the interests of the armed forces be reasonably well protected. They will withdraw from politics only under extreme pressure if their material and ideological interests are obviously threatened by the civilian successor regime, and if their physical well-being is endangered. Finally and probably most importantly, there has to be a civilian counter-elite or elites available who not only claim power for themselves but can convey the message that they would be able to provide stable and ´good´ government (whatever this may mean in the context of a particular polity). This again brings sharply into focus the variable of the autonomous political organisation in society.

POLICY OUTCOMES IN INDONESIA

Now that we have a framework consisting of a number of variables determining civil-military relations, the basic policy options available to a military regime, and the reasons and preconditions for selecting particular options, we may try to bring these factors together in an attempt to suggest the more likely policy outcomes in the near future of Indonesia.

Option One : A Continued Veto Regime
For quite some time, it has been suggested in the literature that the Soeharto regime is essentially a military dictatorship(39) determined to retain power and restrict participation; and indeed, the great power exercised by Soeharto and the elimination of the PKI provide ample opportunity to mount such an argument. More recently, it has been argued that the government´s electoral vehicle GOLKAR has, by whatever means, outpolled the traditional parties so devastatingly that, for all practical purposes, this represents a distinct trend "towards a one-party

authoritarian system".(40)

Certainly, the government has displayed over the last eight years or so a decreasingly tolerant attitude towards dissent. But this toughening, we suggest, is the reaction of a government which, in the face of growing manifestations of dissatisfaction among important sections of society, has been unable to formulate, or communicate credibly, its middle and long term policies. Moreover, the clamour for more participation, the demands to eradicate corruption and clarify the future role of the military in society and state,(41) the proposals for overhauling the whole system of government and for changes in economic policy, have raised the regime's perception of threat from civil society and rendered it largely unable to adjust to new political situations. Yet it is highly unlikely that the regime is consciously heading for the 'permanent veto' option. There are two important factors militating against such a policy.

The first is that the level of autonomous political organisation in Indonesia is too high for a government to set up an effective single party system. Admittedly, the existing political parties are not in good shape, are losing popular attraction, and are riven by internal faction fighting. But all this could change if the government attempted to centralise power even further by pushing the parties completely off the political stage. The problem with parties in Indonesia is that they have rarely, with the qualified exception of the deceased Sukarno, produced politicians of high calibre. They have lacked 'consociational' qualities, and this has prevented them from drawing together in times of crisis. And as long as they continue to see themselves and their party organisations as reflecting the traditional cleavages in society, primarily the Islam versus non-Islam rift, the distribution of power between civilian and military elites will not be the foremost political issue demanding solution. But if the military were to move to eliminate the other parties altogether, and also remove the considerable privileges and incomes which party politicians continue to enjoy, civil-military relations could come to occupy priority over primordial issues, and unite civilian forces in their resistance to an increasingly expansive military establishment. The potential for such a united front of civilian forces should not be

underestimated: if Islamic politicians and their
secular and   Christian   counterparts   combine   in   a
fight   for   survival,   aided   by   the   ever   restive
student community, the new middle classes and the
emergent organised labour, the comparatively tiny
military establishment would be hard pressed to
withstand such a united onslaught.

The   second   reason why a permanent veto regime
is unlikely is that if it came to a situation where
the   military   had to face the general population in
the streets - not just demonstrations and riots
which could always be blamed on particular ´deviant´
sections of society - the unity of the armed forces
would be severely tested. As it stands, the
military   supports   the   government   almost
unequivocally not only because soldiers have become
part of a privileged elite, but also because after
almost four decades of indoctrination they have come
to accept that, in their role as traditional <u>satria</u>
(warriors), they have societal duties vis-a-vis the
civilian population. Abrogating these duties and
abandoning   the <u>Pancasila</u>   would   strain   the
ideological cohesiveness of the armed forces so much
that their unquestioning support for the government
could no longer be taken for granted. In short, the
reasons   advanced   in   the   introductory chapter for
regarding the true veto regime as an inherently
temporary measure seem to us to apply to the case of
Indonesia.   Such a regime would strain the unity of
the command structure, and require both a higher
level of differentiation and a lower level of
autonomous civilian political organisation than
Indonesia provides. Indonesia can no longer be
referred to in a strict sense as a veto regime, and
it is certain that it could not indefinitely remain
one.

Option Two : Authoritarian Clientelism
The authoritarian clientelist option, which seeks to
retain power, and at the same time expand
participation by co-opting the newly emergent or
strengthened middle classes, rural ´kulaks´ and
industrial labour into an increasingly corporate
system of government, represents a ´soft´ option
which should have considerable appeal to the regime.

It enables the present office holders to stay in
power by granting political concessions to those
forces which share a basic interest in maintaining
the existing political and economic order. This
requires a degree of flexibility, and the capacity

to recognise and quickly absorb potential allies. Such a flexibility has not been much in evidence, particularly whenever groups have openly clamoured for a share in power. It has even been suggested that a regime which once started out as a coalition of right-wing forces has "now been reduced to a single element: the military".(42)

Yet in an unobtrusive way co-optation has taken place since the emergence of the New Order. Probably the most publicised case of co-optation was the incorporation of the ´Berkeley mafia´, a group of Indonesian economists trained in the United States, into the economic management of the nation. But a large variety of people who in one way or another have profited from the economic strategies of the New Order are prepared to work with the regime or within the system, some openly and enthusiastically, others tacitly.

The adoption of this option could in the long run, after Soeharto had departed from the political stage and a new political management in the form of the generasi muda had taken over the reins of government, change the political system quite considerably. Civilians recruited in growing numbers into the government may gradually assert themselves. Civilians with political expertise may over a period of time take over GOLKAR from within, pushing aside the retired generals who presently control the government ´party´. Such plans and intentions have existed now for over a decade,(43) and the envisaged retirement of Soeharto in 1988 may provide the right impetus to realise them. If co-opted civilians in government, and a new breed of politicians in GOLKAR, proved to be capable leaders, the new generation of officers might well be prepared to relax their control over the state. But to do so they would require that their civilian counterparts have the expertise and ability to lead, that they be loyal to the Pancasila as interpreted by the military, and that their gradual assumption of more political power would not drastically interfere with the individual and corporate interests of the military.

Option Three : Limited Handback
This, basically, is another ´soft´ option, towards the more liberal end of the scale of available options. It would involve allowing civilian politicians to take over the government, but participation in competing for power would be

restricted to political forces which have the explicit approval of the military. In the Indonesian context, the selection of this option would mean that the PKI remained banned, and that former Masyumi leaders with known sympathies for Islamic fundamentalism, or protagonists of separatist or even federalist views, would still be barred from possible positions of influence and power.

But since civilian governments usually have not the means for control and oppression at their disposal which a military regime commands, they would be under pressure to admit ´restricted´ forces to the electoral competition, especially if they wish their likely claims to provide a more democratic type of government to be taken seriously. This normally brings them into direct conflict with the military, who may keep a close watch on the political performance of their successors. If the military has not insisted on certain veto powers by which they can block constitutionally any further liberalisation, protect the physical wellbeing of outgoing regime leaders, and prevent any significant threat to their corporate interests by radical antagonists, they may feel compelled to re-intervene to enforce their stipulation on restricted participation.

This is however an unlikely option in Indonesia for some time to come. First of all, it would disregard the notion that the military has at least some socio-political role to play. While Option Two is probably reconcilable wih current military doctrine, allowing the presently operative concept of dwi-fungsi to be down-scaled to Nasution´s original Middle Way concept, to retreat from government responsibility altogether would ´retard´ civil-military relations to the unacceptable uncertainty of the late 1950s, when the army was unsure of its role in society.

Moreover, there are no good reasons for recivilianising to that extent. There is no determined opposition clamouring for power, which could force the military to retreat to the barracks. Second, no external power is likely to exert pressure on Indonesia´s leaders to surrender power to the civilians, partly at least because Indonesia obviously would not succumb to such drastic intervention in her domestic affairs.(44) And finally, the unity of the armed forces is not endangered by the military holding on to power: more than twenty-five years after parliamentary democracy rather ingloriously collapsed from within, there is little appreciation for this kind of political system among the soldiers.

Most importantly, the precondition of the availability of an acceptable and suitable civilian ruling elite is not met. Neither the politicians in the traditional political parties, nor the civilians in GOLKAR, have yet demonstrated their determination to demand power for themselves, or the capacity to provide stable government. Under these circumstances, even the most liberal officers would not seriously entertain any ideas of surrendering control over the state to civilians. They would refute the argument that if civilian politicians are never given an opportunity to prove themselves, they simply cannot vindicate themselves: the bickering inside the political parties before or after the ´simplification of the party system´, and their failure to table any significant policy initiative in twenty-five years, do not create confidence in the politicians´ abilities.

Option Four : Full Handback / Civilian Renewal
The selection of this option normally leads to the reintroduction of a fully democratic system. It was a regular feature in Latin American civil-military relations before 1964, when military intervention often led to limited-goal short-term Moderator regimes. More sparingly, it has occurred in Asia and Africa as well, but, as in Latin America, has more often than not resulted in reintervention. It appears that only in societies with a closer cultural affinity to the centres of democratic thought and practice (such as Southern Europe) may this option mark the end of military intervention in politics.(45) By and large, it is not an option sought by Veto regimes such as Indonesia, and only exceptional circumstances may leave a Veto regime with no other viable option.

For Indonesia this policy option could conceivably mean a return to the turbulent years of parliamentary democracy (1950-57). Such a development would be relished by no one except the most idealistic democrats, of whom there have never been many in Indonesia, and those who would profit the most from it, the communists presently banished from positions of influence. If, indeed, it would mean the re-emergence of the PKI, it would not only be the army which would perceive this as an unacceptable threat, but also the existing parties,

117

since all of them, in varying degree, played their part in the massacres of late 1965. It could rekindle separatist or even secessionist sentiments in the Outer Islands, and promote the idea of jihad among the Moslems.

But even if the PKI could somehow be prevented from partaking in the political opportunities fully fledged democracy offers, a return to such a system would be firmly resisted not only by Soeharto and his contemporaries but also by the generasi muda. It would mean losing many of their privileges, and an almost complete loss of influence in the politics of the nation. More fundamentally, the military also fears that politicians in search of a constituency would return to appealing to primordial loyalties and thereby re-activate the traditional cleavages in society which are far from having been overcome. This fear is not completely unfounded. When party politicians prior to the first New Order elections in 1971 were given a freer rein to campaign for support, they immediately set out to exploit these cleavages for their own ends. Given the severity of these cleavages, a degree of authoritarian control has been considered necessary, under both Sukarno's Guided Democracy and Soeharto's New Order, until the simmering primordial values can be considered safely contained, and the dangers of separatism and violent intra-communal strife averted.

Impasse

If none of the four basic options are adopted, or the selection is made on the basis of an incorrect evaluation of the variables at work, the regime may end in impasse. Ultimately, as has been pointed out already, such a regime may be toppled in a coup, or may otherwise be forced into a 'disorderly' retreat to the barracks. There are analysts who have always considered New Order politics to constitute already such an impasse, and for the last fifteen years predicted the immediate collapse of the regime. This was to come about either from a coup originating from the almost proverbial 'young colonels' of the generasi muda, or for authors with a more morbid imagination, from the assassination of Soeharto.(46) These predictions have so far failed to materialise, but this, considering that they reflected wishful thinking rather than insightful estimates, should come as no surprise.

Of course, in an organisation consisting of

several hundred thousand men there are bound to be dissenting voices, even in a body as disciplined as the Indonesian armed forces. But the fact is that dissent has increasingly become manageable. If someone steps too far out of line, he is swiftly neutralised or even sacked. No one, not even the harshest military critics of Soeharto such as Generals Nasution or Dharsono, would ever advocate a coup against the regime. Not only have armed uprisings of any kind never succeeded in Indonesia, though this in itself is a rather powerful disincentive for such an enterprise; but also, according to the political views and values of the Indonesian armed forces, coups by themselves do not solve any problems. On the contrary, coups aggravate problems by breeding counter-coups and counter-counter-coups. Rather, solutions to problems have to be sought by deliberation and the application of newly-won insights. All hopes that the new generation of officers might stage a coup may as well therefore be buried. They have not done so so far, and there is less reason to suppose that they will do so in the near future. They are after all in the process of assuming power in a peaceful, no-risk way within the next few years anyway.

If impasse is not created by interference from coup makers, there is still the possibility that it may come about as the result of imprudent decisions by the regime leadership. The political inflexibility of Soeharto since the middle of the 1970s, already referred to above, is seen even by some close supporters as a potentially fatal lack of statesmanship. Moreover, no clear cut decision seems to have been made in regard to which of our four options are to be adopted for the future, although the efforts made to pass on the values of the 1945 generation of officers to the generasi muda, and the arguments mounted for the prolongation of dwi-fungsi ad infinitum, provide some indication of present government thinking on the issue. Furthermore, the indications given by Soeharto that he may have offered his services for the last time in the presidential elections of 1983, were made in such non-committal terms(47) that few pundits are inclined to take them seriously. But if he is serious, then the fact that no possible successor is in sight so far, enhances the uncertainties regarding the future of Indonesian politics.

But Soeharto, who despite some errors of judgement in the past has proved himself to be an exceptionally astute politician, still has several years to solve the problem of his succession, and thereby set the direction of future Indonesian politics. And given the risks and problems involved in relinquishing power, he can still be relied upon to give the issue his careful attention when the time comes. It appears to be premature to pronounce that the Soeharto regime has already reached an impasse.

CONCLUSION

So far, arguments have been presented indicating that it may not be possible for the New Order regime to opt for the permanent veto strategy, and that it appears to be highly unlikely that it will adopt either the handback/renewal or even the limited handback policies. Nor is present-day Indonesia in an impasse situation, or seriously approaching such a state of affairs. The only option left, then, is that of authoritarian clientelism. There are indications that, to some extent, this policy is already being pursued; there are good reasons why it should be pursued more vigorously; and there are opportunities to create the required preconditions to make such a policy successful in the medium range perspective.

As has been pointed out already, technocrats have been recruited into the political system to take charge of designing and implementing the economic policies of the regime. While they cannot yet be regarded as exercising power independently of Soeharto and the military, they nevertheless have enormous influence. In some very important cases, they have already displaced generals on economic assignments: the fall of Indonesia's autonomous 'oil king', General Ibnu Sotowo, which brought the giant oil concern PERTAMINA under close control by the state (and the technocrats) is a case in point. All kinds of economic, professional, cultural, political and even religious organisations are constantly being co-opted into the system, partly by various pressures but also by material incentives. The Socialist Party (PSI), after its ban by Sukarno in 1960 an amorphous organisation which never regained the status of a recognised party, has become an important ally of the regime leadership; former party stalwarts as well as sympathisers occupy many positions of influence in the economic field and even within GOLKAR. This alliance was consummated in 1982 in a rather spectacular way, when an army major, the son of Professor Sumitro Djojohadikusumo, a former PSI minister and the doyen of Indonesia´s technocrats, married into the Soeharto family.

It would be to the advantage of the regime if the policy of meaningfully sharing some power with the new entrepreneurial and industrial groups or classes could be accelerated. Until recently, it could be argued that business circles were so completely dependent on government initiatives and contracts that they could not possibly be expected to assert themselves vis-a-vis the political authorities; and given the prominent role the government is bound to play in the economic field for a considerable time to come, there is no pressing need as yet to grant these groups wider ranging political concessions. On the other hand, the more successful government policy is in generating economic activities, the less will be the dependence of the entrepreneurs on the government. Increasingly, business opportunities arise which do not require governmental consent or the mediating offices of high officials, generals, or economic power brokers of various kinds. In other words, with the dependence on government weakening, the possibility emerges that the new classes will clamour for a greater say in the polity; and to grant these circles such a greater say before they become strong enough to assert themselves, only makes good political sense. Moreover, since approximately two-thirds of Indonesia´s export earnings are based on oil, the present oil crisis is bound to have a significant impact: it affects not only the economy per se, but also the government´s capacity to buy political support by channelling funds to particular areas and groups. One particularly serious problem area is the unemployment and underemployment question. It is assumed that 17% of the workforce is out of work at the end of a high growth era.(48) To contain unrest especially in the urban labour market, in a period when lower growth rates will be insufficient even to absorb the approximately 3% annual growth rate of the labour force, two high-powered political intelligence officers have been appointed to manage government-labour relations: the former chief of KOPKAMTIB, Admiral Sudomo, has been made Minister for Manpower, with the former head of the state intelligence, BAKIN, Lieutenant General Sutopo Yuwono, as his Secretary General. Both officers are skilled political tacticians who know that dialogue and a measured yielding to demands may sometimes produce better results than an iron fist. They may conclude that at a time of financial stringency, control and even oppression of the labour force may have to be accompanied by political and industrial concessions to keep the aspirations of an increasingly motivated as well as restive labour force within manageable proportions.

Thus there are good, although not yet compelling, reasons to open the political system to a somewhat higher level of participation which, after all, would only be in keeping with the regime´s promises to implement Pancasila Democracy. The preconditions for change, however, are less than favourable. In particular, no socio-political group has emerged which openly clamours for power, and which could credibly be relied upon to provide a stable government. No such civilian force is likely to emerge, and no military elite will place sufficient trust in such a group if somewhat miraculously it were to arise, as long as the 1945 generation of military and political leaders are in control of their respective organisations: their particular experiences, bound up in a rather rigid adherence to political convictions based on primordial loyalties, do not allow for flexibility and the will to experiment with new political ideas and forms of government.

But this generation is fading away in the near future from both military and political organisations. Herein lies the chance for change. This inflexibility however is nothing peculiarly Indonesian. Experience in other parts of the world has shown that a personnel change of at least the regime leaders is normally required before a full-scale or even partial opening of the political system is possible.(49) If Soeharto in 1988 were indeed to decline renomination to the presidency, he would thereby enhance the opportunity for change; besides, his voluntary retirement would be of significance for the political culture of Indonesia, as it would signal that changing the President does not require violence and does not need to constitute a political upheaval. At the same time, the generasi muda, on occupying the centres of power, would have to be willing and able to investigate whether adjustments of the political order to the new social and economic conditions would not be in the best interest of the nation as a whole, and the military as well. Their own political views, which are not determined by the turbulent experiences of the first two decades of the Republic, may allow them to opt for a limited liberalisation of the political system, and a somewhat lower level of involvement in politics on all levels by their profession.

The adoption of such a policy is however far from certain. The longevity of some of the military regimes in Asia may suggest to them that political stability, economic development, and the preservation of the corporate and individual interests of the military may well, or even best, be secured by retaining power without granting any major concessions to other forces. For change to have a chance at all to take place, the preconditions for such a development would have to improve. Most importantly, it is imperative that the younger generation of politicians should articulate views, formulate policies, and display a degree of political competence which would entice the generasi muda to develop sufficient trust in their civilian contemporaries. But if over the next few years they fail to demonstrate credible leadership qualities without antagonising the armed forces, and thereby miss the unique chance which presents itself in the form of the change of generations among the power holders, then the opening of the political system may be retarded for a considerable time to come.

NOTES

The research for this chapter was supported by a grant from the Deutsche Forschungsgemeinschaft, Bonn.

1. It is difficult to pin-point precisely the date of Soeharto´s assumption of power. A letter of authorisation signed by the incumbent civilian President, Sukarno, on 11 March 1966 made Soeharto, then Minister/Commander of the Army, responsible for restoring order in the strife-ridden country and the undisputed strongman in the Cabinet. The June/July 1966 session of the (Provisional) People´s Consultative Congress, MPR(S), the highest policy-making body in Indonesia, legitimised Soeharto as the de facto Prime Minister, there being no provision for such an office in the constitution. In March 1967 the MPR(S) relieved Sukarno of all his functions and appointed Soeharto as Acting

President. Exactly one year later the same body elevated Soeharto to the office of full President. For somewhat different accounts of these processes, see H. Crouch, The Army and Politics in Indonesia (Cornell U.P., 1978), pp.179-220; and U. Sundhaussen, The Road to Power: Indonesian Military Politics 1945-1967 (Oxford U.P., 1982), pp.226-254.

2. Soeharto was born in 1921; for personal details, see his semi-official biography, O.G. Roeder, The Smiling General (Jakarta: Gunung Agung, 1969).

3. For such evaluations of the New Order see, for instance, J.S. Hoadley, The Military in the Politics of Southeast Asia (Schenkman, 1975); M.D. Wolpin, Militarism and Social Revolution in the Third World (Totowa: Allanheld Osmun, 1981); and C.I. Eugene Kim, "Asian Military Regimes: Political Systems and Styles", in M. Janowitz, ed, Civil-Military Regimes : Regional Perspectives (Beverley Hills & London: Sage, 1981).

4. See C. Geertz, The Religion of Java (Free Press, 1960).

5. For a more updated discussion of divisions within Indonesian society, see F. Tichelman, The Social Evolution of Indonesia (The Hague: Nijhoff, 1980).

6. Such a view is taken in R. McVey, "The Post-Revolutionary Transformation of the Indonesian Army", Part I, Indonesia, 11, April 1971.

7. See U. Sundhaussen, "The Fashioning of Unity in the Indonesian Army", Asian Quarterly, 2, 1971.

8. Doktrin Perdjuangan TNI-AD "Tri Ubaya Cakti" (Bandung, Seminar Secretariat, 1966) p.18.

9. For the structure of power in the Soeharto regime see U. Sundhaussen, The Military in Indonesia (Cambridge, Mass., MIT Center for International Relations) pp.22-60. A slightly changed version has been reprinted as "The Military: Structure, Procedures, and Effects on Indonesian Society", in K.D. Jackson & L.W. Pye, eds, Political Power and Communication in Indonesia (Berkeley, University of California, 1978). Since then the regime has not changed its structure substantially.

10. See U. Sundhaussen, "Regime Crisis in Indonesia: Facts, Fiction, Predictions", Asian Survey 21, 8 (August 1981); and General (ret) Dr A.H. Nasution, Memorandum kepada DPR tentang Pelaksanaan UUD 45 Secara Murni dan Konsekwen (Jakarta: Lembaga Kesadaran Berkonstitusi, 1982).

11. See Sundhaussen, "The Military in Research on Indonesian Politics", Journal of Asian Studies

, 31, 2, 1972, p.362; Sundhaussen, <u>The Military   in</u> <u>Indonesia</u>, pp.61-64; and D.E. Weatherbee, <u>The Post</u> <u>1958 Military Generation and the Coming New Order in</u> <u>Indonesia</u>, unpublished paper, University of South Carolina, 1980, pp.22-26.

12. See Nugroho Notosusanto, <u>The Transfer of</u> <u>Values in the Indonesian Armed Forces</u> (Jakarta: Centre for Armed Forces History, 1974) pp.13-14. For the doctrine emanating from this seminar, see <u>Dharma</u> <u>Pusaka 45</u>, published by the Army Headquarters, Jakarta, 1972.

13. Sundhaussen, <u>The Road to Power</u>, pp.122-43.

14. See J.A. MacDougall, "Patterns of Military Control in the Indonesian Higher Central Bureaucracy", <u>Indonesia</u>, 33, April 1982.

15. See, for instance, <u>Djakarta   Times</u>,   7 October 1968.

16. For the long list of the government's favouritism towards GOLKAR, and impedimenta blocking the path of political parties, see for instance K. Ward, <u>The 1971 Election in Indonesia</u> (Melbourne: Monash University Centre of Southeast Asian Studies, 1974).

17. See <u>Harian Kami</u> (independent Jakarta daily), 11 March 1970, 15 April 1971.

18. See <u>Harian Kami</u>, 15 April 1971

19. These figures are compiled from D. Hindley, "Indonesia 1971: Pantjasila Democracy and the Second Parliamentary Elections", <u>Asian Survey</u> 12, 1 (January 1972); B.S. Harvey, "Indonesia: The Search for Stability, the Inevitability of Change", <u>Dyason</u> <u>House Papers</u> 4, 2 (October 1977); and <u>Far Eastern</u> <u>Economic Review</u>, 14 May 1982. The figures for 1982 are percentages based on 91.23% of the votes counted.

20. See C. Geertz, "Religious Change and Social Order in Soeharto's Indonesia", <u>Asia</u>, 27 (Autumn 1972), p.71.

21. D. Bakker, "The Struggle for the Future: Some Significant Aspects of Contemporary Islam in Indonesia", <u>The Muslim World</u>, 62, 2 (April 1972), p.131.

22. A survey among students in the leading universities, usually considered hotbeds for anti-regime critics, showed that 57% rejected all parties. See M. Fremerey, <u>Studenten und Politik in</u> <u>Indonesien</u> (Munich: Weltforum, 1977) p.86.

23. See, for instance, H. Feith, "Suharto's Search for a Political Format", <u>Indonesia</u>, 6 (October 1968).

24. See E. Zimmermann, "Towards a Causal Model

of Military Coups d´Etat", Armed Forces and Society, 5, 3 (Spring 1979) p.398.

25. See U. Sundhaussen, Social Policy Aspects in Defence and Security Planning in Indonesia, 1947-1977, monograph, (Townsville: James Cook University South East Asian Studies Committee, 1980).

26. Ali Moertopo, Some Basic Thoughts on the Acceleration and Modernization of 25 Years´ Development (Jakarta: Yayasan Proklamasi, 1973) p.18.

27. See, for instance, R. Mortimer, ed, Showcase State: The Illusion of Indonesia´s ´Accelerated Modernisation´, (Sydney: Angus & Robertson, 1973).

28. For an overview, see A. Budiman, "The Pancasila Economy, Capitalism and Socialism", Prisma (Jakarta independent quarterly) 26 December 1982.

29. Vice President A. Malik, In the Service of the Republic (Singapore: Gunung Agung, 1980) p.314; or Lieutenant General Widodo, Sinar Harapan (Jakarta Protestant daily), 7 February 1977.

30. World Bank, World Development Report 1981 (Washington 1981).

31. See Kompas (Jakarta Catholic daily), 21 July 1982.

32. R. Robinson, "Culture, Politics and Economy in the Political History of the New Order", in B. Anderson & A. Kahin, eds, Interpreting Indonesian Politics (Ithaca: Cornell Modern Indonesia Project, 1982) p.144.

33. See D.Y. King, "Indonesia´s New Order as a Bureaucratic Polity, a Neopatrimonial Regime or a Bureaucratic Authoritarian Regime: What Difference Does It Make?", in ibid., pp.114ff.

34. See Robinson, op.cit., p.147.

35. See Far Eastern Economic Review, 30 June 1983.

36. See S.P. Huntington, Political Order in Changing Societies (Yale U.P., 1968) pp.233-37.

37. See S.E. Finer, The Man on Horseback (London: Pall Mall, 1962) pp.20-76.

38. See U. Sundhaussen, Military Withdrawal from Government Responsibility, paper delivered at the 10th World Congress of Sociology, Mexico City, August 1982, to be published in 1984 in slightly revised form in Armed Forces & Society.

39. See, for instance, M. Caldwell, ed, Ten Years´ Military Terror in Indonesia (Nottingham: Spokesman, 1975).

40. D. Dhakidae, "Poitical Parties and the

Party System in Indonesia", <u>Prisma</u>, 25 (June 1982) p.14.

41. See <u>Tempo</u> (Jakarta independent weekly), 20 March 1982.

42. Ben Anderson, "Last Days of Indonesia´s Soeharto?", <u>Southeast Asia Chronicle</u>, 63 (July-August 1978) p.14.

43. See A. Bahasoan, "Golongan Karya: The Search for a New Political Format", <u>Prisma</u>, 25 (June 1982) p.79.

44. The influence of the West on Indonesia is grossly exaggerated by those writers who wish to affix to the New Order the label of a comprador regime. While it is true that Indonesia requires foreign aid from the West, the more it borrows the more it can credibly threaten to default on its debts if creditor nations were to attempt to interfere in domestic politics. The muted reaction of the West to Indonesia´s invasion of East Timor in 1975 testifies to the lack of resolve to censure Indonesia.

45. See U. Sundhaussen, <u>Military Withdrawal from Government Responsibility</u>, <u>op.cit.</u>

46. See Anderson, <u>op.cit.</u>, p.16.

47. See, for instance, <u>Kompas</u>, 21 July 1982.

48. See <u>Far Eastern Economic Review</u>, 8 December 1983.

49. See C.E. Welch, "Military Disengagement from Politics: Lessons from West Africa", <u>Armed Forces & Society</u>, 9, 4 (Summer 1983), p.543, citing M.C. Needler and A.H.M. Kirk-Greene.

Chapter Six

MILITARY RULE IN SOUTH AMERICA : THE DILEMMAS OF
AUTHORITARIANISM

George Philip

MILITARY INSTITUTIONALISATION AND POLITICAL
ENGAGEMENT

Practically the whole history of Latin America since
independence has shown that military government is
no guarantee of political stability - indeed, rather
conspicuously the reverse. It is, however, almost a
truism that, within South America at least,
superficial political instability has accompanied
considerable continuity in the nature of the
underlying social order. At one level, military
regimes almost always fail. That is to say, in the
end they are either overthrown or forced to make a
disorderly retreat from power. Yet by this stage
they have often served their purpose - repressing a
challenge from a radical threat to the status quo,
arbitrating among rival political factions, or
breaking through barriers to social and economic
reform. Moreover, their ability to relinquish power
under the right circumstances, even if this is done
in a disorganised way, may be as important to
maintaining an underlying social continuity as the
initial seizure of power.

There are perhaps two main reasons for this
paradox. The first is that South American societies
divide, in cases where they do divide seriously, on
the basis of class rather than religion, race or
(with a few exceptions) region. Class differences
may divide society, but class conflict is likely to
unite the officer corps of any South American army.
Whatever factor is stressed (middle class origin,
dislike of social disorder, opposition to Marxism,
institutional integrity), it is generally agreed
that South American armies have relatively little
patience with autonomous lower class militancy and

still less with Marxist politics. Mass mobilisation is rarely acceptable, and then only when firmly led from above. This military outlook itself relates to the highly developed state of South American military institutions. The high and increasing level of unity and differentiation has undoubtedly facilitated effective military intervention in politics (there is less danger of an attempted coup going disastrously wrong and so weakening the military institution) and has helped the military to maintain a long-term political role, but it may also reduce the chance of achieving political stability in the narrow sense. Before going on to discuss this point in more detail, it is worth briefly outlining the way in which the military institution has evolved throughout South America.(1)

For most countries the immediate post-independence period was one in which informal armies led, usually on a personalist basis, by individual caudillos frequently contested power. A successful caudillo ruled as an individual rather than as a particularly military figure; some held power for quite long periods although most were overthrown, in their turn, by a new military rising. Gradually, however, South American armies did become increasingly professional. The impetus to this was sometimes provided by a successful caudillo anxious not to be overthrown as he had arisen; thus Ramon Castillo reopened the military academy (closed since post-independence days) in Peru. In other countries international conflict played an important role; Brazil's army, which had never gone through a caudillo period as such, developed a strong corporate spirit and began to make professionally-motivated political demands after the 1865-70 war against Paraguay. It was the army which overthrew the Brazilian monarchy in 1889. Similarly, successful wars against Peru in 1837-39 and 1879-83 played a major part in developing a professional military institution in Chile. Finally, military professionalisation was in some cases promoted by civilian political leaders who hoped, even then, that a more professional military would be a less political one. In this, they were to be disappointed: the Argentine President Sarmiento founded his country's military academy in 1869.

One key factor in this professionalisation was precisely the development of military colleges. There was henceforth to be only one means of becoming an officer, namely graduation through a military academy. Promotion from the ranks was largely banned, and entry into the army as an officer was to be undertaken young, in some cases as early as a boy´s mid-teens. Secondary education was made a minimum requirement for acceptance. The ranks, meanwhile, came to be made up of conscripts. Conscription was introduced in Chile in 1900, Peru and Argentina in 1901, Ecuador in 1902, Bolivia in 1907 and Brazil in 1916. Although rules pertaining to conscription were often respected more in the breach than in the observance, this led to an increase in the size of the armies and thus in their organisational complexity and bureaucratic sophistication. Finally, senior European officers were in several cases brought in to organise South American armies. Thus Colonel Korner advised the Chilean military between 1886 and 1910, and the Chileans themselves were then contracted to advise the Colombian and Ecuadorian armies.(2) Argentina was also heavily influenced by German practices, while the Peruvian military was advised by French officers in the country from 1896 to 1940.

By the 1920s, therefore, the military institution in most South American countries was by far the best organised force within each society. Officers´ education levels were, in general, superior to those of their civilian middle class counterparts. Officers, because they were aware of this fact and also because the military career structure involved long postings to often remote parts of the country, developed an increasing sense of being isolated from and largely superior to civil society. Educational and bureaucratic achievements were particularly important to the careers of South American officers because, after around 1880, wars between South American countries became rare. For various reasons, moreover, the military continued to play a political role. On occasions, senior officers acted in politics to protect what had become one of their most important corporate attributes, namely their control over promotion. The position of a professional army within a patronage state would always be difficult, and officers often intervened in politics to keep politics out of the army. (One is reminded here of the Irish playwright who insisted that, far from the Irish being priest-ridden, it was the Irish priesthood which was people-ridden.) On other occasions army officers were invited into politics by civilians eager to settle scores against one another, a practice described in the well-known phrase, "knocking on the doors of the barracks". On yet other occasions, notably during the Great Depression, civilian government simply collapsed and the army was the obvious candidate to fill a political vacuum.

A major "wave" of military intervention therefore took place in South America between 1922 and 1932. In Brazil, an important but failed rising by younger officers (the tenentes) in 1922 was followed by a gradual increase in military involvement in politics, culminating in 1930 when officers helped the civilian President Vargas into power; he remained there, with military backing, until 1945. The military also took power in Argentina in 1930 and did not fully relinquish it until the inauguration of Alfonsin in late 1983. The Peruvian military likewise began a long period of rule in 1930 while even traditionally civilian Uruguay saw a military intervention - that of Terra from 1932-38. Chile entered the Depression with a military president, Ibanez, who had seized power in 1927 and the consequent obloquy of economic failure fell this time on the military. Thus in 1932 a civilian President was elected and the military stayed out of power until 1973.

These military interventions brought to the forefoot certain military-political figures - Vargas (himself a civilian backed by the military), Peron, Ibanez and Benavides - whose careers have provided the subject matter for many subsequent generalisations about military behaviour in politics. It is, however, important to remember the context within which they operated. The armies which (at least initially) supported them were well-organised bureaucracies whose essential cohesion could largely be taken for granted. Moreover, despite the fact that their most important role was often internal, they were organised and structured according to traditional concepts of territorial defence, which were strengthened by the two world wars (Brazilian fighting units participated directly in the second), and by some local territoral conflicts during the 1930-45 period. Officers, while military professionals, were still in some ways political amateurs. At the same time the 1925-50 period, despite (in some cases, perhaps, because of) the Great Depression, was one in which South American economies made considerable progress. The corollary of this was rapid growth of cities and the urban classes (particularly the middle class), social upheaval and political reorganisation.

The dilemmas which faced military rulers under these circumstances were well analysed by Huntington.(3) If military governments sought to hold on to power in alliance only with the traditional classes, they risked being isolated from new groups which were constantly being formed as a result of economic change. Such isolation was plainly dangerous in the long term although undoubtedly viable for short periods. At some point, however, it would be necessary to attempt a "break out" from this isolation, as both Vargas and Peron, in their different ways, attempted. However, a military leader who turned himself into a "populist" - who sought in other words to use his official position to win popular support from below by taking an (at least) rhetorically radical stand against other established interests - risked losing his own military base. The overthrow of Vargas in 1945 and (eventually) of Peron in 1955 gave some substance to this analysis, although it must be said that Peron maintained military acceptance during a ten year period of rule which included a successful re-election in 1951. Alternatively, according to Huntington, the military could assume a "moderator" role; that is to say, it could act as a "participant and arbiter" in civilian politics without taking over the government for long periods of direct rule. This was the pattern subsequently chosen in Brazil (1945-64) and Argentina (1955-66). The difficulty here was partly that the military would make enemies more easily than friends - groups arbitrated against would become increasingly embittered and, if only for this reason, increasingly unacceptable to the military. Polarisation would gradually replace "moderation", as to a great extent happened in Argentina after 1955. Another difficulty was that the military itself would become increasingly faction-ridden and political by being drawn - as "participant and arbitrator" - into civilian politics. Under these circumstances, the virtues of professionalism and military hierarchy would be harder to maintain than ever.(4) For all of these reasons, therefore, these various military interventions - which threw up some striking figures and some important achievements - rarely resulted in political settlements which were satisfactory in the long run. Government continued to be carried out by a series of expedients and durable political order remained elusive.

The post-War period, however, saw some further

developments in the evolution of South American military institutions. In Brazil in 1949, a group of officers who had served in Europe during the Second World War reacted against what they saw as a threat to military hierarchy from populist democracy and set up a Higher War College, the ESG. In Peru in 1950, military President Odria, looking for a way of removing certain suspected opponents whom he could not purge openly, gave them the task of setting up a strategic studies college, the CAEM. Gradually military colleges of this kind, and the viewpoints associated with them, spread through the entire Continent. These colleges ran what were essentially one-year preparatory courses for elite senior officers, generally for those about to be promoted Colonel. It would not be too much to say that the training provided at this level was (and remains) military-political rather than purely military. At the root of it is the doctrine of national security. Post-1945 developments led to a shift in the official concern of South American military establishments from an external to an internal role. Both the French (following their experiences in Vietnam and Algeria) and the Americans (fearing a repetition of the Cuban Revolution in South America itself) helped divert the attention of South American military elites toward the danger of "subversion". Subversion, so it came to be taught, was a natural consequence of underdevelopment whose root causes could be tackled by economic progress (in some countries, economic reforms were also stressed). In the short-term, however, subversion could only be checked by eternal vigilance and, where necessary, determined repression of the subversives. The political implications of this doctrine scarcely need to be stressed.(5) Finally, these higher war colleges often introduced certain elite civilians (mainly economists and technocrats) both as students and instructors. Civil-military contact of this kind would both help to spread the new military world view and would also facilitate alliances helpful to any future military government.

The "subversion" which the military elite was trained to fear duly made its appearance in the 1960s. The success of the Cuban Revolution rather went to the head of various Left-wing organisations throughout South America which, with the support of Cuba itself, sought to overthrow their own governments by direct insurrectionary methods. There were the Montoneros and ERP in Argentina, and

MIR in Chile (a small organisation whose influence was magnified by its links with the much larger Socialist Party), the Tupamaros in Uruguay, the MIR in Peru, and various other organisations in Brazil, Bolivia, Venezuela and Colombia. Moreover, the initial operations of these groups often failed to meet a strong response from civilian Presidents (Peru and Venezuela being exceptions) who proved either ineffectual or, in some cases, actually sympathetic to insurgency. Moreover, while only small minorities were directly involved in these attempted insurgencies, a far larger section of the population supported mass movements which, while largely peaceful, threatened privileged social groups who reacted by perceiving a threat to order and seeking to persuade their military contacts accordingly. In Brazil in 1964, Chile and Uruguay in 1973 and Argentina in 1976 there was economic chaos, mass social mobilisation, and either the threat or the reality of serious political violence.

In these four cases, then, there were "crisis" coups which brought to power military regimes which quickly proved much harder and more uncompromising that their predecessors. These have often been seen, with some justification, as a distinctively new type of military regime; O'Donnell has called them "bureaucratic-authoritarian" and the name has largely stuck.(6) Since the Argentine case is being discussed separately in this volume, and not much serious literature is yet available about the Uruguayan military regime, this chapter will confine its more detailed discussion to the military regimes which emerged from these areas in Brazil and Chile. It will explore the political dilemmas which they have faced, from a roughly chronological perspective. Subsequently it will discuss the dilemmas faced by all four regimes in a more analytic way by raising the question of whether there is a form of social control compatible with maintaining the unity of this type of government.

TWO CASE STUDIES

The Brazilian Military : moderator, semi-totalitarian, or clientelist ?

Many observers, including the US Ambassador, at first believed that the Brazilian coup of March 1964 would be of a "moderator" type.(7) Certainly the ESG-associated officers who assumed the key

positions after the coup (although not the main
conspirators themselves) had intended to return
power to civilians after a somewhat longer period
than usual of "cleaning up" the crisis left by the
overthrown President Goulart. A successful
"moderator" transition, however, requires three
conditions; an officer corps willing to return power
to civilians, a popular civilian candidate at least
minimally acceptable to the military, and an
external social and economic environment which can
be managed. None of these conditions was present in
post-1964 Brazil. To take these points in reverse
order, the post-1964 government embarked on fairly
conventional IMF-style austerity measures to curb
the 100+% inflation rate prevailing at the time of
the coup. These proved far more costly in terms of
growth and far slower to take effect on inflation
than the government had foreseen. While economic
growth and the popularity of a particular government
are not as closely connected as is sometimes
believed, nevertheless the economic environment
could hardly be described as favourable at any rate
until 1968 by which time the "moderator" attempt had
largely been abondoned.

Finding a popular civilian proved to be more
difficult than anticipated. Naturally enough, the
incoming military government was determined not to
hand back power to the leaders of the Brazilian Left
- Brizola or Goulart - whom they regarded as
subversive pro-Communists. These two, and a
considerable number of lesser figures, were banned
from holding public office for a ten year period.
Yet, as these figures were banned, their support
would surely devolve on semi-Left figures such as
Kubitshek (President 1956-60) who might thus be
pushed Left by this new found constituency.
Kubitshek, apart from being regarded with misgiving
by the harder line military officers, was also
unacceptable to various conservative civilians who
also coveted the Presidency but were unenthusiastic
at the prospect of electoral defeat. In June 1964
Kubitshek was banned from public office for ten
years and thus eliminated as a possible president.
The second key civilian, Carlos Lacerda, was a state
governor at the time of the coup; he was an extreme
conservative but with an undoubted charismatic
appeal. For personal reasons, however, he was
unacceptable to Castello Branco - the military
president after the coup and the leading member of
the ESG-linked "Sorbonne group". Castello Branco's
initial promise that presidential elections would be

held in 1965 was therefore quickly modified; gobernatorial elections did indeed go ahead, but presidential elections were postponed for a year. Meanwhile, some trappings of democratic government remained - Congress, for example, remained open although a purge of the Left had given it a conservative majority.

Meanwhile, the Castello Branco government came to be threatened from within the military itself. This threat came from a group of hard-line officers - a more amorphous and less intellectually sophisticated body of men than the Sorbonne group but no less capable of exerting political pressure. Beneath a certain incoherence of expression the underlying perspective of the hard liners was clear enough. These men were suspicious of all civilians and irreducably hostile to civilian politicians - the greater the politician's popularity, the greater the hostility. They had seen the 1964 coup as an opportunity to purge civilian "corruption" (i.e. civil modes of political behaviour) and were afraid of being cheated of their triumph by over-sophisticated political manoeuvering; they were, as Schneider put it "tired of holding the cow while others received the cream".(8) It is not easy to link these hard-liners with any particular branch of the military; they were, rather, unsophisticated authoritarians suspicious of the Sorbonne group. Many of them were relatively junior in the command hierarchy (i.e. colonels or majors). During the course of 1965 the hard-liners began to operate as a distinct tendency.(9)

The "moderator" project progressively unravelled as civil-military (and purely intra-military) tensions grew. In the governorship elections in October 1965 Castello Branco engineered the defeat of Lacerda's candidate in Guanabara. The two men definitively broke, and Lacerda began using his influence on Congress and the military against Castello Branco. Even more important, the election results provided the occasion for openly expressed military unrest from hard line officers. In response to this, and further weakening the possibilities of a moderator pattern, the government passed a law (the Second Institutional Act) which made elections to the presidency indirect (i.e. through Congress) and dissolved Brazil's existing political parties pending re-organisation; the power of Congress was also weakened. In the next few months it became increasingly clear that Costa e Silva, the War Minister and most senior serving officer, but a man without pronounced political views, would succeed Castello Branco when the latter´s term expired at the beginning of 1967. Increasingly this hardening government line drove the civilian Left further into opposition (joined there by Lacerda after the ultimate frustration of his Presidential ambitions); 1968 was a year of urban unrest, strikes and student riots. These developments led to further reaction from the military hard-liners. Finally in October 1968 Congress was suspended (in the event only for a few months) and the Fifth Institutional Act was passed giving the President sweeping power over almost all aspects of Brazil´s social and political life. The "moderator" pattern was definitively broken.

Between the end of 1968 and early 1974 there developed a second pattern of military rule, which can be described as semi-totalitarian. The Sorbonne officers were, for the time being, largely eclipsed by hard liners. The ascendancy of the latter was completed when a small section of the Left resorted to violence in 1969 and allowed the whole military counter-insurgency apparatus to be deployed against them. Within this the national intelligence service (the SNI) played a particularly prominent role. The SNI was created after the 1964 coup by a leading Sorbonne officer, General Golbery do Couta e Silva who became its first director, and it quickly assumed a decisive role (Golbery later told a reporter "I have created a monster"). It´s second director General Medici became president of Brazil in September 1969 after Costa e Silva had been incapacitated by a stroke. Medici was imposed by Brazil´s senior generals without consultation of any kind with civilians. Even during this period the Brazilian regime was perhaps never as brutally repressive as those of Pinochet or Videla, but at the same time it made no serious effort to relate to civil society. The twin ideologies of counter-insurgency and developmentalism were proclaimed, not perhaps with rigid exclusiveness, but certainly in a more dogmatic way than ever before or since.

Yet this pattern also proved transitory. There seem to have been two main reasons for this. The first is that the Brazilian elite as a whole was too amorphous and plural in its outlook to be content with extreme authoritarianism for long.(10) There continued to be differences of view relating to patterns of public expenditure and also to the allocation of regional political office. There even

137

remained some genuine attachment to democracy. Conflicts of outlook within the state of Sao Paulo were particularly acute. Secondly, it became clear in 1975 and 1976 that conflicting groups within the elite were willing to use the security forces against each other. The death under torture of a journalist in Sao Paulo in 1975 made this fact particularly evident. The top political authorities became concerned at the possible undermining of their own position by such methods (General Golbery, who returned to a position of influence in 1974 after losing out with the rise of Costa e Silva, was particularly hated by some of the military hard liners - largely, it appears, for personal reasons) and moved energetically to end such abuses. The SNI remained very much in place, however, at the core of the Brazilian military establishment, although it was less involved in human rights abuses than certain local military commands and appears after 1973 to have become increasingly moderate in its general outlook.

By 1974 the Left-wing insurgency had been decisively defeated and the Sorbonne group had also been able to manoeuvre its way back into power; General Ernesto Geisel, President 1974-79, was a leading member of this group. His politics were broadly similar to those of Castello Branco although the Brazilian state in 1974 was far more authoritarian than it had been a decade before. Geisel began to talk of a political "decompression" and hoped that the years of rapid economic growth between 1968 and 1973 would have redounded to the popularity of the government. Congressional elections were scheduled for November 1974. The government allowed an open campaign and hoped for a decisive victory which might have permitted an early return to civilian rule from a position of strength. In the event, however, the government party suffered some severe defeats although its control over the rural areas was such as to enable it to avoid humiliation.

During the past decade, the Brazilian regime has adopted a strategy of authoritarian clientelism while looking for opportunities to bring about genuine political transformation. Elections have regularly been held for Congress and local municipios and the political opening was extended considerably further in November 1982 when state governors were elected directly; the regime still takes care to maintain control over the presidential succession, although even this has come into question in 1984. Moreover it has undertaken several pieces of electoral engineering, in April 1977 and again in 1979, to place obstacles in the way of the opposition. In 1979 the regime reversed its earlier "reform" of 1965 and encouraged the creation of a multiparty system. Not only would this help government candidates in elections held under a "first past the post" system, but it also allowed the creation of a moderate opposition which could be co-opted into the government system when the need arose, while the more extreme opposition could be kept isolated.

Meanwhile the government has paid considerably more attention to its own electoral performance. Its main weapons are clientelism and co-optation; control over state employment is a major factor here. Political machines, based on favours and influence, can still be maintained in rural Brazil although the urban centres now vote consistently for the opposition.(11) While the technocracy and the military (particularly the SNI) have still continued to play a dominant role in day to day policymaking, the regime is increasingly constrained by the need to avoid provoking an adverse popular reaction.

The difficulty with such a strategy (from the viewpoint of the regime) is that it is permanently unstable. Admittedly, post-1974 presidents have manoeuvred with considerable skill between the Scylla of renewed authoritarianism and the Charybdis of a complete loss of political control. In doing so, however, they have had to dismantle at least part of the authoritarian state - the press and trade unions, for example, are a good deal freer than before - and to extend the scope for directly elected politicians. But the regime cannot go on democratising for ever; eventually the regime will either have to turn back the clock and try to re-impose a cruder form of authoritarianism or it will have to acknowledge that democracy has indeed arrived and accept the consequences.

Chile : the adaptability of personal authoritarianism

The Chilean case is in some ways the reverse image of the Brazilian. Whereas Castello Branco wanted the Brazilian military to adopt a "moderating" role and became more authoritarian than he had intended. Pinochet was always a profoundly authoritarian figure who soon prevailed over various less undemocratic rivals. The 1973 coup in Chile was supported by a range of opinion from the overtly semi-Fascist Patria y Libertad to the Christian Democratic party whose leadership wanted a short military interregnum to be followed by new elections. It is probably safe to say that much of the officer corps, while substantially united on the need to remove Allende by September 1973, were not anticipating a prolonged period of purely military rule.

It is likely that the intensity of the repression directed against the Left itself ruled out an immediate return of power to civilians. Pinochet's own ascendancy within the military, however, was established by his use of the DINA (the military intelligence and counter-terrorist organisation). DINA was only set up in December 1973; up until then Chile had five different intelligence services which tended to operate against each other as well as against civil society. DINA recruited its senior members from the army but also used civilian figures, often right wing extremists active against Allende prior to 1973, for its more "sensitive" jobs such as murdering Chileans in exile.(12) It also made use of a network of informants so that by 1977, when DINA directly employed 9,300 people, there was also "a network of paid and volunteer informants several times as large, honeycombing all walks of life inside Chile and beyond".(13) At the height of the repression, during 1974, DINA was disappearing around 50 people a month.

Pinochet's second main source of support was civilian. It constituted Chile's financial elite which was attracted by the strict "Chicago school" measures adopted in and after March 1975. For this elite, however, repression was only a means to an end and not an end in itself; it was also concerned with Chile's external image and came to dislike DINA's brutality, particularly after 1976 when the main repressive task appeared to have been accomplished. It also happened that Manuel Contreras, the head of DINA, opposed the Chicago economists and sought to undermine them in various ways.

In June 1977, two Chilean newspapers - owned by the Edwards family which was very much part of the financial elite - launched major "investigative" attacks on DINA. It soon became evident that such a course had the support of Pinochet himself, now securely in power and anxious to free himself from his embarrassing ally. US President Carter's "human rights" policy may also have been an important factor in this decision. Thus in July 1977 Pinochet made a speech which called for the "institutionalisation" of the regime and in August 1977 DINA was officially dissolved and replaced by the newly-created CNI; by November of that year Contreras was clearly on the way out.

With DINA no longer a major power centre, Pinochet began to seek explicit civilian support for his rule. In 1978 he fought (and won) a plebiscite against Amnesty International and other subversive influences in Chilean affairs. In 1980 he was ready with a new plebiscite; this was to approve a new constitution and an extra eight year term of office for Pinochet himself. This was passed with 65% of the vote. Although the campaign was slanted, it does not appear that the vote itself was actually rigged. Undoubtedly Pinochet had come by this time to enjoy a considerable degree of popular support, even though much of this appears to have been lost during the slump of 1982-83.

Pinochet´s rule during the last decade has been essentially personal. He himself once told an interviewer that "not a leaf falls in Chile without my knowing about it". He used DINA to consolidate his authority vis-a-vis the military, and then plebiscites to confirm support for his rule among civilians. Personal rule is in many ways the simplest short-term form of counter-revolutionary government. The ruler can project himself onto the population and, with the aid of carefully controlled mass media, maximise such popular support as is available for a government of this type. Even more important, it enables the ruler to arbitrate conflicts within the elite and to change tack when the situation requires, as Pinochet did in 1977 and has tried to do again in 1983. A more institutionalised (i.e. complex, autonomous and predictable) form of government would almost certainly be less effective in these repects. While by no means identical in every respect, Pinochet´s style of rule has evident resemblances to that of Franco in Spain, Stroessner in Paraguay and Salazar in Portugal - comparisons which suggest the potential political longevity of rulers of this type. Yet it is also apparent that long-term personal rule has its drawbacks. A personal ruler who is too closely identified with unpopular or failed policies may provide a focal point for political attack; it then becomes difficult to save the authoritarian system while removing the figure-head. Instead, as may perhaps be seen during the political crisis of late 1983, a political vacuum may be created around the leader which makes it difficult to resist a re-opening of politics when he does die or becomes discredited.

MILITARY AUTHORITARIANISM : REPRESSION AND THE NEED FOR CIVILIAN SUPPORT

Both of these regimes, then, have passed through a series of stages without finding an obvious point of internal equilibrium. They have certainly proved durable and have unquestionably altered the context of politics in both Brazil and Chile. It is not at all clear, however, that they will ultimately succeed in imposing the political settlement that they would wish. It is worth exploring a little further why this should be so while at the same time bringing in the rather less successful military regimes of Argentina and Uruguay.

Linz´ famous definition of authoritarian politics is a good place to begin the discussion.(14) Linz´ three criteria of authoritarianism were mentality rather than ideology, limited pluralism, and practical limits on the extent of police power. Linz has subsequently stressed that informality and unpredictabilty are typical of authoritarian regimes.(15) It will be helpful to discuss the three criteria in reverse order.

One major way in which the two regimes considered above (and also the post-1973 regime in Uruguay and post-1976 regime in Argentina) have departed significantly from the pattern of earlier regimes has been the greater importance of a counter-terrorist apparatus with an acknowledged role within the military institution. For this reason, and also because of the "national security" doctrine which at times comes close to a full-fledged ideology, it might seem that these military regimes had the potential to introduce a kind of totalitarianism. Timerman argued, in the case of Argentina, that a totalitarian state was already in existence.(16) For a limited period of time these regimes did indeed take on some totalitarian characteristics. However in each case powerful forces emerged from within the political system anxious to put limits on the use of state terror. Few supporters of the military governments were deeply regretful at the routine use of torture and disappearance when the victims were believed to be members of the armed Left, or those who had links with them. Yet many were anxious that similar methods should not be used to settle intra-elite conflicts; a number of examples show that these anxieties were not by any means ill-founded.(17) A counter-terrorist apparatus by its very nature is always looking for enemies to eliminate. The DINA in Chile began by repressing the MIR (an insurrectionary Marxist group), went on to harass supporters of the Allende government in general and then, in and after 1975, turned its attention to Christian Democrats and radical members of the Church. Much the same process of escalation can be seen in the Argentine case. Such an apparatus is likely eventually to pick on a target which proves unexpectedly influential with other sections of the government (or the military) and which thus discredits the hard-liners themselves. Meanwhile, if the armed Left is indeed crushed, there will be siren voices from within the system urging a gradual transformation of rule from terrorist dictatorship to a comparatively respectable form of authoritarian clientelism. Such a transition can indeed be made, and will sometimes be successful, but it is not easy to reverse the process subsequently.

Limited pluralism was interpreted by Linz in terms of recruitment into the elite. It may be more fruitful, however, to see this notion in terms of the relationship between the regime and certain sections of civil society. These will be essentially matters of calculation. Although a great deal has been written, particularly from a corporatist point of view, about relationships between the government and organised labour, these appear less important (with the notable exception of the Argentine case) than relationships within the elite itself. To speak plainly, the economic elites´ attitudes to a conservative military government are likely to be based on a mixture of greed and fear. The fear is of the civilian Left in general and the armed Left in particular; the more successful a military regime is in repressing these forces (and the weaker their original challenge), the more this fear will diminish and the less reason there will be for established groups to cling to the military "for fear of finding something worse". Greed is likely to be adquately satisfied by a high rate of economic growth if this is combined with some satisfactory governmental regulation of particular capitalist interests within a viable

overall economic framework. Neither of these two
conditions, however, will necessarily be met.
Post-1974 Brazil provides an example of difficulty
with the balancing of elite interests. Much of the
business community, deprived of a satisfactory means
of communication with the government under the
authoritarian state particularly during the
´miracle´ years of 1969-73, came to suspect that
special favours were being given to state companies
and, through them, to the military institution
itself. (Military officers in Brazil play a
prominent part in many state companies, notably in
the nuclear power industry, although direct spending
on the military is not particularly high.) Changes
in the government at the end of 1973 made matters
still worse by blocking several informal channels
previously used by sections of the business
community, particularly in Sao Paulo. There then
followed some strong press attacks on excessive
"statisation" of the economy and a sharp conflict in
the crucial Sao Paulo state between the appointed
governor (loyal to the regime) and a hard-line
business group allied to local military commanders.
When the latter began to use arrest and torture to
put pressure on the governor, President Geisel
responded by carrying out a thorough purge of the
local security forces.

Chile in 1982-83 provides an example of
difficulty with the economy itself. Without
entering here into the controversy surrounding
"Chicago" economics, it is clear that many wealthy
Chileans came to believe that Chilean monetarism was
mainly responsible for the severe economic slump
affecting the country after 1981. With the regime
itself showing no sign of abandoning its economic
programme, a number of prominent businessmen -
staunch supporters of the regime until then -
suddenly discovered that they had been democrats all
along. In Argentina economic failure also forced
the Galtieri government into a corner, from which it
hoped to escape by pursuing foreign military
adventures - in the event unsuccessfully.

Whereas class conflict has tended to unify the
officer corps in South America, intra-elite conflict
has tended to divide it. This is partly because the
wealthy, in any capitalist system, are better able
to put over their views than the poor; access to the
media may be particularly important in this context.
It is also partly because, for reasons discussed
above, state repression cannot safely be let loose
on critics of the regime when these are within the

144

economic or political establishment.(18) It is true, finally, that even the most highly institutionalised military is not a hermetically sealed unit. Civil-military contact may be deliberately kept to a minimum for junior offices, but senior officers - particularly those in direct government roles - are bound to have contact with civilians on a regular basis. Even "purely" military officers are likely to have wives and children, either savings or a mortgage, and some hope of a well paid civilian job upon retirement (and Latin American officers, by European standards, generally retire early). Simple pronouncements about the need to combat subversion and maintain a high moral tone may not be sufficient to maintain unity if there is a division within the elite on complex economic issues. The mere awareness that there is serious disunity among supporters of the regime will also be a disillusioning experience for the more purist officers.

Once either intra-elite conflict or military-political efforts to rein in the security forces (or a mixture of the two) lead to an initial opening up of politics, opposition is likely to spread. Opponents of the dictatorship - in the Church hierarchy, the press and the trade unions - can make use of relative openness to press for further opening toward democracy. Similarly, if economic failure reveals serious disunity within the military-political elite, militant opponents of the regime may once again feel confident enough to come out openly onto the streets. It may be that, faced with its own discrediting, a regime of this kind finds that it no longer has a hard-line option.

Finally there is the criterion of mentality rather than ideology. One way of interpreting this is to say that military regimes are not legitimate and do not seek their own legitimation with any particular energy. Few governments in Latin America are legitimate in the fullest, most demanding sense of the word; many regimes, however, have survived in office for long periods, being accepted by civil society more on the basis of convenience than conviction. Yet it is not strictly true that legitimacy, as such, is unimportant to these various regimes; it is, rather, sought partially and provisionally with the basis of its (partial and provisional) legitimation being likely to change over time. We have already seen how the Brazilian regime changed from an apparent moderator, to a devotee of growth-with-repression and eventually to an authoritarian clientelist regime pursuing a slow democratisation. The Chilean regime at first sought legitimation through ideas of "national security" and opposition to Marxism and subsequently sought (and received) reinforcement from plebiscite victories. (However true it may be that the plebiscite campaigns were slanted, it is not seriously disputed that Pinochet did enjoy significant popular support at least between 1977, when the economy began to recover, and 1982.) These "weak" sources of legitimation may well prove sufficient when economic conditions are favourable and internal unity strong, but may not be enough to arrest the process of internal fragmentation once this, for any reason, begins in earnest. When conditions are unfavourable, the promise of eventual democracy may prove a strong card in the government's hand (as St. Augustine might have said "O Lord, give us democracy but not yet!"), but if things go badly it will come under pressure to expedite the process and will have to walk very carefully if it is to manage its own retreat from power.

In conclusion, it is worth re-emphasising the point made at the beginning of this chapter. In South America superficial political instability has tended to coexist with an almost remarkable underlying continuity in the pattern of social stratification - remarkable certainly when one considers the extent of the economic and demographic changes in South America during recent decades, and the persistence of extreme inequalities in the distribution of income and wealth. It may well be, then, that the high differentiation and unity of the South American military have been conducive to both of these features. The military may shuffle in and out of power, not always able to control its succession or even to guarantee the length of its term of office, but it is likely to protect the social system even as it fails to stabilise the political process. This point can be made with an example. In 1934 the elder Somoza took power in Nicaragua; only once since then has there been a change in the nature of the Nicaraguan government - in 1979 when the last Somoza was overthrown by Marxist revolutionaries. In Argentina, however, there have been no fewer than twenty governments since 1934 - but there has not been a Marxist revolution and an attempt to promote one during the 1970s was brutally crushed by the military. Thus, whereas Huntington was right to point out that the existence of a purely military constituency (i.e. a highly differentiated and relatively highly united officer corps) is likely to destabilise military regimes, it may by the same token greatly strengthen the social system itself.

If we focus on the narrower question of regime stability, it is clear that the recent military authoritarian regimes of South America, which owe at least something of their character to the very high degree of civil-military differentation brought about by the further development of the military institution, have not escaped the earlier dilemmas of rule faced by their predecessors. The new regimes (Argentina 1966 and 1976, Uruguay 1973, Chile 1973, Brazil 1964 and, although not discussed here for reasons of space, Peru 1968(19)) were all more ambitious in their efforts at social and political restructuring and so either unable or unwilling to pursue the earlier moderator pattern. Even so, in one of the more significant outcomes, attempts to maintain semi-totalitarian forms of rule largely failed. (I define semi-totalitarian rule as government with an important state terrorist presence, an ideologically guided sense of direction - ideology in these cases being a mixture of developmentalism and "national security" doctrine - and with little or no input from civil society beyond a narrowly defined civilian technocracy.) There have been periods in which military rule has indeed been of this nature - Chile 1974-76 being an obvious example - but sooner or later there has been a reaction against state terror either from within the state itself or from the economic elite, and the regime has responded with a search for at least partial legitimation.

Once this search begins, military regimes need a degree of dependable support from civilians which, even when sought strictly de haut en bas, ends any attempt to govern from outside civil society. Both the Brazilian and Chilean regimes have had significant areas of civil society from which they were able to draw support - in contrast to the almost complete isolation suffered by Argentine military governments after a few years of rule. Once this stage is reached, the important thing for any regime is to keep its own supporters and clientele united. Serious internal disunity may otherwise lead important interests to "defect" from the ruling coalition, ally with outsiders and foment political conflict that may well induce the military to accelerate its withdrawal from politics. Moreover, in the absence of a genuinely legitimating formula, pro-regime civilians may easily transform themselves into a fractious and divisive grouping unable to resolve internal differences without serious conflict. Finally, an essential part of the semi-legitimation subsequently pursued by these various regimes has been the promise of an eventual return to civilian rule. Return can then be acclerated if pressure mounts on the regime, or it can be held back a little longer if the political environment appears excessively threatening, but the time must come when the regime must choose to take the process of gradual democratisation beyond the point of no return or revert to a far more naked form of authoritarianism. None of the regimes being considered here has, so far, been both willing and able to revert in this way.

What are the prospects, under these circumstances, for a genuine transformation of civilian politics? All the evidence suggests that old politicians can retain their popularity remarkably effectively during even quite long periods of military rule. Peron and Peronism has survived in Argentina, Belaunde in Peru was returned to power by election in 1980 after his overthrow in 1968. Even Brizola, after being exiled by the Brazilian military in 1964, was elected governor of Rio de Janeiro state in November 1982 - despite protests from a section of the army. The politicians themselves, of course, may have become mellower and more moderate during years in exile - but this is not always so true of their followers. Perhaps the most important change is that, when these military regimes finally do return power to civilians, civilian politicians as a whole may finally take note that it would be unwise to bank on a "moderator" coup in the event of a further military intervention. It would now be a foolish civilian politician who believed that the military could easily be manipulated into doing his bidding. As a result, all civilian politicians may have a real incentive to limit their differences, avoid precipitating confrontation and find a way of working together in order to avoid the return of perhaps decades of dictatorship. It is at least to be hoped so.

NOTES

1. A. Rouquie, L'Etat Militaire dans L'Amerique Latine (Paris, 1982) provides a good general account of institutional development.

2. Frederick M. Nunn, "Emil Korner and the Prussianization of the Chilean Army", Hispanic American Historical Review, 52, 2 (May 1970), pp.300-322.

3. S.P. Huntington, Political Order in Changing Societies (Yale, 1968), Ch.4.

4. On Argentina, see G. O'Donnell, "Modernization and Military Coups: theory, comparisons and the Argentine case", in A. Lowenthal, ed, Armies and Politics in Latin America (Holmes & Meier, 1976).

5. They are, however, interestingly discussed in A. Stepan "The New Professionalism of Internal Warfare and Military Role Expansion", in A. Stepan, ed., Authoritarian Brazil (Yale, 1973), pp.47-65.

6. G. O'Donnell, Modernisation and Bureaucratic Authoritarianism; Studies in South American Politics, (Institute of International Studies, Berkeley, 1973); on the O'Donnell hypotheses about the nature and origin of these governments, see D. Collier, ed., The New Authoritarianism in Latin America (Princeton, 1979), and G. Philip "Military Authoritarianism in Latin America", Political Studies, 32, 1, 1984.

7. On this period generally, see A. Stepan, The Military in Politics: Changing Patterns in Brazil (Yale, 1971); P. Flynn, Brazil: a Political Analysis (London: Benn, 1978); and R. Schneider, The Political System of Brazil: the emergence of a modernising authoritarian regime (New York: Columbia U.P., 1971).

8. R. Schneider, op. cit., p.173

9. A. CIA report, 28 December 1965 (declassified in 1975: Document 14F) says of the hard line that "until recently (it) represented an unorganised small minority of both active and retired officers. During the past several weeks, however, there has been evidence that shortly before the gobernatorial elections a loose organisation had begun to develop among middle-grade officers, some of them reportedly had begun plotting."

10. This has been convincingly documented in P. McDonough, Power and Ideology in Brazil (Princeton, 1981).

11. M.J. Sarles, "Maintaining Political Control through Parties; the Brazilian strategy",

Comparative Politics, 15, 1 (October 1982).
12. J. Dinges and S. Landau, Assassination on Embassy Row.
13. Ibid., p.132.
14. J. Linz "An Authoritarian Regime; Spain" in E. Allardt and S. Rokkan, Mass Politics: Studies in Political Sociology (New York: Free Press, 1970), pp.251-83.
15. Particularly in his later work; see J. Linz "Totalitarian and Authoritarian Regimes" in F. Greenstein and N. Polsby eds., Handbook of Political Science (Reading, Mass: Addison-Wesley, 1973) pp.175-411.
16. J. Timerman, Prisoner without a Name; cell without a number (London: Penguin, 1981).
17. On Argentina, Timerman, ibid.; on Chile, Dinges and Landau, op.cit., especially p.135. The Herzog case, in Brazil, was briefly mentioned above.
18. Graham Greene´s distinction (in Our Man in Havanna) between the torturable and non-torturable classes seems particularly apposite here.
19. There is a voluminous literature on the Peruvian case. See, for example, A. Stepan, The State and Society: Peru in Comparative Perspective (Princeton, 1978); S. McClintock and A. Lowenthal eds., The Peruvian Experiment Reconsidered (Princeton, 1983); and G. Philip, The Rise and Fall of the Peruvian Military Radicals 1968-76 (London: Athlone, 1978).

Chapter Seven

ARGENTINA : THE AUTHORITARIAN IMPASSE

Guillermo Makin

MILITARISATION AND THE BUREAUCRATIC AUTHORITARIAN STATE

The use of force by an Argentine military regime against non-Argentine citizens may yet prove to have a salutary effect, if the advent of yet another military regime is no longer automatically greeted with the expectation that it will be ´good for business´. Considering that since the Argentine military first entered politics in 1930, every military regime has led to impasse, the notion that such regimes are successful has survived longer than many a myth. An explanation of how the military acquire power in Argentina, how they exercise power, and especially how they come to lose power, is therefore clearly necessary.

The political role of the Argentine military is derived both from recurrent elements of the Argentine political structure, and from short term factors appropriate to particular regimes. Most basic among the recurrent elements is the structure of land ownership, which from an early period has been biased against immigrant groups. Other underlying features of the social and economic structure likewise derive from the pattern of immigration and settlement, and from the prosperity which resulted from the varied exports of the humid pampa. They have combined to produce a high level of urbanisation, the formation of a large middle class, and in consequence industrialisation and a large and affluent market. A large, urbanised and literate middle class has then demanded a level of political participation, which has been denied it as a result of the resistance by dominant groups to the practices of universal suffrage.

The first middle class demands for political

participation were spearheaded by the Radicals between 1890 and 1916. Industrialisation further increased these demands, once an organised and unionised labour force came into the political arena as a result of Peronism. The result has been a major conflictive issue at the core of Argentine politics for almost a hundred years. The electoral reform of 1916 produced an outcome which remains unaccepted by the Argentine propertied sectors, which in coalition with foreign interests have brought about military regimes. The organisation of the working class as a consequence of Peronism has been perceived as a further threat by both local and foreign interests. The military interventions of 1930, 1943, 1955, 1962, 1966 and 1976 can therefore be seen as a continuum in the sense that, for all their varied forms, they constitute slightly different reactions by the same political and social actors to the same longstanding problem: the refusal of coup organisers and their supporters to accept the consequences of popular suffrage.(1)

An additional long term characteristic of Argentine politics strengthening the trend towards militarisation is the presidential system. In such a system power sharing is extremely difficult. A president stands or falls: never does he share power. The scarcity of coalition cabinets provides one indication of this feature, the operational weight of which is further strengthened by what has now become another long term element in Argentine politics, the precedent set by previous military interventions themselves. Given such a precedent, those who obtain power as a result of elections are unwilling to share it with those who obtain it as a result of coups, and vice versa. Power sharing has thus been impeded by the presidential system, and this has been reinforced by the precedent set by coups. At the core of the political system lies a sharp differentiation between the military and civilian political authority as sources of political power.

The military interventions of 1966 and 1976, with which this chapter will be particularly concerned, are undoubtedly at base the result of the unresolved status of the crisis of representation, and the enfeeblement of political institutions aggravated by repeated interventions in the past. Where both of these cases differ from previous interventions is in the military diagnosis of the situation, arising from their much greater corporate assurance, which in turn is the consequence both of previous interventions and of the reprofessionalisation campaign of 1963-66. These have brought to the fore an element in military doctrine, present but covert and unsuccessful in 1930 and 1943, which sees the military as the proper institution for achieving the political and economic reordering of society. This corporate assurance of the military is expressed in the ´doctrine of national security´, whereby the military believe themselves to be the true and only valid interpreters of the national interest. Along with this goes a scathing dismissal of the mechanics of democratic consultation as ´demagoguery´, ´partidocracy´, or ´electioneering´. At the time that they seize power, the military claim a consensus for their actions; as their initial popularity diminishes, their reasoning becomes more elitist and dismisses popular opposition as a ´misunderstanding´ by the majority of the national interest. It is therefore not surprising that an authoritarian incumbent never calls elections in Argentina, unless either political pressure from the parties and trade unions makes them unavoidable, or else the incumbent believes that given control over the resources of the state, the elections can be won, negotiated, rigged or ultimately ignored.(2)

Guillermo O´Donnell has written on regimes of this type in Latin America and southern Europe, and has classified them as ´bureaucratic authoritarian´, because of the role of technocrats blended with military tendencies, which since 1940 have aimed at ´demobilising´ the popular sector. We may note in passing that this is the feature of military ideology regarded as commendable by big business, while the military tendency to co-opt trade union leaders may also render it acceptable to them. There is little place in such a regime, however, for political organisation. Rather, it is hoped that after placing politics and politicians in some kind of institutional attic for two or three decades, they may eventually be dusted off and all will be well.(3)

O´Donnell elaborates his conception of bureaucratic authoritarianism both from Huntington´s concepts of mass praetorianism and mobilisation,(4) and from Juan Linz´s typology of authoritarian regimes.(5) In his earlier work, he concentrated on the economic and political circumstances leading to the establishment of bureaucratic authoritarian regimes, while in his most recent book, published in 1982, he also examines their fall. Briefly, it could be said that, for O'Donnell, this kind of regime is brought into existence by the requirements of late and dependent capitalism. The reasons for the establishment of such regimes are a fear of the popular sector (hence the importance in his scheme of the military's perception of threat from civil society), and inflation. He has also used the concept of alliances to explain re-interventions, and to analyse the support which the bureaucratic authoritarian regime receives from the 'internationalised bourgeoisie', the transnational corporations, the big landowners, and of course the military.(6) In his most political vein, O'Donnell could be said to argue that such regimes come into existence to reverse popular mobilisation; in his most economic vein, he argues that they come into existence to allow a 'deepening' of industrialisation. The remainder of this chapter will seek to examine the Argentine military regimes of 1966-73 and 1976-83 in the light of these ideas, and of the points made in the introduction relating to the importance of the military institution itself.

THE 1966 COUP AND MILITARY REGIME

The Origins of Bureaucratic Authoritarianism

A brief account of the origins of the bureaucratic authoritarian state may start with the overthrow of Peron by the army in 1955. The resulting 1955-58 period of military rule severely increased the factionalisation of the military. From their pro-Peronist position prior to 1955, purges of the officer corps shifted the armed forces to a position of strong but diffuse anti-Peronism, and led to a drop in the cohesiveness and discipline of the officer corps, resulting in factional struggles between the 'reds' and 'blues' in the army, and the navy.(7) In the process, officers who had lost their posts because of the failed coups of 1951-52 were reinstated. This intolerant anti-Peronist posture of the armed forces also meant that whenever politicians attempted to incorporate the electoral majority, they were always liable to overthrow by a veto coup. This was the fate of President Frondizi, a Radical elected with Perón's support in 1958, who had to cope with endless military complaints and conspiracies because of his, to the military, suspiciously pro-Peronist policies.(8) When the

Peronists won the provincial elections in 1962, the military could take no more, and Frondizi was deposed, leading to the next period of military rule.(9)

Unlike the three previous interventions of 1930, 1943 and 1955, the 1962 coup did not result from the actions of one fraction of the military, while the majority of the officers stood by or even opposed it. On this occasion, intervention was decided upon by the chiefs of staff, and in this sense it reflected an increased level of military unity. However, once Frondizi was out of the way, there was little the officers could agree on, apart from handing over the management of the economy to the usual pro-foreign capital economists. There were conflicting views concerning the length and purpose of military rule, and the way in which Peronism should be dealt with. Should it be banned or co-opted, and if the latter option was chosen, what form should co-optation take ?

One general, Juan Carlos Onganía, emerged as the most influential man in the armed forces. His initial diagnosis was that elections could only be called if the Peronists were allowed to participate, but he was soon dissuaded from this, and other aspects of his beliefs had greater repercussions. Onganía believed that the officer corps, like society as a whole, had been damaged by politicisation. For the army, he proposed 'reprofessionalisation', or as expressed here, an increase in the unity and differentiation of the military. In practice, this meant that Onganía himself dealt with the politics, and the uninvolved officers obeyed his orders. He could take the contaminant: they were to remain unpolluted in their barracks. For society he likewise came to prescribe an abstention from politics,(10) but this came after 1966, once the reprofessionalisation campaign had strengthened his hold on the armed forces. After toying with the idea of lifting the ban on Peronism, this was once more imposed in the 1963 general election, but the 1962-63 military regime may be placed within the moderator category, though not without tottering dangerously close to impasse, given the confrontations between army and navy factions. With Peronism out of the way, the Radicals obtained - with only 23% of the vote - the presidency and most governorships, as well as a working majority in Congress. This was not a recipe for political stability or legitimacy, and the Radicals' hold on power was precarious. It was nonetheless a prosperous and tolerant period, now regarded with nostalgia by most. By 1966, however, Onganía had attained an undisputed supremacy within the military, and the time was deemed right to get rid of President Illia, and cast political parties and politicians into oblivion for what Onganía hoped would be two decades or more.

The Military Regime of 1966-73

The military regimes of 1955-58 and 1962-63 may be regarded as attempted Moderator regimes, at least in the sense that the military sought to hand over to civilian politicians untainted by the threat of Peronism. The Handback option failed, because regimes which by definition excluded the dominant civilian political movement in the country could neither gain effective legitimacy themselves, nor therefore protect themselves against further intervention. The fifth military regime, however, did not even seek to establish a Moderator pattern. The 1966 coup was, like its predecessor in 1962, planned by the chiefs of staff of the three armed forces, rather than by one faction within the military, and the new regime indicated its shift to a straightforwardly Veto pattern with its proclaimed aim of holding power for several decades. The ostensible purpose of this was to reform political practices in some unspecified manner, while it was also held that ´economic development´ would result from the political and social ´order´ which the new regime confidently expected to result from its ban on politics. One feature of the 1966 intervention which distinguishes it from its successor of 1976 is however the low level of perceived threat from civil society, before the emergence of guerilla opposition in 1969.

The new regime initially enjoyed the backing of the trade union leadership (which expected various favours from it), as well as of big (foreign) business, and was staffed by technocrats. Between 1966 and 1973, as in 1932-43 and again in 1955-58, the influence of foreign capital (now in the guise of transnational corporations) in determining policy amounted to corruption. A series of scandals relating to undue foreign influence did little to improve the standing of a regime already unpopular due to its prudish ban on films and books. By 1969, it was the middle classes and the best paid workers who took to the streets. Successive upheavals in major and minor cities made it clear that military rule had brought disorder instead of order. Inflation was higher in 1972-73 than in any earlier period, and guerilla surfaced in 1969. Such was the legacy of the 1966-73 experiment: guerilla, inflation, and the politicisation of the middle classes.

Thus, a bureaucratic authoritarian regime of the type which brought about the "Brazilian miracle", ran aground in Argentina on the rocks of the large middle class and labour movement which moved in with strikes and demands. The 1966-73 regime never graduated into authoritarian clientelism, its collapse catalysed by urban reaction. This resistance of the urban sector is largely to be expected, and given the virtual absence of a peasantry in Argentina, a military regime cannot find an effective counterweight to urban opposition.

By 1971 the policy of the armed forces since 1955, namely to ban the Peronist party, had failed and had rendered Argentina ungovernable. As is sometimes the case, only the Right can change such deadlocks. Onganía was deposed in 1970, and after a brief interlude during which General M.T. Levingston was made President, the commander in chief of the army, General A.A. Lanusse, a prominent anti-Peronist, succeeded to the presidency. It should be noted that Lanusse became President because of his position as the Chairman of the junta of commanders in chief of the armed forces. Thus the institutional arrangements prevalent after 1976 began to crystallise: lack of unity within the military led to government by junta, even occasionally featuring assemblies of high ranking officers to reach some particularly painful decision.

Lanusse, given his anti-Peronist credentials, was in a strong position to implement a change and allow the Peronists to participate in politics. As with all such gestures, in 1916, 1931, 1946 and 1955, the incumbents believed that the electorate would vote them in. Lanusse planned to lift the ban on Peronism, but the price was to be that Peron should allow Lanusse to become the constitutional president. Hence a two year struggle between Perón and Lanusse, in which Perón emerged the victor.

The 1973 Demilitarisation

The failures of eighteen years of military guardianship and government had made Perón popular once again. His return was widely regarded as signifying a healthy return to consensus politics. There were other problems which led even the propertied groups to want Perón back: consensus politics were expected to end the guerilla activities which had begun after 1969, and it was confidently hoped that Perón's union connections would end plant level radicalisation, regarded as dangerous by both big business and the trade union bureaucracies. Perón's return in 1973 therefore seemed to have something in it for every relevant social and political actor. The press and old political foes regarded the return as something of a national healing and reconciliation process. To workers, Peron's return was a guarantee that working conditions and wages would again be protected by the state. To the middle classes and to nationalists it meant the possibility that undue foreign influence would be curbed. Paradoxically, the despot of old had come to symbolise tolerance to the intelligentsia. To bankers and factory owners, Perón was a guarantee against radicalisation. The catalogue of expectations is long but not necessarily incompatible.

Providing substance to this bewildering array, there was every indication that during his years in Europe Perón had absorbed pluralism. However, much more ominous signs began to indicate that ghosts from the political past would return to haunt Argentine politics. Ten years of charismatic rule (1945-55) had failed to create a political party, and eighteen years in the wilderness had further weakened what remained of the Peronist movement. Peronism was now attractive to a larger portion of the electorate, and indeed to portions of the electorate which had previously opposed it, but popularity was not the same as coherence or organisational force. Whatever the nature of the flaws of Peronism as a party, whether inflicted by third parties or self-inflicted, after 1973-74, it was precisely these organisational flaws which would help cause the downfall of Peronism in 1976; most of the hopes of 1973-74 proved illusory.

Power was too briefly in the capable but enfeebled hands of an ailing Perón. Although Perón did not wish to become President, Mrs. Perón forced the resignation of President Cámpora,(11) and according to the constitution new elections were called in which, this time, Perón was allowed to stand. The strain of office was too much for a man in his seventies. The personalist features of Argentine politics surfaced again with Peronism in power, and help to explain why his third wife became his running mate, and on his death his constitutional successor.

By July 1974, after Perón's death, members of the financial establishment began to plan a new military takeover. Again the coup was to be of the 'new' type. It would not be temporary, it would be directed at altering political and economic malpractices, and hence power would have to be held for several decades. Since assertions to this effect had infuriated the press and the liberal middle classes after 1966, it was decided that this time the new regime would criticise neither democracy nor the politicians, but would justify military rule as aiming at a 'stable' democracy in some unspecified future. Yet again the military takeover was planned by the general staff of the three armed services, and the well-tried system of power sharing between them was once more to be resorted to. The management of the economy would be given to 'liberal' (in Argentine politics a synonym for undemocratic) economists, with good international connections so as to attract foreign capital. Education was left to the traditional Catholics, but this time there would be more officers in control of other ministries.

Although the ineptitude of Mrs. Perón and her supporters contributed to her downfall in 1976, a further complicating factor relates to the manipulation of political violence by the armed forces so as to legitimise their intervention. Since the guerilla movement did not fade away after Perón returned to power, Peronism in government came to be blamed both for backing it and for denying budgetary aid to the army. The support of Congress and the Executive for legal repression was subject to innuendo in the closing months of 1975, while the role of the armed forces was played up. The mutually dirty war between guerillas and the armed forces was by no means a symmetrical conflict between extremes, since the centre of the political spectrum and civilians accounted for 41% of the dead, while army casualties amounted to only 5%.(12)

Even before the military takeover the army began to

form illegal death squads. Radical and Peronist politicians began to disappear or be killed. Members of both political parties were tortured, and scores of bodies appeared riddled with bullets at the roadsides. In all this was a pattern of demobilisation lending credence to the link made by O´Donnell between demobilisation and the rise of the bureaucratic authoritarian state.

The development of the 1973 demilitarisation certainly illustrates the contention in the introductory chapter that key factors for the survival of a Handback regime are the "skill and luck of the successor administration". Mrs. Perón seems to have been poorly endowed with both, and this, in a markedly presidential system, is bound to affect the prospects of the regime. Even though the vigour of Argentine secondary institutions was enough to prevent an initially strong bureaucratic authoritarian regime from graduating into bureaucratic clientelism, these were not enough to prevent or withstand the military takeover itself.

Desperate to regain the consensus which she had frittered away by the close of 1975, Mrs. Perón tried to avoid a coup by bringing forward the date of elections, announcing in March 1976 that they would be held in December, and that she did not intend to stand for re-elecion. It was a case of too little, too late. By December 1975 the military had defeated the Trotskyite ERP guerilla in Tucuman, and had infiltrated the Marxist (but still Peronist) Montoneros. However these developments were concealed in the run-up to the coup in March 1976. It was too embarrassing to admit that the legally ordained fight against the guerillas was beginning to work. The military preferred to show that they could be defeated only by a military regime.(13)

THE 1976-83 BUREAUCRATIC AUTHORITARIAN REGIME

Origins and Transformations

As already noted, the 1976-73 military regime belongs within the Veto category, at least in its initial stages. However, it could certainly be argued that the unity of the armed forces was low, even if their differentiation vis-a-vis civil society remained high. In spite of repeated references to unity in the discourse of the military, recurrent difficulties over policies, such as the trade union ´law´, and the replacement of presidents, meant that interservice rivalry reached an all time high. The personal ambitions of the comparatively grey military leaders of the period also played a not inconsiderable role in making it clear that the military were far from united. It would therefore be possible to characterise the 1976-83 regime as semi-factional.

Given the fear of the threat posed by the popular sector, coupled with the desire to co-opt it - two contradictory features of the aspirations of all military regimes - the military after 1977 began covertly to contemplate the launching of a political party which would succeed the regime in the unlikely event of elections needing to be called. Past political history indicated the difficulty of such a design, which has repeatedly been mooted, only to be hurriedly dropped again as soon as political and social displeasure. indicated that it lacked political feasibility.

By mid-1980 the regime was clearly in difficulty. The military underwrote the free-market and high domestic interest rate policies so dear to international bankers, as applied by Mr. José Alfredo Martínez de Hoz. In spite of ample warnings, in the Argentine quality press as well as by civilian politicians, that such policies would not only destroy Argentine industry but that Argentina's ability to pay would be undermined, the lending by international bankers continued. Thus Argentina's foreign debt climbed from US$9 billion in 1976 to $43 billion by 1983 - this in a country which is self-sufficient in oil and which built no infrastructure with such borrowed capital. GDP remained at its 1974 levels, and the profitability of big and small corporations was eroded by a shrinking local market (the real income of the salaried sector plunged by 40% after 1976) and high interest rates (32% p.a. in real terms), leading to a wave of bankruptcies after April 1980. Whatever remained of industry operated with ruinous idle capacity for several years.

The strength of the human rights lobby in Argentina, another indicator of strong autonomous political organisation and one which had been reinforced by the ´dirty war´ fought against the guerillas, created a ´Nuremburg mentality´ among officers of the armed forces. Officers and NCOs embarrassingly involved in disappearances, torture and deaths, have been posted abroad, their identities changed, and financial security provided by ample endowment. In other cases diplomatic appointments were resorted to. Simultaneously the military, knowing that one way or another elections would eventually have to be called, repeatedly tried to negotiate the non-investigation of repressive excesses. The politicians refused to reach any agreement, and it is generally accepted that until the 1982 invasion of the islands, the question of what would be done about military repressive excesses was the most important issue in Argentine politics, and one of burning importance to the military regime.

Military Adventurism and the Crisis of the Regime

As in 1966-70, the 1976 regime soon showed signs of veering towards impasse. No specific plans emerged, only sporadic and provocative statements, such as Galtieri´s well known dictum that the ballot boxes were best locked up. Such statements aroused little support, owing to the high level of autonomous political organisation in Argentina already noted.

President (and General) J.R. Videla and his Minister for the Economy, Martínez de Hoz, stepped down as scheduled in March 1981. General Viola replaced Videla, and for a time the crises of the regime were held in abeyance due to the change in its top personnel. A moratorium was expected to rescue landowners, industrialists and commercial debtors. Months went by and no specific measures emerged. Proposal followed proposal and nothing was decided. Disillusion was widespread even among allies of the military when President Viola appeared to be taken ill in November 1981. The Junta, which had with difficulty agreed to appoint Viola, could not easily bring itself to replace him. After a month-long period of military intrigue, Galtieri, the army representative on the Junta, ensured that the members representing the navy (Admiral Anaya) and the air force (Brigadier Lami Dozo) would allow him to become President while remaining a member of the Junta. Galtieri therefore seemed to be in a stronger position than Viola, who had held both positions but not simultaneously.

The economic measures announced late in 1981 by the newly appointed Minister for the Economy, Dr. R.T. Alemann, a ´liberal´, were not opposed by the corporate organisations representing landowners, businessmen and industrialists. The changes proposed by Alemann essentially entailed continuing with the orthodox policies of the Martínez de Hoz period, while adding a new austerity in state spending and proposing a privatisation of mineral resources. In the past, similar policies had caused political earthquakes which helped to topple Perón and undermined Frondizi. Since the civilian political spectrum was certain that the military regime was close to collapse, the 1981 proposals in contrast merely resulted in assurances that any contracts generated by the new policies would be reversed, along with most of the other policies of the military regime. Though the Galtieri phase of the military regime enjoyed an initial and brief respite after attaining power in late 1981, trouble from the opposition could confidently be expected with the opening of the political season in March 1982.

It would appear that the military regime meanwhile set in motion a series of policies which, it hoped, would help it to withstand the storm of dissent to be expected after March. From early January and through February 1982, authoritative journalists known to be military mouthpieces began to mention that the Falklands/Malvinas might be recovered by military action, and that negotiations with Britain on the issue should be terminated since they could lead nowhere. All these ´noises´ were unprecedented, in that negotiations had been regarded as desirable and praiseworthy since Britain had begun to negotiate in 1965. Secondly, the Argentine ambassador in London, C. Ortiz de Rozas, was recalled in late January for unprecedented, long and publicly announced consultations with President Galtieri on the Malvinas. Finally, when the conversations in New York were regarded as unsatisfactory in Buenos Aires, the Argentine Foreign Office issued the unprecedented threat:

"Argentina reserves (the right) to terminate the working of this mechanism and to choose freely the procedure which best accords with her interests."(14)

General Galtieri had been dismissive of President Viola´s gradualist approach to most problems, and on this issue he believed in adopting a position of strength. Such was likewise the Galtieri approach to the issues of military responsibility for repressive excesses and the future role of the military in a process of demilitarisation and democratisation: to negotiate with the civilian political parties and pressure groups from a strong position, discarding the ineffective compromises of the brief Viola interlude.

Accordingly, Galtieri resurrected the idea of a political party which was to be ´friendly´ towards the military and their allies. In the midst of the tense but politically quiescent southern summer months, the project was relaunched with a much publicised barbecue in Victoria, La Pampa province. Public employees were coerced into attending to simulate popular enthusiasm, though those politicians who only lose elections needed no coercion to attend. The new political party would be an alliance of centrist votes (which go to the Peronist and Radical parties when permitted to do so) and the electorally weak regional parties. Even with the resources of the state, such a party could not have commanded more than 10% of the vote under open conditions. In contrast, the strongly critical Multipartidaria (comprising Peronists, Radicals and other smaller parties) could easily poll about 80% of the vote.(15)

On 30 March 1982, as summer drew to an end, the military regime for the first time since 1976 faced a massive public demonstration of discontent with all of its policies. By then, the tactic publicly under consideration within the regime since at least early January was ready to help defuse internal problems. At this stage, it is relevant to bear in mind that none of the previously considered military regimes had fallen so low in popular esteem, even among the usual local and foreign backers of such regimes. None of the five military predecessors of the 1976-83 experiment were faced with a united civilian political spectrum toying with the idea of reforming the military and investigating the past policies which it had espoused. Every previous post-military constitutional regime had compromised and accommodated, but even before the events of April to June 1982, this stance no longer seemed to be repeatable.

The unprecedented political decision to use military means to regain possession of the Falklands/Malvinas, given the strength of Argentina's historical claims and the problems faced by the military, cannot but be seen as yet another attempt to prevent elections or determine their result. It should be noted that the political parties, the trade unions, and the local human rights lobby made it clear that the invasion neither solved nor postponed other issues. The regime, as both Peronist and Radical politicians argued at the time, would simply be pushed into paying a dear price for the support which it needed, and demands for liberalisation would be exacerbated. The regime would also be judged for its performance on this additional issue. In other words, the precarious standing of the regime was not improved, even before its military defeat.

Since the top priority of any military regime is the preservation of its corporate autonomy, any concession to the British which imperilled military interests could simply not be entertained if the internal risks were thereby increased, especially if the military administration was seen to lose or negotiate fruitlessly. In other words, the military could not back down where the democratic forces would not back down either. Backing down, that is dropping or imperilling the claim to sovereignty, would entail for the military a loss of power: in short, their careers might be endangered, and their institutions reformed. As it turned out, however, military defeat was a massive blow both to the autonomy of the military and to the generals´ hold on power.

During the conflict, and even while the disinformation spread by the regime still deluded most of the population (but only some of the politicians), leaders of the Peronist and Radical parties, as well as trade unions, insisted on a return to the rule of law, constitutional observance, the investigation of the disappearances, and the reversal of economic policies.(16) The military, having haughtily refused to meet civilian politicians and trade unionists since 1976, called them for a series of meetings in 1982, only to be told by a leading trade unionist, Triacca, that "if we are seriously into the business of regaining sovereignty, we must next invade the Ministry for the Economy".

If it is accepted that military regimes as they have appeared in Argentina (and most of Latin America for that matter) are demobilising, then (especially given their practices and policies) it must be accepted that extended and repressive demobilisation can contradict the prevalent military discourse which holds that the armed forces are the people in arms. The military in Argentina have always wanted to be popular and to be at one with the people. However, the policies of successive military regimes meant that military dreams of popularity and communion with the people had been postponed to fight the military conceptions of demagoguery, subversion and Communism, and to promote an equally military perception of economic development. The latent contradiction could be ignored if the degree of unpopularity or of economic malaise was slight. As from the late 1970s the unpopularity of the Argentine military was greater than ever, and the economic mess was without precedent. The only option open to save the corporate interests of the military and commensurate with Galtieri´s inclinations was therefore to embark on a foreign policy adventure dear to all Argentines. The enterprise failed to end strong and public dissent with the military, even when defeat and confrontation with the British seemed improbable. Pressures and strident criticism calling for democratisation continued unabated throughout April, May and June 1982. After the defeat of 14 June, the threats which the regime had sought to dispel by placing Argentine national interests at risk had increased manifold. An international conflict, a recession affecting local and foreign investors in Argentina, and a possible default on Argentina´s international debt, were the tangible result of a military regime which also happened to kill so many of its citizens.

1983: A Transient or Permanent Demilitarisation ?

It may be worth adding a word on the differences already apparent in the present Argentine process of demilitarisation. As has already been noted, civilian politicians are considering, for the first time since 1932, plans for the reform of the armed forces.(17) Secondly, there is none of the overconfidence of previous attempts at democratisation between 1932 and 1973. There is instead a healthy scepticism, an awareness that democratic politics requires organisational efficiency and a prevalence of democratic practices throughout society, that the economic problems posed by an unnecessary international debt will condition the democratic attempt, and that the longstanding problem of the acceptance of democratic practices by the Argentine propertied sectors is by no means resolved. The prevalent assumption among democratic politicians is that the new attempt to set up a democratic regime faces a formidable array of difficulties, as well as the usual, but it would appear this time less sullen, internal and external adversaries: those defeated by universal suffrage.

However, should the democratic experiment fail yet again, a right wing military regime - or even a now not so inconceivable left wing military regime - will not allow the Malvinas issue to drop. As in the case of the military regimes reviewed here, a now less likely re-entry of the military into politics can be expected to attempt to succeed in those policy areas in which the military see the 1976-83 experiment as having failed. It is thus entirely plausible that the steady economic, social and political deterioration, resulting from a succession of both military and civilian governments, may well lead in the event of any reintervention to an attempt at a military breakthrough regime.

An extremely relevant development, in weighing whether the 1983 demilitarisation is likely to be longlasting, is the extent of civilian renewal. Perón and Balbín, the long dominant leaders of the Peronist and Radical parties respectively, are dead. Both main political parties have made dramatic progress towards change. The Radicals have rejuvenated and dramatically expanded their membership, enabling them to win the 1983 presidential elections under the leadership of Dr. Raúl Alfonsín. The Peronists have completed their first ever democratic internal contest which featured a rejection of Mrs. Perón. Linz notes that one crucial value unleashing a civilian renewal is the mere passage of time, adding that the civilian leadership must also have internalised the reasons for the previous breakdown of democracy.(18) Though Linz had the Spanish and Portuguese cases in mind, a sequence of failed civilian and military regimes may well have the same didactic effect on a political class. Interviews with presidential candidates, presidential hopefuls and their advisors indicate that perceptions have certainly changed.

NOTES

1. See Alain Rouquié, _Pouvoir Militaire et Société Politique en Republique Argentine_ (Paris: FNSP, 1978).

2. See D. Cantón, _Elecciones y Partidos Políticos en la Argentina: historia, interpretación y balance, 1910-1966_ (Buenos Aires: Siglo XXI, 1973).

3. See Guillermo O´Donnell, _Modernization and Bureaucratic Authoritarianism_ (University of California, Berkeley: Studies in South American Politics, 1973): for other works by the same author published in English, see "State and Alliances in Argentina, 1956-76", _J. Development Studies_, 15, 1,

1978; "Reflections on the Patterns of Change in the Bureaucratic Authoritarian State", Latin American Research Review, 12, 1, 1978; and "Tensions in the Bureaucratic Authoritarian State and the Question of Democracy", in D. Collier, ed, The New Authoritarianism in Latin America (Princeton, 1979). Of O´Donnell´s work in Spanish, three books and several essays, his most recent book published in 1982 contains an up-dating of his theoretical approach, as well as a detailed account of the rise and fall of the 1966-73 Argentine regime.

4. See S.P. Huntington, Political Order in Changing Societies (Yale, 1968); and S.P. Huntington & C.H. Moore, eds, Authoritarian Politics in Modern Societies: The Dynamics of Established One-Party Systems (New York: Basic Books, 1970).

5. See Juan Linz, "An Authoritarian Regime: Spain", in E. Allardt & S. Rokkan, eds, Mass Politics (Free Press, 1970).

6. O´Donnell, J.Development Studies, loc.cit., 1978.

7. There is no political connotation attached to either colour, which were those used by the army on manoeuvres; confrontations in September 1962 and April 1963 were no war game however.

8. See Roberto Roth, Los Años de Onganía: relato de un testigo (Buenos Aires: La Campana, 1980); Roth was Onganía´s trusted adviser and is regarded as a well informed observer.

9. Dr. Arturo Frondizi was elected for the usual constitutional term of six years, so that having been elected in 1958 he should have left office in 1964. A coup cut his tenure short on 28 March 1962, ten days after the Peronists had won several provincial elections. This the military could no longer tolerate.

10. For a fuller description of this corporate ´state of mind´, see Guillermo O´Donnell, 1966-1973, el estado burocrático-autoritario (Buenos Aires: Belgrano, 1982), pp.85-95.

11. Interview with Dr. Angel Federico Robledo (Buenos Aires, Sept-Oct 1980): he was Peronist Minister of Defence (1973-74), briefly Foreign Affairs (August 1975), and Interior (1975-76). After the forced departure of José Lopez Rega, Mrs. Perón bowed to pressure within the Justicialista (Peronist) party and made Robledo Vice-President of the party. Against the opposition of the Peronist right wing (verticalistas), Robledo sought to democratise the organisation along the lines of a political party proper. His analysis was that

charisma and proscription had deformed the party. The reasons for his failure, which would go a long way towards explaining the 1976 coup, are too complicated to allow for discussion here.

12. Information compiled from the Buenos Aires dailies, La Prensa, La Opinión and La Nación, gives 816 deaths, 4.9% from the military, 9.7% from other security forces (mostly police), and 44.1% from the guerillas, the remaining 41.3% being civilians; Ministry of the Interior figures for total deaths are much higher at 1358, but the percentage breakdown is strikingly similar.

13. Interview, Teniente General (R.E.) Alberto N. Laplane, London, October 1979. He was General Commander of the Army from March to August 1975, when he was ousted by pressure exerted on the President (then Mrs. Perón) by Generals Videla and Viola, as well as by the then head of the navy, Admiral E.E. Massera. The form of this pressure was confirmed in further interviews with Dr. A.F. Robledo and Dr. A. Cafiero (Buenos Aires, Sept-Nov 1980); Admiral Massera refused to grant an interview once the questions were made available to him.

14. See G.A. Makin, "Argentine Approaches to the Falklands/Malvinas: Was the Resort to Violence Forseeable?", International Affairs, 59, 3, 1983, pp.391-403; see also Falklands Islands Review: Report of a Committee of Privy Councillors (The Franks Report), London: HMSO, 1983, p.41.

15. For the coverage the development received in the Argentine press, see La Nación, Clarín, La Prensa, 11, 12 & 13 February 1982; the barbecue for 13,000 guests, with the speeches and other announcements, were regarded with considerable disquiet.

16. Material derived from several extensive telephone interviews with former President A. Illia, Dr. R. Alfonsin, Dr. A. Troccoli, Dr. A. Cafiero, Dr. A.F. Robledo, Mr. Andres Framini, Dr. Oscar Albrieu, and Gen. A.N. Laplane, April-June 1982.

17. See Clarín, 14 June 1983, p.8; not only is the issue unprecedented, but the fact that it has been accepted and enthusiastically taken up by all members of the political spectrum, from the left to the right, would only leave open the question of the efficiency of the reform.

18. See Juan Linz, "Crisis, Breakdown and Re-Equilibration", in Linz & A. Stepan, eds, The Breakdown of Democratic Regimes (Baltimore & London: Johns Hopkins, 1978); and also G. O´Donnell, "Notas

para el estudio de procesos de democratización política a partir del estado burocrático-autoritario", <u>Desarrollo Economico</u>, 22, 86, 1982.

Chapter Eight

CENTRAL AMERICA: COLLAPSE OF THE MILITARY SYSTEM

James Dunkerley

ARMY, SOCIETY AND EXTERNAL INVOLVEMENT

At the end of 1983 only one Central American state - Guatemala - was ruled by a military government. However, as the extended and increasingly acute political crisis in Central America has demonstrated, formal tenure of office constitutes only one aspect of political activity by the local armed forces, which, even when they are out of power, exercise authority over policy to a greater degree than do many of their counterparts in other third world countries. Moreover, the proclivity of the armed forces to wield power behind the scenes has never been more marked than in the early 1980s. As a result, we will be concerned here less with the problems of specific military regimes than with outlining the nature, historical conditions and present breakdown of a regional politico-military system.
     The collapse of this system has been uneven in pace and character, but it has become sufficiently generalised to compel major external intervention. In the case of El Salvador, such intervention has undoubtedly served to salvage - for a while, at least - a military apparatus that had held power directly since 1932, and established its own protocols and governmental traditions to a significantly greater degree than had the local civilian elite. Had the United States not intervened progressively from 1980, the Salvadorean armed forces would, in all probability, have been destroyed within the space of a few months. One of the ironies of their corporate salvation is that it has combined both massive logistical reinforcement and an expansion in operational capabilities with a withdrawal from government. The case of Honduras is

somewhat similar but appreciably less acute, if only because the army began to take a direct political role very late in the republic´s history. There elections for a civilian administration were forced by Washington on a military regime in 1981, shortly before the United States massively enhanced military aid. In both instances the military presence in public administration was reduced, but its residual political role was not decisively altered. The new civilian regimes were not endowed with independent powers, and existed as manifestations rather than embodiments of formal democracy. In neither case was there any substantial military opposition and, indeed, it was the politicians who increasingly found themselves embarrassed by the new and unfamiliar situation. The Guatemalan army, significantly larger, more efficient and independent, has so far resisted such a move and retained a more traditional format for applying its solution to the crisis. It too, however, continues to be the object of pressure to return formal control over government to civilians.

The need for such extensive dependence on the United States and the form it is taking betoken the severity of the collapse of the longstanding system of government and socio-economic organisation accelerated by the overthrow of Somoza´s Nicaraguan regime in July 1979. The Sandinista (FSLN) revolution has established a form of polity and society profoundly different from those in the rest of the region, and effectively represents the margin by which the contemporary conflict has been drawn. For our purposes here, the principal feature of the Sandinista revolution is the manner in which it succeeded first in effecting a comprehensive defeat of a force distinct from but comparable to most Central American armies, and then in subordinating military activity to the dictates of the political party holding state power. The complementary suppression of an institutional monopoly on coercion through the creation of popular militias and a general militarisation of civil society has further sharpened the threat posed by this alternative model, and undoubtedly heightened the apprehension and corporate cohesion of those institutions battling guerrilla forces attempting to repeat the FSLN´s example. It is, of course, of marginal value to view these features divorced from their wider socio-economic framework, but it cannot be denied that the sharp military character of the challenge to the established mode of political power has weighed heavily in the deliberations of those who uphold the status quo. Since it is so distinctive, we shall not consider the Sandinista military apparatus here. Yet we should note that it possesses a number of characteristics which are as traditionally Central American as they are radical and innovative. Many Central American officers (but few of their North American advisers) view the FSLN with trepidation less for its claimed ties with the Soviet bloc than for its successful realisation of popular and indigenous military customs which first contributed to the formation of regional forces and then, in the early years of the twentieth century, came into conflict with them. If senior officers in El Salvador and Honduras have accepted withdrawal from the absolute direction of civic affairs, and those in Guatemala have shown themselves at least prepared to consider such an eventuality, it is very largely because the United States has made this the condition for supplying greater professional means with which to eradicate a guerrilla challenge.

Before we return to a more detailed discussion of these cases, a number of general points should be made. The first is that since Central America is essentially a balkanised region, its unity and internal variations need to be treated with a degree of sensitivity. At times of crisis general laws become less efficacious and should be interrogated with some insistence. With the exception of Panama, the creation of the Central American nation states was not a colonially supervised process, but rather a local response to the collapse of colonial authority. As in much of Africa, the delineation of frontiers was undertaken along already established lines of imperial administration, but since this took place in the first half of the nineteenth cenury the formation of the nation state as an entity replete with ideological apparatuses and a historical lineage is, in the last quarter of the twentieth century, sufficiently advanced for the defence of such identities to be an authentic figure of civilian and military consciousness. This is not, of course, co-substantial with the formation of the nation as a viable socio-economic unit, or the completion of the many tasks central to military activity that this entails, but it does have emphatic effects in terms of political comportment, and has generated a deep-seated nationalism. However, both aspects of this phenomenon - conservative nationalism as embodied in the formal military apparatus and radical nationalism represented by the guerrilla forces - have developed with a pronounced and increasingly acute appreciation of the fact that the small size of the region and its relatively homogeneous socio-economic fabric facilitates interaction between social and political currents to such a degree that the 'nationalisation' of problems is rarely viable even if constantly sought after. As a result no military - whether in government or not - has ever retained a purely nation-based focus. At an administrative level this acceptance of a certain supra-national cohesion was formalised in the establishment of CONDECA (the Central American Defence Council) in 1964, linking the various forces into a tenuous operational collaboration under U.S. tutelage. CONDECA effectively came apart in 1969, due to the short but vicious border war between Honduras and El Salvador - a conflict generated by internal tensions rather than the minor border dispute invoked as justification for hostilities, but nonetheless a conflict indicative of a strong element of inter-elite competition that remained something of a trauma over the following decade. The 1980 peace treaty that finally closed this period of national antagonism was compelled by greater threats posed from below, and signalled the emergence of a less formal but more substantial series of regional understandings between general staffs. The success of this new pact was illustrated by its firm support for the August 1983 coup of General Mejia in Guatemala, suggesting that by that stage senior officers - if not their entire corps - felt obliged to engage fully in political as well as military operations at a regional level. We might also note that while there are few more ardent advocates of the domino theory than staff officers of Central American armies, those who are fighting against these men in the name of national liberation depend equally heavily upon extra-national support and pay scant respect to formal frontiers. As a result, soldiers whose avowed mission up to the 1970s was integrally bound up with the defence of national sovereignty and unity, and the exertion of pressure on neighbouring states from an essentially external perspective, have been progressively drawn into a much more systematic collaborative enterprise.

Against this tendency both to view and to practice political and field operations on a wider scale, there exist several historical points of difference within the region. The popular vision of a 'banana republic' that might be said to be drawn from an amalgam of Honduras with El Salvador is in need of more than usual rectification with regard to Costa Rica, and to a certain degree with regard to Panama. In these countries it is the differentiation rather than the uniformity of the region that is most evident in terms of military affairs. Within a strictly geographical definition of Central America one would also have to include Belize as an exceptional case since it is now an independent state. However, Belize is being accepted as an integral constituency of the zone only very slowly because, despite its progressive involvement in international military operations, its distinct colonial trajectory encourages a linkage with the Caribbean community in a manner similar to that by which Guyana is analytically and culturally if not physically detached from the South American mainland. Many of the Atlantic provinces of the Central American states also conform to this type and have exhibited a quite potent localised resistance to the hispanic political culture that dominates them, but although these provincial peculiarities have occasionally extracted discrete concessions, they have registered a minimal impact on a national scale. In all events, there is little likelihood of the germinal Belizean Defence Force acquiring many of the attributes of its regional conterparts, and we may confidently exclude it from our discussion here.

The origins of Costa Rican civilism, which has been qualitatively more important and enduring than in any other Central American, or even Latin American, republic, are normally held to lie in the even distribution of land inside the republic. This is not strictly the case, and today Costa Rica has one of the most uneven structures of tenure in the hemisphere. However, what does appear to be a compelling contributory cause is the fact that from well before the establishment of the republic, this zone had an extremely sparse population and a minute indigenous community. Moreover, once coffee began to be cultivated on a significant scale (from the 1840s), a relatively balanced system of small-scale freehold enterprises worked by waged or family labour did prevail. For a critical period there was a marked lack of reliance on either forced labour or the progressively exigent and exploitative labour rent systems which underpinned the agrarian organisations and public order problems of the other states. As a result, the central condition for the formation of military institutions elsewhere was

absent in Costa Rica. The original distinctiveness
has since disappeared, but many of its effects
persist. Even before the formal abolition of the
Costa Rican army after the 1948 civil war, political
conflict in the country was markedly civilist in
tenor. Once the army was done away with, to be
replaced by a lightly armed paramilitary police
force, open competition between political forces was
endowed with a secure basis, and the division of
powers became an authentic aspect of the
governmental system rather than a borrowed norm.
This system has survived for over thirty years, and
represents a kind of permanent ideal type for
civilian politicians in other states, while from
time to time providing a wishful model for officers
casting about for positive rationales for
withdrawing from power. It cannot, however, be
reproduced, and there are disturbing signs that, as
in the case of Uruguay which exhibited similar
characteristics from the turn of the century up to
the coup in 1973, both escalating internal tension
and the pressures of external conflicts are
undermining a parochial anti-militarism.

The distinctiveness of Panama within the
Central American system lies in the manner by which
the National Guard has exercised its influence in
political affairs. The key factor in this regard
is, of course, the Canal Zone and its large
contingent of U.S. troops, which have resulted in
the development of the Panamanian nation and state
being distorted and exceptional by any standards.
The strong and often provocative presence of a
foreign power and the manifestly strategic factors
that underlie its tenure of a critical swathe of
national territory have been responsible both for
the formation of the National Guard - currently in
the process of exchanging the formal persona of a
paramilitary force for the full impedimenta of a
military apparatus with distinct services and
autonomous hierarchy - and also for leading it to
take the initiative in renegotiating the terms of
U.S. occupation. Although General Torrijos´s
intervention in 1968 was motivated in the first
instance by oligarchic in-fighting and corruption of
a type discernible elsewhere in the region, it soon
became apparent that the Guard would have to develop
a relatively independent policy on the question of
the Canal if it was not to be badly outflanked by
increasingly widespread and threatening indignation
at Washington´s ´colonialism´. Torrijos thereby
became the most consistent and serious advocate of

military reformism and nationalism in the region, although the thrust of his policies was always strongest in foreign relations. The pursuit of this line was sufficiently muscular to instill alarm in the United States, and bestow upon the charismatic officer a reputation which compares with that of any Latin American figure in the last decade. The fact that the existence and control of the Canal fractured the country in a political rather than a geographical manner by itself goes a long way towards explaining why the Panamanian National Guard's own authoritarian and not very innovative regime enjoyed popular acquiescence for so long. One can locate the termination of this period in the signing of the Canal Treaty in September 1977, rather than in Torrijos' death four years later. Since 1981 there has been a continuation of the formal civilian government to which the country returned in 1978, but in practice the Guard's power and scrutiny of authority has not diminished one iota. Indeed, six years after the resolution of the Canal issue, the military seemed poised not only to put another general in the presidency but also to retrieve direct corporate authority over public administration. The fact that this seems likely to cause only minimal readjustment amongst the civilian elite reflects the weight of constabulary-centred traditions and consciousness throughout the course of the country's history. This is evident elsewhere, the most vivid example being Somoza's Nicaragua, which, like Haiti, Panama and the Dominican Republic had its militia formed during periods of direct U.S. occupation. But Panama is unique in that it was directly created by Washington's fiat. Elsewhere U.S. intervention has been constant and has generated considerable effects at the military level, but has occurred at a crucial historical distance from independence and the establishment of indigenous political traditions and administrative norms. It has, in essence, been overbearingly corrective and reactive in character, whereas in Panama, on the other hand, it has existed precisely at the centre of national life, to which it gave birth. Thus the National Guard is confronted with a contradiction not dissimilar to that which dogged Somoza's apparat: the formal mandate to defend the nation is bestowed upon an entity which was forged by and is critically dependent on the very power which is perceived by a significant sector of the population as the greatest threat to nationhood. Panama is perhaps the only

Latin American state where a national liberation movement - none is yet in existence - might acquire a strength around the motif of authentic sovereignty to the same degree that the Sandinistas did in Nicaragua. Thus the upper echelons of the National Guard have in recent years demonstrated an anti-Sandinismo as virulent as that of any of their regional confreres; but it has perforce to be coloured by a certain domestic moderation instilled on the one hand by the tangible dangers of exchanging a tactical dispute with Washington for unconditional parasitism, and on the other by a recognition that the margin of the Guard´s distinctiveness from their erstwhile namesakes in Nicaragua resides only in the absence of a family dynasty, greater institutional autonomy, and a potent foreign garrison.

To conclude this section, a number of general statements can be made about the core Central American military institutions and their practice of political power. Although these might be perceived as being largely based on ´common sense´, they bear restating if only to clarify general tendencies, and to signal those features that need some elaboration. They also serve to underline some critical comparisons with the structure of the military regimes in South America discussed in Chapter Six, which while they might appear quite similar are different in some key respects. Our broad observations here apply in general to the cases of El Salvador, Guatemala and Honduras, which will be discussed more closely in the final section of the essay.

1. These forces retain important characteristics bestowed upon them during the formation of the republics in the nineteenth century. Their outlook and modes of operation as well as their political instincts are significantly determined by pre-professional requirements of social control in plantation economies. Economic development, the growth of the middle class, and urbanisation have not fundamentally transformed a historical role determined by the dragooning and subsequent control of a rural labour force.

2. Although they were the objects of externally directed efforts at modernisation and professionalisation from the mid-twentieth century onwards, the Central American forces continue to exhibit an uneven but generally low level of professional conduct with respect to efficiency, and

a relatively high one with regard to caste cohesion. This is due to the narrow ecological limits of both state and civil society, which has required only limited administrative capacity in political affairs, but strengthened group solidarity in the face of scarce resources. The capacity of the armed forces to exercise internal control is more variable and cannot be directly related to externally determined norms of professionalism.

3. The outer parameters of military political activity remain constricted by the economic veto of the landed elite. No major incursion into the power of this class has been sustained for any length of time under military supervision. The terms on which this oligarchical veto is held are not, however, homogeneous or identical in all cases.

4. The general social pact implicit in this last point has given the army substantial freedom in operational matters, and frequently conceded it direct political administration of the state, but has frequently limited the forms by which the military may engage in politics. The principal restraint here has been that democratic formalities be observed. This complements the institutional and structural incapacity to forge authoritarian military regimes of the Southern Cone type by facilitating regular changeovers of ´elected´ presidents and administrations, and has simultaneously tended to reduce the damage that could be caused by the coup d´etat. Thus, the coup remains an integral part of local political discourse but not the primary mechanism for the distribution of power and largesse, as it is for example in Bolivia.

5. In times of generalised crisis (1944-50, 1960-63, 1967-72, 1979-) the landlord-officer alliance is invariably tightened, but lacks the fluidity or political weight to sustain itself for long without external aid on both the military and economic fronts. Its continued survival has depended on an increase in United States assistance, which in the most recent instance has produced a quantitative expansion in repressive capacity rather than a qualitative alteration of political forms. The military, being incapable of a coherent alternative policy at a corporate level for a sustained period, have been obliged to adhere more closely to their constabulary role.

6. Under conditions of escalating guerilla warfare, the military´s capacity to withdraw from the US-landlord pact has effectively evaporated.

Adherence to policy initiatives that extend beyond the traditional mandate (for example, fiscal and agrarian reforms) is only secured in the context of counter-insurgency operations and under international pressure. Resistance to such proposals is entrenched in so far as the social base and political logic of the military as an institution is founded upon established agrarian patterns and modes of control.

In terms of the basic variables outlined in the introductory chapter of this volume, it is evident that the Central American militaries have a markedly lower level of unity than their South American counterparts, since such unity as they possess is the result much more of their narrow social base and pronounced sense of threat than of the level of professionalism evident, say, in Chile or Argentina. Differentiation between the military and civil society is weak, but a measure of autonomous political organisation is evident both in the capacity of the landlord class to control the military, and in the emergence of armed opposition forces whose challenge to the regime constitutes the major source of threat. At the same time, the regime types to which this pattern of variables might be expected to lead are influenced by an exceptionally high level of external dependence.

These general observations are subject to a number of specific qualifications, but it should be apparent that they have a close bearing on the context in which military regimes operate and on how they act. All our statements indicate that the Central American crisis of the 1980s goes to the roots of a deeply structured system.

GUATEMALA

Except for the period 1944-54, the government of Guatemala, Central America's largest and most powerful state, has been militarised almost constantly since independence. The form has, of course, varied, but so great has been the proximity between the army and political power that one can properly speak of a national tradition of military regimes. Senior officers have rarely faced problems that derive from the anomaly of the institution holding power; perhaps the only comparable example in the hemisphere in this regard is Paraguay. The principal issues with which they have had to deal since 1954 have been concerned with fielding the longest and most demanding counter-insurgency campaign in the Americas, and with the precise distribution of power within the institution and the negotiation of its terms with a relatively strong entrepreneurial sector. Difficulties in both these fields have led a long-established system to enter a profound crisis in recent years, a crisis marked by two coups, in 1982 and 1983, and the failure of the ´managed´ presidential poll of 1982. In the sense that the army has held power either to thwart the emergence of, or to deal directly with, a guerrilla challenge, its problems have been relatively familiar, and seldom the subject of extended negotiation either inside the military or with the civilian elite. The crisis that confronts the power bloc at present is, it should be stressed, one that takes a military form but extends throughout an entire socio-economic system; since 1954 military government has become structurally inseparable from that system.

Under the Spanish empire, Guatemala was the military and administrative centre of Central America, a ´kingdom´ in its own right, and it continued to play a similar role during the early republican period. The trajectory of this military tradition was altered somewhat by developments at the end of the nineteenth century, when the Mexican-influenced liberal revolution broke the back of clerical and protectionist resistance to open up religious and communal lands to private ownership, and expand the market for land during the ´take-off´ phase for coffee. This both fuelled peasant discontent and underpinned the erosion of the old republican elite whose principal ecomomic base had been the cultivation of crops for the dye indstry. Very schematically, one might say that the capitalist coffee farmers, many of the most powerful of whom were foreign settlers, desisted from taking up the direct management of the state, seeking instead powerful, military based leaders who might ensure the maintenance of public order, the implementation of free trade policies, and the upkeep of basic infrastructure on their behalf. The Guatemalan oligarchy was both maintained and transformed, but instead of developing a political tradition of its own, it moulded one around its patronage of the army. Thus, although it is frequently stated that the relatively modernised Guatemalan military of today bears no resemblance to the rude levies of the nineteenth century or the constabulary force of the early twentieth century, the social context within which it exercises power is at root little different.

In political terms, the system was one of extended personalist dictatorship whereby the army did not rule in a properly institutional sense, but provided the means by which one of its number might uphold the landlords´ mandate. Thus, although government was not fully militarised, the ideological and cultural apparatus of civilism was weak, and the army had a high profile in administrative affairs. This system was fractured, but not fully broken, during the reform period of 1944-54. This decade-long hiatus remains highly relevant to the present crisis, because it represents the historical ´working through´ of an option that henceforth disappeared from the vocabulary of the Guatemalan military, restricting it to an essentially reactive and entrenched position. Towards the end of the Second World War a burgeoning middle class, expanded by relatively high economic growth but severely hampered by the authoritarian Ubico regime (1930-44), and significantly affected by United States democratic influences to counter the dictatorial models of the axis powers, effectively undermined the landlord-military pact from both within and without. The ruling class´s reliance upon personalism exacerbated this movement for reform, and expanded its constituency to include many officers who sought some form of change, however limited. At the same time it was precisely the narrowness of the system that served to politicise an officer corps that, heavily influenced by the United States and partially so by Mexico, was manifesting the first signs of a professional discontent with backward and inefficient methods. Developmentalism, statism and modernism, the incipient features of which were evident by 1944, thereby became incorporated into the reformist cause, and contributed towards opening the breach for a civilian administration. The Arevalo government (1945-51) was far from immune to military threats, which effectively stifled any substantial reforms in the economic field and placed the government upon a permanently defensive footing, but its survival in the face of such a challenge from those for whom an entire political modus vivendi was at risk was in itself something of an achievement. The strength of the reaction required that the junior officer corps that had done much to sponsor and protect the 1944 movement either commit itself fully to consolidate the reforms or withdraw completely; it took the former course. The government of Colonel Jacobo Arbenz (1951-54) was unique in Guatemalan history in that it attempted to modify relations of production in the countryside by fundamentally non-coercive means. In doing this Arbenz necessarily eschewed liberal methods, but he relied less on the questionable advice of the small Communist Party than on a ´neutral´ and ´professional´ military to oversee and constrain a measured campaign of popular mobilisation around a goal of agrarian reform, as well as more democratic motifs such as universal suffrage, which had been introduced but hardly effectively implemented by Arevalo. The project failed because, at the peak of the cold war, Washington was totally unprepared to tolerate such a risk-laden endeavour, and sought to overthrow the regime. The military institution, insecure about its new and apparently secondary role, edged firmly towards neutrality. One should not underestimate the profound impact and implications of the final CIA-backed invasion of 1954, but in hindsight it is clear that the passing of a window of opportunity for the armed forces was no less critical. Arbenz established the rudiments of a ´democratic revolution´ and therefore drew Guatemala into a new era, but in doing so he provided for his own downfall and the rapid reversal of the gains that had been achieved. The post-1954 regimes have thus been restorationist in a general sense, but they have also registered the changes that took place over the reformist decade.

The effects of the 1954 counter-revolution were to make the military the country´s leading political force in a positive sense rather than by default, to refine the army´s methods of holding power through the establishment of closely ´managed´ elections, whereby one minister of defence succeeded his predecessor as president, and to constrain military dissidence very tightly indeed. Naturally, the consolidation of such a system took some time, and required a degree of negotiation which involved occasional outbreaks of sectional coups, but by the mid-1960s the format had become regularised. The survival of personalist elements has meant that various senior officers have been able to form their own parties, but the effect of this in terms of civil-military relations has rarely gone beyond short-term tactical conflicts, the maintenance of localised spoils circuits, and the incorporation of factions of the civilian elite into military negtiations over office. At no stage have these electoralist vehicles genuinely disturbed entrenched military power. They have served to formalise the high command´s dealings with its civilian allies, and to provide a form of buffer zone between the military and various interest groups with which it cannot deal directly without prejudicing key elements of the corporate structure. It is unlikely that such political forces, which are without exception lodged on the extreme right of the political spectrum (notably in the MLN), could take advantage of the US-sponsored trend towards refurbishing formal democracy and establish a genuinely competitive system against the military veto.

Civilian scope for resisting such a veto is limited by the structures outlined above, but it is also restricted by more recent developments which have situated the military at the centre of the existing socio-economic network in more than its purely coercive aspects. Both as an institution and in terms of its individual members, the army has come to acquire important economic interests. This process has linked the more common statist ideas of junior officers with the less official and more directly remunerative forms of accumulation and social mobility evident in the upper echelons of the corps. These two currents do, of course, manifest contradictory aspects and are always subject to negotiation, but their overall effect has been to brake any tendency to revert to a genuinely civilian regime. In so far as the inclusion of economic interests within strictly institutional objectives is relatively common in the third world, this is not an anomalous feature, but the phenomenon has been taken so far in Guatemala that the country´s military have acquired a certain notoriety even in Latin American terms for their entrepreneurial brio. Short-term commodity booms and the discovery of oil in the 1970s consolidated such a tendency at the very time that the post-1954 system came under concerted popular pressure.

No less important as a factor in maintaining the military in office is the singularly extended and taxing anti-guerrilla campaign fought by the army over the last fifteen years. This campaign has arguably given the Guatemalan military greater experience in the field of counter-insurgency than any other in the Americas bar that of the United States and possibly Colombia. Although there was a marked hiatus in the mid-1970s, the insurgency that expanded at the end of the decade was in many respects a continuation of that which had been fought by different methods in the late 1960s. In the first phase there was a heavy reliance on United States skills and advice; in the more recent period this feature is much less marked, in clear distinction to developments elsewhere in the region. The principal reason for this lies in the breaking of all but formal diplomatic relations with Washington as a result of the Carter administration´s policy on human rights. Having successfully contained the guerrilla threat at the turn of the decade, a relatively powerful army and state responded to US pressure in a manner more akin to that taken in Chile and Argentina than to that evidenced in El Salvador or even Nicaragua.

The exceptional path that was followed at the end of the 1970s - that of accepting diplomatic isolation, seeking alternative military sponsors, and deepening right-wing nationalism - owed much to the basic logistical necessity of maintaining an all-embracing repressive posture if the incipient peasant war was not to break beyond containable limits. The fact that the local capitalist class failed to supplement US pressure, and, indeed, rallied round the ultramontane colonels, demonstrates that such a threat was widely perceived and not simply a function of military perpetuationism. There was no major internal dispute on the question of democracy or the form of maintaining public order even before Somoza´s fall. Once the FSLN had come to power and the Salvadorean civil war attained its present dimensions, this tendency further to restrict the scope of political debate was accelerated. Thus those conflicts that have since occurred have taken place within a very narrow political field. This does not necessarily reduce their critical character, but it does represent an aversion to reconsidering the full gamut of social policy, as well as indicating that the bases of internal polarisation over the last five years have been determined by external influence only to a certain degree. The issues facing senior Guatemalan officers in the mid-1980s are principally of a tactical nature; their strategy for confronting a profound social breakdown is not the subject of dispute and is broadly accepted as a historical necessity.

The debate over the counter-insurgency campaign itself has not been particularly heated, but it does feed into and to some extent derive from more disturbing disputes at government level. The origin of these may be located in the wake of the Nicaraguan revolution, although they did not fully break on the surface until the elections of Spring 1982. This poll was handled with remarkable ineptitude by the ruling bloc, which sought simply to continue the tradition of placing the minister of defence in the presidency without allowing for a fuller debate with the civilian parties of the right (the centre and left boycotted the poll), or within the officer corps as a whole. There emerged, as a result, a discernible generational split in the army with important sections of the middle officer corps distancing themselves from the high command, in support both of the extreme right, pledged to a more emphatic military campaign and a greater civilian voice in affairs of policy, and of greater flexibility in the structure of command. This split never acquired a properly political character, but it did fuel demands for adherence to formal democracy and an end to fraud, as well as indicating that changes in administration were necessary after July 1979. General Rios Montt´s coup against the ´continuist´ bloc ushered into prominence those who supported a higher nationalist profile, more flexible (but no less violent) counter-insurgency methods, and a move to rationalise the mechanism by which senior office was allocated. No significant social reform was placed on the agenda, and once it was clear that the parties of the extreme right had no real influence, the new regime seemed to reflect little more than a fairly predictable response to excessive concentration of spoils, and a complementary loss of political nerve and touch in the upper reaches of the institution. Montt´s personal eccentricities (centred upon a fundamentalist protestantism) played little part in the making of the coup and were not central thereafter. What soon became the object of dispute was the degree to which a polity on a war footing should be aligned with Washington, and how far an economy that was under no less stress should be organised in the short-term interests of private capital. As Rios Montt began to retreat from the obligatory early promises to hold fresh elections, he also began to implement policies that put the centralist and statist traditions of the military above those of its no less strong laissez faire traditions. In short, he moved to maximise the military´s advantage at a time of war to extract minor but still appreciable concessions from the private sector. This served to reinforce the tattered alliance between the civilian elite and the bulk of the high command, for which the spoils system and close relations with the United States were so important. Thus General Mejia´s coup in August 1983 was not at root prompted by Montt´s insensitive anti-catholicism: it reasserted the US mandate, revitalised the old internal alliance, and opened up the military to a greater regional role. The fact that Mejia could oust Montt within fifteen months and with little difficulty indicates the extent to which these differences were ones of style and tenor rather than of substance. Were it not for the pressing external circumstances, it is probable that such a dispute would have taken place without recourse to changes in government. Nevertheless, Mejia´s takeover was not simply a restitution of the status quo ante. It reflected a recognition inside the majority of the officer corps that the pseudo-democratic channels that had always existed should be reopened, and the civilian political formations given greater space within them as an overture to Washington.

The difficulties of giving such an ´opening´ both some substance and firm limits will without doubt add to those that stem from the military´s role and methods to complicate any major alteration of the diplomatic isolation in which Guatemala has existed for the better part of the last decade. The slow but apparently relentless aggregation of mass opposition to the post-1954 system has accentuated tension in the negotiation of relations inside a narrow power bloc. This bloc possesses by virtue of its greater institutionality more scope than did the dynastic structure of the Somozas in Nicaragua, but it still remains the most politically restricted target in the zone, despite its undeniable logistical strength. The Guatemalan armed forces have moved with greater caution than their less confident and weaker regional allies, and are now engaged in a war of position in which radical tactics are employed but with little option of changing strategy. The progress - or otherwise - of this campaign is now the most important single factor in determining the political role of the Guatemalan military.

EL SALVADOR

The breakdown of the Salvadorean political system

has proceeded by stages, but became completely irreversible in 1980, by which time the United States was committing itself to a major salvage operation without which the military and its allies would certainly have been overthrown. Nowhere else in the region is fighting so intense and widespread, having escalated beyond discrete outbreaks of insurgency into a nation-wide campaign in which large formations are involved. Unlike Guatemala, this is a relatively new phenomenon in El Salvador, and has thrust the army into a series of acute crises for which it lacks an adequate response in either political or military terms. As a result, it has acquiesced in an only marginally qualified US direction of affairs. There have been a number of contradictions in this process, but they are largely of a secondary order. For the first time in its history the Salvadorean military has become a truly constabulary force, reserving unto itself merely the rights to implement US policy in its own less than efficient manner, and to retain a voice in political matters that might still remain undetermined in the face of unpredictable metropolitan expansiveness and civilian insecurities.

On the face of things, the Salvadorean politico-military tradition is very similar to that of Guatemala. For two decades the army has controlled the government through managed elections, in which civilian parties have been allowed to participate whilst always being forestalled from posing any genuine threat to the monopoly of the institution's own political power. However, both in the detail of this arrangement for distributing power and in its more distant antecedents there exist important differences.

Although El Salvador possesses a productive structure very similar to that of Guatemala, and has mirrored the phases of its economic development quite closely, the country has always been overpopulated and there have rarely existed substantial problems with respect to the provision of a rural labour force. Thus, while it has always been necessary to regiment seasonal labour and uphold the rights of the large commercial estates, the profile of the military as an agent of rural control has been somewhat lower, more localised, and generally oriented towards intermittent outbreaks of discontent rather than a crisis that oscillated eternally between productive needs and public order. The difference is one of quantity rather than quality, but it has proved important in defining superstructural and political roles. Moreover, while the break-up of indigenous and municipal common lands towards the end of the nineteenth century dynamised a highly competitive market for land, as well as social discontent to no less a degree than in Guatemala, it did not have such an all-embracing effect on the republican oligarchy, which retained its direct control of the state and its hegemony over the military.

This system lasted until 1932, when the world economic crisis propelled a complete breakdown of the longstanding system of authoritarian but civilian rule, prompted an untenable stab at reform, and then provoked a short-lived but extremely violent peasant rebellion (January 1932). This uprising incorporated the efforts of the small and inexperienced Communist Party, adding an ideological element to an otherwise traditional peasant jacquerie. The ´communism´ of the 1932 revolt was in practice absolutely minimal, but was sufficiently discernible to enable the rising to be depicted as ´red´, thereby further justifying an unmitigated jettisoning of civilism and formal democracy. The price the landlord class paid for the military´s extraordinarily violent and utterly decisive suppression of the rebellion was formal political power. After 1932 there was no civilian government for fifty years. Thus the terms of the ruling coalition in El Salvador were that the landed elite retain its veto over economic policy and be allowed to sponsor tame political groupings, but that it surrender formal direction of government to the armed forces. Although this system was destabilised in 1944-48 under Guatemalan influence, and underwent certain modifications in the 1950s and 1960s, it remained intact and unquestioned from within the army and the rural oligarchy.

It was precisely the scope of the defeat of the left and the peasantry in 1932 that enabled the military to hold on to power for so long and, after a decade, to experiment with various subordinate forms of relaxation and very tightly controlled reforms. The historical timing of the major shift in the balance of forces therefore determined a different development from that in Guatemala. The military had space to tinker with the dictatorial apparatus, and gradually refine it with democratic trimmings, low level co-optational elements, and a degree of negotiation with the political forces of the elite and the managerial middle class. Thus, although the Cuban revolution prompted an interruption along democratic and reformist lines in 1960-61, this was reversed without a retreat into the pogrom-based government evident in Guatemala after 1954, or indeed that which had prevailed in El Salvador itself for ten years after 1932. The army had institutionalised its rule sufficiently to allow it to be mediated by its own political party. Furthermore, it passed responsibility for the maintenance of public order to the paramilitary police, creating an important division of repressive labour. There was, until the mid-1970s, a more delicate balance between fraud and repression, and a greater emphasis upon the necessity for a democratic facade, than that which existed in Guatemala.

The effects of this more negotiable system were to broaden internal debates over its orientation, and to exacerbate popular expectations of a genuine participationism. As a result, first the left and then the authentically reformist forces within Christian and Social Democracy entered into sharp antagonism with the landlord-military pact. By the early 1970s the system was confronted by a major social challenge, as well as by the opportunity to bleed off many of its more critical features by permitting in practice the reforms for which the formal space and disposition already existed. This opportunity was never taken up, revealing the true superficiality of the refinements to the post-1932 regime. In 1972, electoral fraud prompted a significant section of the junior officer corps to join with the democratic opposition and attempt a coup. In 1977 it incited discontent and mass mobilisation which were so widespread that they were only controlled with great difficulty. Already badly fractured, the 'guided democracy' of the colonels collapsed extremely rapidly in the wake of the Nicaraguan revolution. Although the army had long held power, it only engaged in counter-insurgency operations with reluctance, since these were left (in their early stages at least) to the National Guard, Treasury and National Police, all of which preferred an unsophisticated brutality and possessed few properly professional characteristics. Thus the military had become distanced from its formal mission, almost as a result of its historic success. Moreover, while the paramilitary forces retained close relations with landlords on a local basis, and the senior commanders interacted with them in terms of government and the state spoils system, large sections of the junior officer corps had become critically dislocated from the traditional alliance because they were involved neither in low-level repressive operations nor in the 'mixed economy' of state administration. It was this professionalised and generational sector that attempted against all the odds to forge a reformist alternative to the ossified pseudo-democracy on its right, and the escalating threat of marxist guerrillas on its left. The potential that such an option offered for braking polarisation and stemming the post-Somoza tide commended it to Washington, which, if only by dint of non-intervention, aided the coup of October 1979 staged by colonels and majors who forwarded a programme as radical as any held by Central American officers since 1954.

This initially effective move sought to meet democratic and reformist demands made highly popular precisely by the disappointments of pseudo-democracy, through the creation of a strong centrist regime that incorporated both officers and civilian technocrats of the political centre. It failed because Salvadorean politics had already become too polarised to sustain mediation, despite the quite genuine statist aspirations of the reformist officers and the appreciable good will of the reformist parties, including the Communist Party. Thus, in its efforts to block the powerful left, the junta was obliged to make increasing recourse to the repressive organs and political forces which it had just suppressed. The civilians, on the other hand, were driven further to the left by the continued belligerence of the right wing, and the apparent acquiescence in this of the junior officers.

The form in which the first junta of October 1979 to January 1980 presented a number of democratic and structural reforms served as the model for all succeeding regimes, but these were and continue to be contolled by the extreme right, which succeeded in forcing the United States to redefine all its ambitious reforms in terms of the counter-insurgency campaign, and halt any substantial inroads into the authority of the landlord class. By mid-1980 the political centre had allied itself firmly with a left wing pledged to armed struggle, its rump remaining only to provide the kernel of a number of 'democratic' civilian administrations that survived only by courtesy of the US embassy. The reformist current in the army neither retained its impetus nor transferred its loyalties to the left; it simply became marginalised. On the other hand, the senior officers who retrieved their old positions of influence were obliged to yield up their veto over operational affairs, albeit slowly and as a result of the aggregate effects of their own inefficiency. This dual process incorporated a number of crises and might have prompted further divisions, but the tight links between the senior political managers of the armed forces and the landlords were too strong for Washington to break without running a major risk of the complete implosion of the dominant bloc. The United States therefore mediated in favour of the old alliance, and desisted from implementing the changes it had tabled as a resolution to the conflict. By doing so it effectively committed itself to an extended military campaign, and a dangerous dependence on a force that was not well equipped to fight it.

The failure of the centrist initiative which seemed for some time to be a potential option for military government in El Salvador underlines the extreme fragility of the old landlord alliance when it comes under armed challenge. It has proved to be too cumbersome and entrenched to sustain the kind of reorientation and manoeuvre necessary to stall polarisation and avert widespread rural warfare. The peculiar weakness of the Salvadorean military is that it tried to undertake such a transformation, but when it was far too late. This tardiness was in fact determined by the system itself, even though it possessed more fluidity than did that in Guatemala. For a while the very ability of the guerrillas to sustain a long campaign and outfight the army in tactical encounters suggested that with its critical ´formative experience´ as distant as 1932, and in the wake of the frustrated experiment of 1979, sections of the military might still opt in extremis for a negotiated solution before the war became total. However, the preponderant US role has effectively ruled this out, other than as an irreversible act of dissidence. A pessimistic interpretation of the lessons of Nicaragua would suggest such negotiation to be essential, but an optimistic reading of developments in Guatemala would obviate it as a feasible option for a junior officer. Yet while the possibilities of restoring some genuine debate over policy inside the armed forces seem minimal, they do exist to a greater degree than in Guatemala, and may be kept alive by the burdens of a war that is gradually being lost in local and strategic terms.

With this somewhat muted caveat, we can say that the failure to realise the objectives of October 1979 committed the Salvadorean military apparatus to the dictates of Washington, and to its traditional alliance with rural oligarchy, the only viable social force for the counter-revolutionary endeavour. Such a state of affairs is underpinned by the fact that by mid-1983 the local logistical resources for countering a geographically expanding and operationally more efficient guerrilla threat were effectively exhausted. Not even the despatch of thousands of troops to foreign centres for intensive training, the increased employment of borrowed air power, and the introduction of Vietnam-style methods, could compensate for a depleted manpower base and ingrained resistance to the adoption of the methods of modern warfare, as opposed to those of traditional repression that coexisted for decades with pre-professional deportment. Moreover, as a result of the considerable difficulties encountered by the United States in its efforts to overcome these structural impediments, the Salvadorean military is liable to come under even closer external supervision, and be more tightly incorporated within a regional collaborative enterprise. Such a prospect embodies a surrender of sovereignty that the Guatemalans have already shown themselves prepared to resist at some length. The Salvadorean military, which has never played a constabulary role in the same mode as did its counterparts in Honduras and Nicaragua, and is constructed around traditions that emanate from fifty years in virtually undisputed power, may yet baulk at this option even though it is manifestly counterposed to the threat of extinction.

HONDURAS

The case of Honduras differs significantly from those of Guatemala and El Salvador in that the military only entered politics in a unified and effective manner in the 1950s. As a consequence, the army has no deep-seated set of political traditions to fall back on, although it has been engaged in government with growing commitment and confidence since the mid-1960s. This distinctiveness derives very largely from the belated adoption of coffee, the lack of an authentic liberal revolution, and the dominance of the banana enclave controlled by foreign enterprises. Thus the

economy, backward even by local standards during the
colonial period, jumped from virtual autarky to a
deeply imbalanced structure wherein a rural
subsistence economy surrounded but was critically
dominated by highly capitalised plantations directed
by companies which provided basic infrastructure and
determined political development. Nowhere else in
Central America did a local political economy
manifest such a complete internal imbalance, with
both poles being more extreme than in other
countries. Such a combination - a classic case of
combined and uneven development - led to frequent US
intromissions to protect company interests, regulate
fiscal matters, and tutor politics into a more or
less compliant succession of civilian figureheads
overseeing a thoroughly threadbare and corrupt
administrative apparatus. The United States never
occupied Honduras militarily for any length of time,
but its influence was sufficiently strong to imbue
both civilian and military elites with what may
impressionistically be termed sepoy tendencies.
Equally, the enormous weight of the fruit companies
in local affairs hampered the emergence of an
authentic domestic landlord class, and thereby
closed off a line of development evident in the
neighbouring states. The spoils system, established
in the periphery of the companies and through their
relations with the state, compensated for this to
some extent as a low level source of accumulation,
but it also held back a genuine class-based
politics. Moreover, this system was not exclusive
to the civilian or military spheres, and restricted
the emergence of a clear corporate constituency in
economic as well as professional terms.

When combined with the fact that the relatively
small and dispersed population did not require
excessive coercive management to bring it into the
labour market, or regiment it once it was there,
these factors served to delay the construction of a
coherent military apparatus, let alone its
politicisation, until the middle of the present
century. Used as a paramilitary police to back a
formidable company apparatus to control plantation
labour, the army was denied any substantial
state-forming function, grew accustomed to a
mortgaged sovereignty, and had minimal purchase in
the formation of political alliances.
Paradoxically, it was only in the wake of a major
strike movement in the mid-1950s, itself manifestly
influenced by the example of military reformism in
Guatemala, that the local armed forces properly

194

entered the field of politics. The form in which they did so was essentially as an arbitrator between various civilian factions loosely based on nineteenth century ideologies, but fundamentally seeking control of the state apparatus as a source of income and sectional employment. The insecure landed groups and even weaker industrial sectors lacked the ability to stage an independent political project outside the orbit of the multinational enterprises, but by the same token, they were without the resources to sustain a military that might, by virtue of its coercive strength, do so decisively on their behalf. As a result, the military existed on a state of relative parity with civilian forces, and tended much more towards an arbitrational role exercised over short periods, than towards extended collaboration based on a clear division of administrative labour. Such a tendency can be perceived even within periods of military government, which, given the small size and poverty of both civil society and state, frequently incorporated extensive concessions to civilian needs and pressures, even though from the late 1960s the army held onto power for longer periods and shied away from embracing formal democracy in the manner of their neighbours. In all societies, it is the military´s monopoly over coercive action that ultimately functions as its decisive characteristic, but in Honduras this is much more obvious than in most of Latin America because many of the political, ideological and administrative facets of such a monopoly have never developed to provide the army with an extended identity or supra-logistical tradition.

Even in the 1960s, senior officers were principally concerned to exercise their corporate advantages to secure a claim to scarce resources, maintain public order, and provide a rudimentary national defence. These broad objectives did not compel significant alterations in the form of government, and were maintained within a general framework of exchangeability with the civilian elite. The weakness of civilism matched that of militarism to such a degree that the real absence of democracy was not counterposed strongly against the relatively lenient application of dictatorship. Inside the upper reaches of local society, such distinctions were generally considered a function of direct sectional interests and proclivities rather than wholesale models. The middle class was too marginalised to launch an independent alternative,

and the local masses too little affected by the
minimal alterations in the balance of local power
structures to mobilise in a determinant fashion.

This rickety system came to an end in 1969 with
the war against El Salvador, which resulted in large
part from Honduras´ weakness inside the Central
American Common Market, and a need to redirect
growing domestic discontent. The trauma caused by
effective defeat at the hands of a more powerful
force accelerated an incipient tendency towards a
muscular and independent arbitration based around
agrarian reform and an institutionalised statism.
This current was most manifest among junior
officers, for whom the principal motifs of the
professional mission had been badly tarnished in the
war. Although their influence was to be curbed as
polarisation deepened first abroad and then at home,
the young field officers exhibited a more enduring
and resolute adherence to state-based reformism than
any of their regional counterparts between the two
peaks of this current - 1944 (Guatemala) and 1979
(El Salvador). They compelled at least the partial
implementation of an agrarian reform, and hindered
an institutional retreat from power that was
presented as a concession to democracy, but was
intended to avoid involvement in structural reform.
Yet the reform had little effect, being limited in
scope and brought to a precipitate halt once its
social consequences were fully appreciated. The
senior officers, closely connected with the United
States, inextricably bound up in the spoils system,
and resistant to any nationalist assault on foreign
enterprise, regained their authority without major
difficulties.

Thus the relative delay in the impact of the
Nicaraguan revolution in Honduras was only partially
due to the effects of local military government. In
fact it was only after the United States had
sponsored new elections in 1981, and guided the
military out of power, that the armed forces began
to threaten the Sandinistas and aggravate border
tension, as well as imposing sharp repression at
home. None of this would have been possible for any
length of time had the military not been the
recipients of considerable logistical support and
firm political guidence. In so far as these have
brought with them massive financial inputs, they
represent a very important compensation for leaving
government, which would anyway have been less a
traumatic defeat than a measured settlement. The
outstanding problem for the Honduran military chiefs

may be denominated political only in the extended sense of the term. Yet as their country becomes militarised under US tutelage, they face the uneasy prospect that the rationale for this militarisation may become a self-fulfilling prophecy. Previously untouched by guerrilla activity, Honduras has now weaned a domestic armed challenge. Decisively beaten in its only international conflict in the twentieth century, it now finds itself obliged to taunt a neighbour which possesses military and political resources far greater than its own. Removed from government, the military are placed in a position where the application of dictatorship is far more complementary to their escalating field campaign, than is the lame formal democracy which was set up as a quid pro quo for being able to stage precisely such a campaign. Having accepted their centrality in forcing through these manifest contradictions, local commanders lack well-grounded domestic models by which to realign their political instincts.

CONCLUSION

Although there are a number of patterns in Central American politics, the most typical is the alternation of factional military (or military-backed) regimes whose potential for collapse results from a general lack of social support. The underlying bases of factional politics can be found in the social structure, in latent racial conflict (at least in the case of Guatemala), and above all in both the need for and the willingness of the US government to come to the support of entrenched elites at times of crisis. The officer corps is not highly differentiated from dominant civilian groups, although the perceived threat of insurgency has tended to foster unity in all fundamental military and military-political matters. Moreover, among a variety of military interventions in politics, the most decisive landmarks in the history of the area have been veto coups, in El Salvador in 1932 and in Guatemala in 1954.

Panama provides an interesting contrast to this general picture. It is all the more striking because Panama itself, and not just the Panamanian National Guard, owes its very existence to US policy. Yet in 1968, after a ´breakthrough´ coup, the Guard leadership was able to use a negotiated

nationalism to build a clientele and stabilise its
own rule. It is of course true that the United
States had to appear more amenable to the pressures
of a Central American government than did (or do)
local landed elites. Even so, Panama suggests that
there is a clear relationship between the factional
exclusiveness of other military establishments in
Central America, and the political and guerrilla
threats which they now face. From a different
angle, the eventual fate of the Somoza dynasty in
Nicaragua indicates the same conclusion.

The vicious circle of factionalism, isolation
and violence can be seen, in somewhat different
ways, in both Guatemala and El Salvador. Both have
been, ultimately, under military rule for decades,
although with a formal electoral facade in which
general elections have been no more than elections
among generals. The military has not looked hard
for a civilian clientele, fearing that this would
lose landlord and United States support - as
happened in Guatemala prior to 1954 - and has
certainly shown no interest in returning power to
authentic civilian rulers. Civilians who appeared
to provide an electoral alternative have instead
been subject to routine assassination. This form of
rule, allied to a virulent form of state terror, has
left these regimes with a guerrilla threat which
cannot be co-opted, and an absence of credible
civilians to whom government could be handed over.
The result has been at best a loss of national and
institutional independence to the United States, and
at worst could yet mean defeat by the Marxist left.

Honduras has not suffered factional military
rule in so brutal a manner. Instead there was,
until the 1969 war against El Salvador, a moderator
pattern. Subsequently the military attempted to
develop a clientelist system, an attempt which was
largely abandoned when social conflict began to
increase. Instead, government was returned to
civilians while the military continued to play a key
role behind the scenes. The danger here is that a
more exclusivist and factional form of military rule
might result from a counter-guerrilla campaign
which, because it stems more from the global
priorities of the United States than from conflicts
within Honduras, could both divide the military and
isolate it from potential civilian allies. Such a
development may be held back only temporarily by the
US government's present support for the maintenance
of formal democracy in that country.

BIBLIOGRAPHICAL NOTE

I have included no footnotes in this chapter since the sources used are very wide-ranging, and frequently do not present consolidated information on the military establishments themselves. For readers who do not have Spanish, investigation of this topic in any depth is extremely difficult, but in spite of their obvious bias the US army handbooks on the republics provide a useful starting point. There is only one English language monograph on a Central Americal army, Richard Millett´s excellent Guardians of the Dynasty (Maryknoll, 1977), which traces the background of the Nicaraguan National Guard in close detail. More thematic in style, in need of some revision and as yet unpublished, but full of useful ideas, is Stephen C. Ropp, In Search of the New Soldier: Junior Officers and the Prospect of Social Reform in Panama, Honduras and Nicaragua (PhD thesis, University of California at Riverside, 1971). Part of this thesis has been developed in Ropp, "The Honduran Army and the Sociopolitical Evolution of the Honduran State", The Americas, 30, 1974. Interesting material on the Guatemalan military may be found in Kenneth J. Grieb, "The Guatemalan Military and the Revolution of 1944", The Americas, 32, 1975; the chapter by Jerrold Buttrey in Richard Adams, ed, Crucifixion by Power (Austin, 1970); and Jerry L. Weaver, "The Political Style of the Guatemalan Military", in Kenneth Fidel, ed, Militarism in Developing Countries (New Brunswick, 1975). For a useful wider context that contains appreciable material on the army in Guatemala, see Susanne Jonas and David Tobias, eds, Guatemala (Berkeley, 1974). There is now considerable material on the Salvadorean armed forces, but it is dispersed in general studies. Central to these are the two works by Thomas P. Anderson, Matanza: El Salvador´s Communist Revolt of 1932 (Lincoln, Nebraska, 1971), and The War of the Dispossessed: Honduras and El Salvador 1969 (ibid, 1981). Important less for the information that it imparts than for the viewpoint (and epoch) that it reflects is Charles W. Anderson, "El Salvador: The Army as Reformer", in Martin C. Needler, ed, Political Systems of Latin America (Princeton, 1964). My own The Long War: Dictatorship and Revolution in El Salvador (London, 1982) presents some material, but the forthcoming study by the historian Dermot Keogh promises to provide the fullest account of the contemporary Salvadorean military. All these texts

contain useful bibliographies of further and more
detailed material in Spanish.

Chapter Nine

RIDING THE TIGER : INSTITUTIONALISING THE MILITARY
REGIMES IN PAKISTAN AND BANGLADESH

Gowher Rizvi

INTRODUCTION

In marked contrast to India, the two partitioned
states of Pakistan and Bangladesh have (except for
one brief spell in each) been under military rule
since 1958. So long a period of military government
indicates both that the armed forces have attained
an entrenched position in the political structure of
the two states, and that it has been exceptionally
difficult to combine this position with the
recognition of civilian political forces within any
generally acceptable constitutional structure. It
will be argued in this chapter that military
intervention was precipitated not by a failure of
parliamentary democracy - which, it is true, was far
from functioning satisfactorily - but by the desire
of civil-military elites together with a faction of
unrepresentative politicians to control decision
making power by keeping it out of the hands of
representative elites. Any attempt to
institutionalise must, under the military
dispensation, ensure the exclusion of
´representative politicians´ by creating a patronage
network capable of shoring up support for the
regime. The rules of the game were developed by
Pakistan´s first military ruler, General Ayub Khan,
and have been followed with almost mechanical
precision (with local modifications) by his
successors in both Pakistan and Bangladesh. For
convenience of analysis, this chapter will examine
this theme with reference first to the united
Pakistan up to 1971, and then to Pakistan
(previously West Pakistan) and to Bangladesh after
the 1971 partition.

THE MILITARY IN UNITED PAKISTAN, 1958-1971

Military and Politics in Pakistan, 1947-58

In the recent history of decolonisation, few states
have been born with such problems as Pakistan. The
Pakistan that emerged in 1947 was a "truncated and
moth-eaten" version of that demanded in March 1940.
East Punjab had been sliced off from the West, and
Assam and Western Bengal, including Calcutta, from
East Pakistan. The eastern wing was separated from
the western by eleven hundred miles of ´hostile´
India. The surgery of the partition had left
Pakistan anaemic and incapacitated. Virtually all of
the industries both in the east and in the west had
fallen within the Indian sphere, Pakistan inheriting
the agriculturally productive but backward
territories. Commercial life was similarly
dislocated by the migration of the mainly Hindu
capitalists to India.

The one area in which Pakistan inherited a
disproportionate share of the legacy of British
India was the military. Even though only 23% of
India´s population was Moslem, the Moslems made up
nearly 40% of India´s army. When following the
partition the army was divided, these forces fell to
Pakistan. In the circumstances of the birth of
Pakistan, this was almost considered providential.
It was widely believed that India had only accepted
the partition to get rid of the British, and would
attempt a merger as soon as the British troops had
left.(1) This was given some credence by the
outbreak of hostilities with India over Kashmir. In
the euphoria of independence and a popular distrust
of India, there was almost a general consensus that
defence must have priority. This is clearly
reflected in the defence expenditure for the period
1947-57, when an average of nearly 60% of the total
government outlay was spent on defence. The army,
with a high level of internal unity derived from its
long tradition under the British imperial regime,
and with its self-esteem as the guarantor of the
independence of a fragile and artificial state,
enjoyed from the start a dominant position.

The Prime Minister, Liquat Ali Khan, had
antagonistic relations with the provincial
politicians and army officers, but was fortunate in
that many of the senior civil and military officers
were fellow refugees from the United Provinces. As
was _o be expected, he involved the civil and
military bureaucrats increasingly in decision
making: the provincial cabinets in the Punjab and

Sind were dismissed and placed under governor´s rule. In the army he picked Ayub Khan to replace the British Commander-in-Chief. From a Lieutenant Colonel in 1947, Ayub was within four years made a General. His main qualification was that he was neither a Punjabi nor a Pathan. He was a Hindko speaker from Hazara, unaligned with the provincial political and military elites, and Liquat hoped to use him to keep the army loyal. Liquat had succeeded in putting down a plot for a military coup in 1950, but was assassinated in October 1951 in Rawalpindi, not far from the army GHQ. During his lifetime, he was able to exercise some control over the civil-military officers. His death unleashed the beginning of intrigue and conspiracy by the civil-military elites which were eventually to lead to the demise of parliamentary democratic institutions.

General Ayub was a clever manipulator.(2) He was unabashedly ambitious, and realised the importance of building up a strong army to achieve his political goals. Since the country´s economy was inadequate for the purpose, he needed to achieve this goal through foreign policy, and at a time when the United States was looking for Asian allies in the Cold War, and India would not play ball, his overtures fell on willing ears.(3) With U.S. military aid, Ayub was not only able to create an effective modern army, but also established his own position within it. He was also shrewd enough to realise that his effectiveness depended on his ability to influence foreign policy to suit the needs of the defence ministry. It was largely at Ayub´s instance that Pakistan rejected Nehru´s offer of a plebiscite in Jammu and Kashmir in return for an unarmed and neutral Pakistan. For Ayub, continuing hostility to India provided the <u>raison d´etre</u> for the existence of a vast army. When Pakistan joined SEATO and CENTO, Ayub killed two birds with one stone. He had secured a generous source for military equipment and ensured a perennial hostility to India, thereby making sure that no government would attempt to cut defence expenditure. His chance to exercise supreme power came in October 1958, when President Mirza declared martial law in order to ward off a general election, in which both his own and Ayub´s position would have been in jeopardy. Mirza abrogated the constitution, dismissed the cabinet, banned the political parties, and cancelled the elections, while Ayub, who was appointed Chief Martial Law Administrator (CMLA), soon disposed of Mirza.

Ayub and Basic Democracy

The carefully nurtured plan of the civil-military bureaucracy to overthrow democratic institutions was obviously kept a secret. In public Ayub posed as an honest soldier doing his duty and started a barrage of propaganda both to discredit the political elites and to demonstrate that parliamentary democracy was unsuited to the conditions of Pakistan.(4) In time this view became widely accepted, and Ayub began to describe his action as a 'revolution'.(5) That Ayub ushered in some reforms or that the streets of the cities were cleaner is not disputed. But the implication that Ayub was a reformer trying to sort out the political mess both misses the nature of Ayub's coup and ignores the continuity of civil-military dominance in the pre- and post-1958 period.(6) The coup was little more than a pre-emptive strike to prevent a general election which might have cost Ayub his job and the civil-military bureaucracy their ascendancy in decision making. If we accept this interpretation, the policies of the Ayub regime become more comprehensible.

Behind the military facade the old civil servants, now freed from any control by their political masters, ran the administration in conjunction with army colleagues. The Deputy C.M.L.A. was Aziz Ahmed, the Secretary General to the Government of Pakistan. He and his colleagues from the ministries of Defence, Interior, Finance, Industries, Commerce, Economic Affairs and Irrigation Power formed the advisory council to assist the CMLA. Although the constitution was abrogated as unsuitable, it was paradoxically announced that "Pakistan shall be governed as nearly as possible in accordance with the abrogated constitution". When, after Mirza's resignation, the advisory Council was dissolved, Ayub's new cabinet consisted predominantly of civil servants. There were nine civilians in his cabinet holding important portfolios like Finance, Communications, Commerce, Information, Interior and Labour.

The new regime's close alliance with civil bureaucracy was also revealed by its attitude to corruption. A high-powered screening committee was set up in January 1959 to investigate the charges of corruption among civil servants, but in the event only thirteen officers were dismissed, more than half of whom were migrant Moslems who had now fallen foul of the ruling Punjabi dominance. Ayub Khan had clearly seen the danger of biting the hand that nurtures. By contrast, and as was to be expected, Ayub acted ruthlessly against the politicians. The terms of the existing Public Regulation Order (Disqualification) Act were considered inadequate and he therefore introduced two new orders, the Public Offices (Disqualification) Order (PODO) and Elective Bodies (Disqualification) Order (EBDO). Under these orders anybody found "guilty of misconduct" could be barred from politics; and to make sure that no-one slipped through the net, the two orders were given retrospective effect from 14 August 1947. It was an effective exercise, and although exact numbers of politicians barred under these orders were never made public, informed estimates vary from six to seven thousand.(7)

Barring the politicians from public life or banning political parties was easy. But to prevent them from returning required some careful social and political engineering. Ayub's two main sources of authority remained the civil service and the army, but in the long run if his regime were to survive he would have to obtain legitimisation through greater participation. Political parties were anathema to him. Before he could launch himself in national politics he realized the necessity of creating a strong local base which could be controlled through the government apparatus. This also fitted in with his military belief that the people of Pakistan were too unsophisticated and illiterate to exercise their democratic rights.(8) His response was the establishment of a system of local bodies which came to be known as Basic Democracies (BD). While this system received favourable comments at the time,(9) it was a shrewd device which, while giving the impression of establishing popular institutions, ensured they would remain under the firm control of government officials.

The system was intended to perform multiple functions: it would secure a clientele for the regime, undertake developmental works and provide units of local government. And after the introduction of a constitution in 1962, it would have important constitutional functions as an electoral college for presidential and assembly elections, and as an arbiter in case of conflict between the President and the National Assembly. It was a five tiered institution (the highest tier, the Provincial Council, was abolished in 1961) with the Union Council in the rural areas (Town Committees in the towns) as the basic unit. Two-thirds of the Union Council members (who popularly came to be called the BD members) were elected by adult franchise for a period of five years and the remaining one-third of its members were to be official nominees.(10) They elected their own chairmen. At the next level was the Thana Council, one half of which was made up of the chairmen of the Union Councils within the jurisdiction of that Thana, while the other half consisted of officials nominated by the Deputy Commissioner. The third tier, where the bulk of the patronage lay, was the District Council. It was presided over by the District Commissioner with a ´safe´ membership: half were officials and the rest were ´non-officials´ appointed by the deputy commissioner. The Divisional Council was composed on the same basis as the District Council except that its members were drawn from all the districts within the Division.

Despite much publicity and patronage from the government, the BD system failed to establish itself as a popular institution. The majority of those who found a niche in the system were neither ´political´ nor ´professional´ but were businessmen, contractors or landowners, and touts who jumped on the bandwaggon, seeing in the new institutions the opportunity for securing government benefits particularly under its works programme.(11) It is true that the BDs were given much greater power and involvement than ever before, but they failed to generate the new cadre of leadership, or bridge the gap between elites and masses. At all levels the official stranglehold was such that BDs dared not take initiatives lest they antagonize |the ´Sarkar´. Most of them, particularly in West Pakistan, lacked the level of eduction or training which would have enabled them to conduct their business. As was inevitable they relied on government officials: the bulk of the budgets were prepared by circle officers and the items on the agenda also mostly originated from official suggestions.(12) Even though the system eventually collapsed, in the short-term it served Ayub well. He had created a base of whose support there could be little doubt, since the BD members, aware that their existence depended upon the survival of Ayub, remained firmly loyal to him; and by confining the exercise of mass adult franchise to the local level he had fragmented political conflict and diverted popular participation away from the national level. "The Basic Democracies system devised to recruit a base of popular Bengali support for the regime, and not to make the Bengalis equal sharers of power in the central decision making process, deliberately isolated and disfranchised the Bengali counterelite and its most active group of supporters."(13) This new system also made party politics obsolete. In the BD elections, given the small numbers of voters involved, what mattered was personal contact, influence and money rather than any party affiliation or adherence to a political philosophy. The system, through the works programme, remained staunchly loyal to the regime, even in East Pakistan. In the 1965 Presidential election, Ayub won handsomely in both wings.(14) But it should be stressed that Ayub´s support among the 80,000 BDs was not a correct reflection of his popularity in the country as a whole. The BD system, nevertheless, gave Ayub a base from which he was able to call a referendum on 17 February 1960 to demonstrate popular support for his regime. Armed with 80% backing in the referendum, Ayub proceeded to the second phase of the institutionalisation of his regime: the inauguration of a constitution.

Like the BD, the constitution was made to measure to fit Ayub´s requirements. It was introduced on 8 June 1962 by Ayub´s fiat. The constitution as it emerged was very much Ayub´s brainchild which neither reflected popular consensus nor always accepted the recommendations of his own constitutional inquiry committee.(15) The demands for a federal parliamentary system of government, direct election by adult franchise, granting of fundamental rights, and the existence of political parties had commanded sufficient support as evidenced by the findings of the Constitutional Commission, but failed to find favour with Ayub. The constitution provided for a government which an opposition leader described as being, of the President, by the President, for the President.(16) The BD system, Ayub reckoned, could be depended on (or coerced) to elect the government candidate for the presidency. But Ayub was not willing to tolerate a parliament which could curb or restrain his authority. The President was elected for a fixed term of five years by an electoral college formed by the 80,000 BDs and was not dependent on the confidence of the National Assembly. The central and provincial executives were responsible to the president and held office during his pleasure. The assemblies could discuss but had no control over recurring expenditure (accounting for over 90%), their control being confined to voting new expenditure. Ayub also made sure that his constitution would not be tampered with easily. The constitution could only be amended if a bill was passed by a 2/3 majority and approved by the President. But if the President disagreed, the bill was referred back to the Assembly for re-consideration and it could only be sent again to the President if it was backed by three-quarters of the Assembly. And that was not all. If the President still refused to give his assent, the bill could be put to a referendum of the electoral college, whose verdict would be final, in this or any other conflict between the President and the Assembly. Although the constitution had a quasi-federal structure which assigned to the provinces jurisdiction over a greater number of subjects than allowed in the 1956 constitution, the central government had overriding control over the provinces. The provincial governors, appointed by the President, were responsible to him and not to the provincial assembly; even the appointment of a provincial minister required presidential approval. The emergency powers equipped the President with powers to rule the country through ´ordinances´, the validity of which could not be challenged in a court of law. The President could proclaim an emergency if there was a threat to the external or internal security of the state, and the proclamation would remain in force for as long as he desired. The ´ordinances´ could not be challenged by the Assembly but if it approved the ordinance it became an Act of Parliament. Otherwise it would remain effective as a presidential ordinance.

Even after the introduction of the Basic Democracies and the constitution, the political parties were not allowed to be revived. Ayub harboured an inborn fear and distrust of politicians, particularly those with a popular base, and had therefore endeavoured to create a system which would do without organised political parties. Although members of the first National Assembly had sought election as individuals, two inferences were inescapable. First, most of the members were either newcomers or were politicians of the second echelon. Second, EBDO and PODO had barred many leading politicians, but it was noticeable that representatives of the two most popular parties - the Awami League and the National Awami Party - were conspicuous by their absence. It naturally robbed the regime of some of the legitimacy it had hoped to gain through the establishment of representative assemblies. The experience in parliament revealed Ayub´s fallacy of doing without political parties. Without a party of its own, the government had to ´buy´ support of the assembly members, but the arrangement was far from satisfactory.(17)

Ayub was reluctant to launch his own political party, and given the fact that most of his supporters were former Muslim Leaguers of the second rank, it was not surprising that Ayub was persuaded to take over a revived section of the Pakistan Muslim League. This proved to be a blunder. The Muslim League had been largely discredited before 1958, and although it had the prestige of the Pakistan movement, it lacked grass root workers and organisation. After Ayub joined the League in May 1963 and became its president, the party enjoyed all the advantages of being the party of government. It secured access to large funds, set up impressive offices in the cities and towns, and BD members flocked to join it. The workers could ensure a rapturous welcome wherever Ayub visited but could not generate popular enthusiasm or loyalty. It became the party of the Basic Democrats, it secured little new accretion of popular support, and its fate became linked to that of the system itself. No leader with mass support actually joined Ayub´s party.

Ayub´s constitutional engineering bore the imprint of a soldier´s battle plan. He had achieved the objectives he had set out to win. Or, to change the metaphor, Ayub had turned a full circle from 1958 to 1962. His military coup had been timed to pre-empt a general election which might have removed the initiative and decision making from the civil-military-political faction to the leaders of a genuinely broad based political party. The BD system and the assemblies provided a democratic facade for his regime, and the effective denial of universal adult franchise rendered the popular politicians impotent.(18) The status quo ante 1958 had been restored: the civil-military bureaucracy was ascendant and the unrepresentative rump of the old Muslim League was back in the ministerial chair.

While Ayub had established a political foothold, the army and the civil service remained his bulwark. Ayub remained mindful of his dependence on them and carefully cultivated their good will. The bureaucrats were well represented both in the central and provincial ministries, and "of the 280 members of the thirty-three major commissions formed by the regime for the purpose of suggesting substantive policy changes, nearly 60% were members of civil bureaucracy".(19) They continued to monopolise not only the headships of ministries both in the centre and in the provinces, and the forty lucrative chairmanships of autonomous bodies, but also secured for their members appointments for which they had little technical knowledge. Their privileged position increased their stakes in the stability of the regime - a role they adequately fulfilled through the control and manipulation of the BD system. With vast sums of money at their disposal for works programmes they kept the Basic Democrats in line: the police, judicial litigation or forfeiture of land, or the denial of irrigation water, brought the recalcitrant into the fold. The reliance of the regime on the civil bureaucracy was clearly demonstrated, when during the absence of the Governor abroad, the Chief Secretary of the province acted as the Governor and presided over cabinet meetings. Similarly when Ayub was taken seriously ill for over six months, he refused to part with authority for fear that under the constitution the Speaker - in this case a Bengali and a politician - would become the Acting President.

Once the constitution had been introduced, Ayub was anxious to rid his regime of a military image. The soldiers were withdrawn to their barracks and Ayub himself donned civilian clothes. But having himself come to power through a military coup and having been a party to much intrigue in the GHQ,(20) he was anxious to prevent its repetition. Also his hold over the country, despite institution building, was still dependent on his ability to command the loyalty of the armed forces. He achieved this both by keeping a very close eye on the armed forces and by continuing their privileged position. Under the constitution the Ministry of Defence was removed from civilian control (Article 17) and remained directly under his personal supervision. The capital was moved to Islamabad, in close proximity to the GHQ in Rawalpindi and, to prevent too close a liaison between the army and the air force, the Air HQ was moved to Peshawar. The two Commanders-in-Chief who followed Ayub were ´safe men´; both the generals, Muhammad Musa and Agha Mohammed Yahya Khan, belonged to the minority Shia community, which Ayub could exploit should they display any personal ambition. Indeed Yahya was given an accelerated promotion and by-passed several generals. The expenditure on defence, which, as has been noted, was phenomenal in the pre-1958 period, continued despite the fact that external threat was remote. In 1958-59 the defence expenditure stood at 966 million rupees and at the end of Ayub´s period it was 2760 million,(21) an increase of 200%. The increased expenditure enabled the regime to increase the pay of the armed forces and provide other facilities and perks. Settlement Training Centres were established for the benefit of retiring soldiers and under the Veteran Settlement Programme land was granted to them, varying from 240 acres for a Major-General and above, to 100 acres for Lieutenants, 64 acres for JCOs, and 32 acres for NCOs. Even officers on active service were given land for valour and outstanding services - 50 acres for officers and 25 acres for JCOs. The continuing loyalty of the officers was ensured by their appointment to the chairmanships of autonomous bodies, embassies, and corporations. General Musa was given the governorship of West Pakistan, Air Marshals Asgher Khan and Nur Khan became the chairmen of Pakistan International Airlines, Admiral Aheau, Chairman of Water & Power Development Authority and Governor of East Pakistan. Military officers were also in demand for highly paid sinecures in the private sector once it became obvious that they could be useful in manipulating decisions in favour of their clients. And many, like the President´s son and father-in-law, used their connections to set themselves up as industrialists.

The edifice which Ayub had so carefully built ostensibly worked well. In 1968 the regime could look back with satisfaction and celebrate its "decade of development". On the positive side - even if superficially - the country had enjoyed stability and a government had been in power uninterruptedly for ten years. The regime had launched two five year plans and Pakistan´s economic achievement was widely hailed as a model for developing countries. The BD system showed it was capable of delivering the goods: it had won for the regime two assembly elections (1962 and 1965) and one presidential election; and through its works programme had begun to gather for the regime a new network of clientage.(22) Most important of all, the politicians seemed to have been tamed.

In the very year in which the regime celebrated "the decade of development", signs were discernible that all was not well. With the expiry of the EBDO´s ban on politicians on 31 December 1966, many of the politicians who had been waiting in the wings made their entrance and launched their demands for a restoration of democracy. While divisions amongst politicians continued, their demands were not far dissimilar: reintroduction of adult franchise, restoration of fundamental rights and a revision of the constitution to reflect popular aspirations. The beginning of political agitation also coincided with a number of developments which gave it an impetus. The success of the regime in accelerating economic growth created problems which eroded the regime´s bases. The ´economic miracle´ of Pakistan had been achieved by the government´s policy of encouraging and subsidising the private sector without any consideration for income redistribution or the workers´ rights.(23) The wealth became concentrated in fewer hands and the gap between the rich and the poor widened. The disclosure by Mahbub ul Huq, the Chief Economist of the Planning Commission, that twenty families in Pakistan controlled 60% of the entire industrial capital, 80% of the banking and almost the entire insurance capital, gave substance to the allegation of inegalitarianism and identified the regime as a tool for the rich.(24)

Perhaps most crucial of all in undermining the regime´s institutions was Ayub´s endeavour to keep out the politicians. Its effect was particularly disastrous for the regime in East Pakistan. The exclusion of politicians from participation in decision making meant that East Pakistan´s involvement in the regime was virtually non-existent. This was particularly so because East Pakistan´s share in the middle and higher ranks of both the civil and military establishments was woefully small. The East Pakistan counterelite felt excluded and joined ranks with politicians who emphasised the need for East Pakistan autonomy. And still more significantly, the absence of East Pakistan elites at decision making levels created a dent within the civil-military bureaucracy. Most of the benefits and plum appointments which accrued to the bureaucracy went to the senior officers where the Bengali presence was conspicuously thin. It is not surprising therefore that the Bengali civil-military component who were the beneficiaries of Ayub´s regime should have felt alienated. The failure to incorporate the counterelites within the fold weakened the regime in East Pakistan.

The regime was also losing its grip in West
Pakistan. The September 1965 war between India and
Pakistan had been enormously ruinous and ended in a
stalemate. The Ministry of Information's propaganda
had been successful in convincing the people that
Pakistan had actually won the war. The people were
given to understand that Pakistan captured 1617
square miles of Indian territory, killed 95,000
soldiers and destroyed 475 tanks and 110
aircraft.(25) But disillusionment and resentment
developed fast when in January 1966 Ayub signed the
Tashkent Declaration which provided for a military
disengagement without resolving the Kashmir issue.
With the armed forces largely drawn from the West,
the emotional involvement of the people who had lost
their kith and kin in the war was understandably
greater. There was at once an outburst of anti-Ayub
sentiment throughout the province. The resentment
against Ayub also penetrated the armed forces, who
had only recently been rewarded for their gallantry,
where there was a feeling that their sacrifices had
been in vain. But perhaps more disastrous in the
long term was the economic effect of the war. The
U.S.A. cut off military aid to Pakistan. Pakistan,
like India, had suffered heavy losses in arms and
equipment and these had to be replaced. The country
which had long been groaning under the burden of
defence expenditure was now asked to tighten its
belt even further. Many development and welfare
plans were scrapped, and more and more funds and
precious foreign exchange were diverted to buy
expensive French Mirage aircraft and other
equipment. The support which Ayub had built through
public spending and works programmes withered away
rapidly.

Ayub tried to stem the tide by ruthless
suppression of the opposition. Sheikh Mujib
ur-Rahman had launched his six-point campaign for
East Pakistan's autonomy, and almost overnight had
caught the imagination of the Bengalis. The
government, rather than negotiate with Mujib,
arrested him and thirty-four others (who included
senior civil servants and defence officers) on a
trumped-up charge of conspiracy to secede. In West
Pakistan the regime pursued a similar policy of
arresting Ayub's former colleague Zulfiqar Ali
Bhutto, now the recalcitrant leader of the newly
established Pakistan People's Party. The arrest of
the two main rivals gave the regime a respite but
the lid could not be held down indefinitely. With
the approach of the elections in 1969 the political

activities heightened. The students in both wings launched a popular movement, and the edifice of the regime began to show signs of cracking. The Chief Justice of East Pakistan, Syed Mahboob Murshed, a respected figure for his learning and integrity, resigned to join the opposition. In quick succession several senior defence personnel also joined in. Faced with a popular uprising and his support slipping within the armed forces, Ayub belatedly sought to reach a political accommodation. Bhutto and Wali Khan were released and the conspiracy charges against Mujib were dropped in February 1969. Ayub announced his decision to withdraw his candidature from the forthcoming presidential election and after further arm-twisting conceded the two main demands of the opposition: restoration of the federal parliamentary system with regional autonomy and universal adult franchise. He also agreed that the new parliament could deal with the other demands of the various groups. But having got in the thin end of the wedge, the opposition pressed on: not only must Ayub go, but also the constitution and institutions devised by him. With popular wrath turned against the Basic Democrats, they resigned in thousands, others ran away and some were burnt alive. The government's authority disappeared fast. Yahya, the Commander-in-Chief, made it clear that if the army was to intervene it would not do so merely to bolster Ayub's regime, but would do so under his own leadership.(26) Ayub, having lost his only remaining base of support, decided to abdicate. Ironically, however, Ayub left as he came: by breaching the constitution. Rather than hand over power to the Speaker as provided by the constitution, he wrote to Yahya, that having "come to the conclusion that all civil administration and constitutional authority in the country has become ineffective" he would hand over to "the Defence Forces of Pakistan ... the only effective and legal instrument".(27) Ayub had buried the institutions he had created.

For all its eventual collapse, Ayub's was the most successful attempt to impose some form of military political settlement on Pakistan. This attempt came very close to the pattern of authoritarian clientelism described in the Introduction. Its base was a united army whose sense of national mission was reinforced by the privileged position which it received from the regime. The system of Basic Democracies through which the regime sought to create a political base was thoroughgoing and extensive. It failed partly because of the drying up of the funds needed to maintain so large a patronage network, especially after the 1965 war, but more basically because it could find no place for the politically mobilised population, especially in the towns and in East Pakistan. As is often the case with regimes of this kind, its collapse in the face of large scale urban opposition was sudden, and all attempts to preserve it through political bargaining failed.

The Yahya Interregnum

The Yahya regime inherited the impasse left by the ruins of the political institutions which the civil-military bureaucracy had attempted to impose. The continuation of martial law would have been ineffective if not impossible. Nor could Yahya have retracted the political concessions which Ayub had been forced to concede. In the circumstances Yahya realized that the only way to defuse political tension was to call for a general election and let the Constituent Assembly frame a new constitution for the country. For the first time since 1947 Pakistan would have a general election on the basis of adult franchise. Did this mean that the experience of the Ayub era had convinced the civil-military bureaucracy that they must withdraw from decision making and return the powers of policy making to the elected representatives of the people? Not quite so. It was widely assumed that no single party would emerge with a clear majority in the Assembly, and in the ensuing squabbles, the civil-military bureaucracy would be able to return to the centre of the stage by playing one faction against the other as in the 1951-58 period. Yahya Khan, through the Legal Framework Order, firmly kept the initiative in his hands by requiring that the constitution would have to be approved by the President. Moreover, it was laid down that if the Constituent Assembly failed to produce a constitution within 120 days, it would be dissolved. It had taken Pakistan nine years to frame its first constitution in 1956. If the election failed to give a clear majority to any party (as it was assumed it would) the possibilities of meeting that deadline seemed remote. The army could yet show that ´clubs are trumps´.

The results of the election upset Yahya´s apple-cart. Mujib´s Awami League, campaigning for provincial automomy on his six-point programme, won 167 out of 169 seats in East Pakistan. This gave

him an overall majority in the Constituent Assembly,
and by parliamentary convention power both to frame
a constitution and form the government. But there
was a problem. Bhutto´s PPP had won 88 seats in
West Pakistan and this gave him a majority in that
province. Mujib sought to by-pass Bhutto by allying
himself with some of the smaller parties in West
Pakistan, especially NAP and Jamiat-i-Ulema Islam
(JUI). Bhutto, however, was not a man to let
history pass him by. He had not brought down Ayub´s
regime simply to remain the leader of the
opposition. Bhutto claimed that a constitution
based on the six points would lead to the
disintegration of Pakistan and therefore he refused
to participate in the Constituent Assembly until
Mujib and he could agree on the outlines of the new
constitution. Bhutto´s demands were cleverly
calculated to win the support of the West Pakistani
civil-military establishment and the industrialists.
There was a widespread fear that Mujib´s accession
to power would be detrimental to West Pakistan
interests. The industrialists recalled the
Suhrawardy regime when permits and licences were
granted to East Pakistan traders; the generals were
apprehensive that not only would Mujib insist on
parity in recruitment of the defence services, but
also give accelerated promotion to Bengali officers;
the civil bureaucracy likewise feared Mujib´s wrath
against them. There were also rumours that Mujib
would shift the capital to Dacca and Naval HQ to
Chittagong. By posing as the champion of Pakistan´s
integrity, Bhutto made himself the leader of the
diverse interest groups of West Pakistan. The
massive electoral victory had given Mujib a mandate
to frame a constitution on the basis of his six
points but he was in a predicament. He needed the
good will of the army if power was to be transferred
to the elected representatives, and yet to
compromise his six point programme would make it
impossible for him to fulfill his election pledges.
Given the predominance of the West Pakistani
capitalists and their stranglehold on the
civil-military bureaucracy, any weakening of
provincial autonomy seemed out of the question. The
essence of the six points was not greater help from
the centre for the province but to free the province
from the centre, so that it could help itself.
Moreover, Bhutto had been a member of the Ayub
government for eight years during which he had
forged close relations with the civil-military
establishment and was for all practical purposes

considered an ´insider´. For Mujib to have formed a
coalition with Bhutto would have undermined the
authority of his government from within.
     As prospects of sharing power slipped, Bhutto
prepared to deal his last card with the help of his
military supporters. By threatening to boycott the
National Assembly he persuaded Yahya to postpone the
opening of the session of 3 March 1971. The
reaction in East Pakistan was as was to be expected.
 Mujib accused the military junta of attempting to
sabotage the popular will and launched a
non-cooperative movement to force the transfer of
power to the elected representatives. Meanwhile in
West Pakistan Bhutto and the Generals had come to a
bald conclusion: to let Mujib form a government
would give him the legal power to end West Pakistani
domination. A desperate situation called for a
desperate solution.(28) The Awami League and its
supporters would be militarily subdued and once the
province had been pacified, the support of the
defeated Bengali leaders could be shored up to set
up a coalition government. At this stage no serious
thought was given to the possibility of a popular
liberation war, or intervention by India. Besides,
it could be argued, if East Pakistan managed to
secede, at least West Pakistan would have been
spared the drain of resources and subordination to
the East. For Bhutto such an outcome would even be
beneficial: he would become the leader of the
majority party and legitimately the head of the
government. Once the decision was taken to effect a
military solution, the ground under Yahya and Mujib
had slipped. Yahya and Mujib negotiated and even
Bhutto joined in, but when agreement seemed in sight
the army launched its onslaught. As the cannons
opened up on the night of 25 March, it was the
beginning of the end.
     The break-up of Pakistan was largely the result
of the failure to build institutions based on
popular consensus and the determination of the
civil-military bureaucracy to monopolise decision
making to the exclusion of political elites with a
broad base. The secession of East Pakistan and the
defeat in the war discredited the military leaders
and forced them to hand back the power to the
people´s representatives to pick up the pieces. In
the next two sections we shall examine, first in
Pakistan and then in Bangladesh, the overthrow of
the popular regimes by the military and renewed
attempts to institutionalise their regime.

PAKISTAN AFTER 1971

The surrender of the Pakistan army on 15 December 1971 and the secession of the eastern wing from Pakistan made the position of Yahya and his generals untenable. The military and political debacle of the regime was complete. Opinion within the military leadership was divided and was not immediately agreed on the transfer of power to the elected representatives of the people. It was not until public opinion, stunned and humiliated by Pakistan's military defeat, turned its popular wrath against the armed forces, that the generals decided to vacate the presidential palace. While a few generals were convinced that the situation was beyond the control of the armed forces and only a popular government could salvage the wreckage, others saw it as a tactical retreat to the barracks to bide their time.

When Bhutto assumed the presidency on 20 December 1971 he had two enormous advantages. He was the first elected head of government since 1947 and had a well established political base, particularly in the Punjab and Sind. And perhaps more important was that the armed forces following their humiliation stood discredited and demoralised. While ostensibly it seemed that Bhutto's position was secure, to the more perceptive observers the question remained whether the anti-democratic forces which had thwarted the development of popular institutions during the last quarter of a century would allow power to slip from their hands. A conflict became almost inevitable in view of the PPP's socialistic programme. In the long run it was possible that the PPP might secure a broad popular base, particularly among the poorer section of the population, but the problem was whether it could survive long enough to see the fruits of its efforts. The spate of reforms launched by Bhutto seemed to indicate his desire to take the bull by the horns.

Bhutto had been long enough in the confidence of Ayub Khan to have gathered sufficient insight into the workings of the military mind. He pressed home his advantage to establish civilian ascendancy and to create a legal and institutional framework to make it impossible for the armed forces to interfere in politics. While the armed forces were still in disarray, Bhutto struck sharply. He sacked forty-three senior officers of the three defence forces and introduced some far reaching reforms. The positions of commanders-in-chief were abolished and instead three chiefs of staff were appointed on fixed tenure. The head of state would become the Commander-in-Chief of the armed forces. Bhutto further sought to prevent a reintervention by clearly defining the functions of the armed forces in the new constitution of Pakistan adopted on April 10, 1973. It was laid down that the duty of the military was to "defend Pakistan against external aggression or threat of war", and, subject to law, act in aid of civil power when called upon to do so.(29) The constitution also defined as ´High Treason´ any attempt to subvert the constitution, and required the members of the armed forces to take an oath to refrain from taking part in political activities.

For the moment the armed forces had no option but to acquiesce in the popular will. Similarly, the civil bureaucracy which had dominated policy making under Ayub and Yahya was purged and a large number of senior officers were removed from the services. Bhutto carried out the long awaited merger of the central services into a unified administrative cadre, thus depriving the elite Civil Service of Pakistan of its monopoly of key postings. The civil and military reforms were indicative of Bhutto´s desire to establish the supremacy of the popular institutions and the principle of public accountability.

Whether or not the spate of reforms ushered in by the Bhutto regime was well conceived or properly executed, or whether they at all alleviated the miseries of the common man, is not the concern of this analysis. What is relevant is that Bhutto´s programme of nationalisation and redistribution alienated not only the big business and influential section of the population, but also the small town traders who had been his enthusiastic supporters. These small traders, stung by nationalisation of rice, wheat and cotton spinning factories and export trades in cotton and rice, now formed the nucleus of anti-Bhutto agitation.

The opportunity for which the anti-Bhutto group had been waiting presented itself in March 1977 when Bhutto´s party won a landslide victory in the general election. Bhutto´s political opponents who had formed the Pakistan National Alliance (PNA) and had fared poorly at the polls, now raised the cry that the election had been rigged. Bhutto´s more enthusiastic supporters may well have used unfair means to manipulate votes, but it is clear that the allegations of rigging alone would not explain Bhutto's handsome victory. Such charges are familiar in South Asia, where parties and individuals rejected at the polls often use them to explain their failure. But in the case of Pakistan (and Bangladesh) there was almost a pattern whereby the unrepresentative politicians sought to negate the popular will through an alliance of anti-democratic forces. The opposition came to some bald conclusions: Bhutto, like Mujib in Bangladesh, could not be challenged in a free poll and given his comparative youth was likely to outlive his main rivals. As another general election was unlikely to produce any different result, the leaders of the PNA sought military help to get rid of Bhutto. It was very probably hoped that once Bhutto was out of the way, they could work out some arrangement with the armed forces as under the Ayub-Yahya administration.

From the military point of view such an opportunity was heaven sent. Given Bhutto's personal stature and his popular support, the military leaders could not afford an open confrontation, particularly as the memories of 1971 were still fresh in people's minds. But when the PNA appealed to the army and a well orchestrated disturbance broke out in different parts of the country, the army chief of staff, General Zia ul Huq, had no hesitation in staging a coup on 5 July 1977. Overthrowing Bhutto proved easy enough, but could he be kept out of office for long? It was clear that a free election would return Bhutto and the armed forces would not only be sent back to the barracks but would also face his wrath. Elections were out of the question until Bhutto was safely out of the way. The military leaders opted for a solution with an obvious appeal to their simple minds: Bhutto was executed. The charge that Bhutto conspired to kill an opponent may or may not be true. But that was not the real cause of his hanging. Bhutto was the only national leader who could keep the armed forces under political control and his extermination was therefore considered essential.

Once Bhutto had been dealt with, Zia was in no hurry to restore power to a civilian government. The promise of a general election was dropped and the 'operation fair play' has turned into the longest spell of martial law in the history of Pakistan. When Zia took power he disbanded the Cabinet and the central and provincial assemblies, but unlike 1958 and 1969 he did not abrogate the constitution. He proclaimed himself the Chief Martial Law Administrator (CMLA) but allowed the civilian President to continue in office. The real power remained in the hands of the CMLA, advised by a four-man military council consisting of the three chiefs of staff and the chairman of the Chiefs of Staff Committee. In real terms the responsibility for administration reverted to the civil-military bureaucracy with the Secretaries becoming the heads of their ministries. The four provinces were placed under military governors and in September 1978 Zia dropped the mask by declaring himself President in addition to being the CMLA.

Zia´s dilemmas were similar to those of Ayub: to find an acceptable formula which would avoid the need for a nationwide popular election based on mass franchise. To prop up popular support Zia used Islamic rhetoric and promised to introduce a government based on Quran and Shariah. In Pakistan the slogan of Islam has been repeatedly used and can always be relied upon to provide a considerable political mileage. Particularly in the aftermath of the loss of Bangladesh, Islam provided an important force for cohesion in Pakistan´s search for identity. It also had the immediate effect of bringing much needed Arab money into the national coffers to pay for the increased military expenditure. While Zia pandered the Islamic ideology to the masses, he was working towards a political settlement based on limited political participation by the masses and providing a permanent ´constitutional role´ for the military. To this end Zia enacted a Provisional Constitutional Order in March 1981, providing for the appointment of a Vice President and a 350-member Federal Council (Majlis) composed of such persons as were determined by the CMLA-President.

The Majlis became operative in January 1982 but failed to bring any fresh support for the regime. While local elections on a non-party basis had been allowed in September 1979, a national election was postponed indefinitely as all indications were that the PPP would still emerge as the main political force. Although Zia has shown himself - despite his image as a simple and pious Muslim - an adept manipulator, his attempt to institutionalise his regime continues. The Soviet imbroglio in Afghanistan was almost providential for Zia. It brought him much international support and more important, military and financial aid from the

U.S.A. Pakistan has never been concerned with the
´cold war´ but has made good use of the military
aid, ostensibly to fight communists, in suppressing
political dissidents at home. While the Afghan
crisis temporarily distracted attention from
domestic problems, Zia is acutely aware that he must
shore up support for his regime before he is
engulfed by another popular uprising. The attempt
to set up a half-way democratic house by-passing the
masses and populist leaders is unlikely to be any
more successful than Ayub´s Basic Democracies. In
the meantime Zia´s support is beginning to wither.
The PNA which had urged the army to overthrow Bhutto
is now drifting into opposition: only the right-wing
fundamentalist Jamat-i-Islami, drawing its support
from the urban lower-middle class and the refugee
population, is still willing to throw in its lot
with the regime.

The remaining political parties of all shades
of opinion are sceptical, if not openly hostile, and
prefer to remain aloof. In February 1981 the
Movement for the Restoration of Democracy (MRD) was
established, and is increasingly demonstrating its
popular support, although many of the opposition
groups have refused to join in because of the PPP´s
predominance in the movement. The division of the
opposition obviously remains Zia´s trump card, but
disillusion with Zia is spreading fast. While
Islamic slogans won some initial support, it is now
clear that while Islam can be a force for cohesion
it can also be divisive: it ignores regional,
linguistic and ethnic differences; it has opened up
the old controversies between modernists and
traditionalists and worst of all between Shias and
Sunnis. The women are dissatisfied because of the
lowering of their political status, while the Ulemas
are angered by Zia´s failure to bring about an
Islamic revolution. Zia had to abandon his plans
introducing Zakat (wealth tax) because of the
Shia-Sunni differences on this issue, and similarly
Ushr (tax on agricultural produce) had to be
abandoned for fear of alienating rural supporters.
In the urban areas discontent is rife: the lawyers
have lost their practices, the intellectuals have
been gagged, newspapers have been ruthlessly
suppressed, and student demands have been stifled;
regional conflicts and grievances have intensified.
Army rule has meant Punjabi domination, with the
result that the lack of political participation by
regional leaders in the NWFP, Baluchistan and Sind
has heightened the sense of alienation. The

businessmen have obviously found in Zia´s regime a respite from Bhutto´s nationalising programmes, but are apprehensive because of the uncertainties of the future. Zia´s regime has not been able to denationalise many of the industries, as their incorporation into the public sector has opened up fresh avenues of jobs and opportunities for the professionals. To return these industries to the private sector would at once cause a storm of protest.

Zia has failed either to institutionalise his regime or to win support, and yet has managed to hang on to power. This is not entirely surprising. His main constituency, the armed forces, have remained consistently loyal and disciplined. Despite some rumblings and rumours of attempted coups, the officers and men know that the only way to maintain their privileged position is to stick together. The reward for this is not insubstantial. Clearly this position cannot last long, but in the short term, at least, Zia knows that the fear of a PPP victory at the polls will keep the unrepresentative leaders away from joining in any movement aimed at restoring democracy. The military, the bureaucracy and the unrepresentative leaders have one thing in common: the fear of the masses.

BANGLADESH

Background
Bangladesh came into existence in December 1971, under conditions quite as traumatic as those which had attended the birth of Pakistan twenty-four years earlier. The economy was in tatters after nine months of civil war, while hundreds of thousands of youths, who had acquired arms during the war, did not easily settle back into their old way of life, but went around the country terrorising the population. For three weeks between the liberation of the country and the return of Sheikh Mujib ur-Rahman from prison in Pakistan, it was only with the help of the liberating Indian army that some semblance of authority was maintained.

In one critical respect, however, the inheritance of Bangladesh was very different from that of Pakistan. Bangladesh did not have a united armed force. The original army was formed from some thirty thousand men who had deserted the East Pakistan Rifles, together with the Mukhti Bahini, freedom fighters from the independence war who were under the nominal control of the Awami League. To these were then added some 28,000 Bengali soldiers repatriated from Pakistan. The Mukhti component were mainly young, not well trained or disciplined, but highly politicised and publicly idolised as heroes of the freedom war. The Pakistan returnees were professionals, with longer training and service, who having been posted to Pakistan at the time of the war had been denied the role in the freedom struggle which they might otherwise have played. At the same time most of these officers and men shared the standards and values of the Pakistan army. Most of their formative experience had been under the Ayub-Yahya martial law regimes, and had reflected the armed forces´ contempt for politicians and a rabid anti-Indian feeling; many, even before their repatriation, thought in terms of a military solution to Bangladesh´s problems. On their return, they not only had to face a screening committee and sullenly watch their juniors from the Mukhti supercede them, but in many cases they were relieved of their commissions and eased into civilian jobs. Bangladesh was born with a military both highly politicised and badly divided.

This is not the place to discuss the problems and achievements of the Mujib regime. What matters for our purposes is that he came to power with a profound distrust of the civil-military elite under which he had suffered during the Ayub and Yahya regimes. In addition to Mujib´s suspicion of the armed forces, he was keenly aware of the wasteful extravagance of the military in developing third world countries. His own experience of military rule and the recurring phenomenon of army intervention in many Afro-Asian states convinced him of the necessity of reducing the army to a position where intervention in politics would be difficult. His position vis-a-vis the army was thus quite straightforward: as a force against external threat it was useless; poor countries like Bangladesh could ill afford to maintain large standing armies, and foreign aggression could be checked only by popular resistance. He saw the army as a white elephant which he was powerless to disband, and which must therefore be incorporated into the more productive sector of the economy. In the meantime, he was building up a stong police force and the Rakhi Bahini. The creation of a privileged Rakhi Bahini was much resented by the army, which feared that it might one day be used against itself. The army was as yet too divided and faction-ridden to strike, but when Mujib announced that it was to be decentralised and placed at the disposal of the district governors for employment in rural development programmes, their resentment reached bursting point. The new arrangements were scheduled to come into effect from 1 September 1975. They must either act or would perish.

The fatal attack came from an unexpected quarter. On 15 August 1975, Mujib and almost all of his family were massacred by a group of young army officers, some of whom had been dismissed by Mujib and therefore harboured a personal vendetta, and who did not appear to be connected with any larger group in the army or outside. The killers had acted on their own, and not even their senior officers had been aware of the impending massacre. The young officers then barricaded themselves in the President's house, and backed by the armoured corps attempted to run the government behind a civilian cabinet. The situation remained confused and tense for nearly three months. The senior officers were not directly involved, and were now in the difficult position of either having to join hands with the killers who seemed to hold actual power, or else attempting to dislodge them by force. Major General Zia ur-Rahman took over as Chief of Staff from Major General Safiullah in an attempt to restore discipline in the armed forces and persuade the coup leaders to return to barracks, but had little success. In the meantime the pro-Mujib forces in the army under Brigadier Musharraf were able to organise themselves, and by skilful show of power on 3 November forced the coup leaders to leave the country, while Zia was placed under house arrest. The pro-Mujib triumph was however short-lived. On 7 November yet another uprising took place in several cantonments, and by the end of the day Musharraf had been killed, and Zia ur-Rahman restored. In the struggle some army officers, fearing that the arrested Awami League leaders might pose a serious threat, killed five of them in cold blood. With their killing, Mujib's entire inner cabinet, save one, had been wiped out, and a real political void created. While the rebellious junior officers had been sent abroad, and the pro-Mujib section of the army routed and dispersed, the events of 3-7 November had destroyed what discipline the army possessed; the privates who had been responsible for restoring Zia were highly politicised, had killed a large number of their own officers, and were unlikely to return to barracks without extracting their pound of flesh.

Zia ur-Rahman: The Failure of Factional Clientelism

Zia ur-Rahman faced a difficult task. He stood as the de facto military ruler of the country, and yet his authority within the army was far from secure. But having acquired political authority, the army was not likely to relinquish it easily. Civilianisation, when it came, was the result more of the internal weakness of the army than of the military's desire to withdraw from politics or pressure from the politicians. Zia attempted to create a civilian power base only when he failed to achieve the united support of the armed forces. The timing and manner of civilianisation was largely determined by Zia's need to seek non-military support.

Restoring discipline in the army was to prove difficult, as the number of attempted coups, mutinies and cases of insubordination after August 1975 witnesses, but Zia moved shrewdly and by using a policy of carrot and stick he established a semblance of authority. The officer cadre, unnerved by the mutinous behaviour of their men and fearful for their own lives, closed ranks around Zia. Zia's next move was to win the soldiers by increasing manifold their salaries and providing many of the fringe benefits which until then had been reserved for officers. They were promised subsidised rations and accommodation for their families, and a greater say in future policy making. The more extreme demands for the abolition of the distinction between officers and men were stonewalled for the moment, but a promise was given that more officers would be recruited from the ranks as the army expanded. The economies effected by Mujib in defence budgets were thrown overboard, and despite pressing claims for funds in other sectors, expenditure was lavishly increased. Mujib's 1974-75 defence budget of 750 million taka was raised to 2063 million, from 13% to nearly 29% of the total revenue budget, and a new army division was raised to provide both a loyal force for Zia and promotions for the officers. Intelligence systems were geared up, a special combat force of 12,500 men raised for counter insurgency duties, and the Bangladesh Rifles, an adjunct of the army, raised from 40,000 to 70,000 men. With the carrot came also the stick. The Bengal Lancers tank regiment, which was the stronghold of the junior coup leaders, was disbanded. Troops in Dacca cantonment who had been actively involved in coups and counter-coups were regrouped and despatched away from Dacca. The newly raised 9th Division, with known loyalty to Zia, was given the task of defending the capital. Zia´s early success increased his confidence, and he next cracked down on the military section of the Jatio Samaj Dal (JSD). After a secret trial its leaders were hanged and some 1,500 of its supporters dismissed from the army.

While Zia was consolidating his position in the armed forces, he also sought to mobilise popular support for the military regime by stepping up pro-Islamic sentiments and launching vocal anti-Indian campaigns. It is now commonplace to state that in Islam there is a built-in political message which can be mobilised by portraying a threat to Islam, imagined or real. In the case of the Bengali Moslems, this feeling can be played up more easily because most of them, in fact almost all, are converts from the Hindus, and therefore suffer from a sense of doubt about their identity for which they may attempt to compensate by making a greater show of their faith. Even immediately after independence in 1971, one could notice among the intellectuals a crisis of identity and a concern to reconcile the tensions created by the duality in their identity, that of being a Bengali and a Moslem at the same time. Zia, who came from the more backward and conservative northern Bangladesh, had all the virtues and prejudices of rural Moslems and showed an instinctive ability to make political use of the Islamic factor.

The military government started accusing India of interfering in Bangladesh´s sovereignty by providing sanctuary and facilities to those supporters of Mujib who had fled the country. At the same time, by playing up the Farakha water dispute with India, an impression was created by the media that India might militarily intervene in Bangladesh. In the field of foreign policy, the regime made overtures towards Islamic and other countries which were traditionally hostile to India, thereby giving the impression that the military regime was bringing Bangladesh out of Indian tutelage. A number of joint communiques were issued after meetings with foreign leaders which stressed "the efforts made and the marked success achieved by the Government and people of Bangladesh in opposing interference from outside, defending national independence and state

sovereignty". The rhetorical claims that Bangladesh
was "now in a position to make her own decisions and
formulate her own independent policy to serve her
national interest" might not have meant much in
reality but won some support for the regime.

With the army partially contained, and public
minds diverted against ´foreign enemies´ and ´enemy
agents´, the military sought to entrench its
position by drawing in the civilian bureaucracy. The
civil servants who had been disgruntled with Mujib
now naturally responded enthusiastically in a mood
reminiscent of the Ayub and Yahya era in Pakistan.
Presidential Order No.9 of 1972 under which
officials had been dismissed was rescinded, as a
first step towards the establishment of a
civil-military bureaucracy. The former members of
the civil service of Pakistan now emerged from
obscurity, and again proceeded to occupy all the key
positions in the secretariat, the autonomous
corporations and the districts. The powerful
Planning Commission was taken over by bureaucrats,
and despite lip-service to socialist principles, the
new strategy encouraged private investors in
preference to the development of a public sector.
Some of the nationalised industries were restored,
the ceiling for private investment was raised from
30 million to 100 million takas, and the government
gave pledges against a policy of nationalisation. In
November 1976 President Sayen appointed a council of
advisers which included the three chiefs of staff
and four bureaucrats; its size was later enlarged to
fourteen, but it retained its essentially
bureaucratic character. The restoration of
bureaucratic rule, whatever its defects in the long
run, did however provide stability and continuity,
and perhaps saved the country from further
mismanagement by an inexperienced and indisciplined
army.

Zia could not ignore the power of students in
Bangladesh politics. They had spearheaded the
movements against the various Pakistani regimes, and
despite their support for Mujib, were the first to
raise their voice against the corruption and
mismanagement in the Mujib government. Zia made a
blatant attempt to buy his way out of trouble: he
sanctioned 40 million takas for a student ´work
company´, and import permits began to find their way
into the hands of student businessmen.

Although both the military appointed
Presidents, Khondokar Mushtaq Ahmed and Justice A.M.
Sayen, had promised the restoration of political

activities by August 1976 and fresh elections six months later, it was clear that the military authorities would resist it. However, in view of the divisions within the army, Zia was at first reluctant to provoke a conflict with President Sayen, who despite being a military appointee commanded respect. Zia and his fellow officers insisted and obtained from the President a Political Parties Regulation, which laid down the rules for political activities, and made the military the referee in the game. But it soon became apparent to the 'referees' that the ghost of Mujib still had a hold over the electorate which could not be offset by its alliance with anti-Awami League parties. Indeed, many of the leaders of some sixty parties were like chiefs without indians, and those including Awami League and JSD which commanded support showed no sign of coming to terms with the military. By November 1976, the military leaders abandoned hope of creating an anti-Awami League coalition with electoral support, and therefore called off the elections because of "external threat" and "danger to national unity and solidarity". On 30 November Zia relieved President Sayen of his duties as Chief Martial Law Administrator, and now openly assumed the powers which he had hitherto been exercising not entirely invisibly from behind the scenes. To his relief there was no reaction from the chiefs of the other services. This no doubt encouraged him some five months later to assume the Presidency himself.

Zia projected himself as a middle of the road and pragmatist leader, and was increasingly acceptable to the middle class who feared that the country might be reduced to anarchy. He sought to regularise his assumption of the presidency through a referendum, the results of which must have made even Zia blush: of the country's 38 million voters, 88.5% turned out to vote and 98.88% cast votes in Zia's favour! That a majority had given Zia an affirmative vote need not be seriously questioned, but in a country where there had never been more than a 60% turnout of voters even in general elections, before or since, 88.5% must remain a record.

Zia's 'overkill' in the referendum robbed him of much satisfaction. It was becoming apparent that if his regime was to gain legitimacy he must call a general election. There was no denying that the Awami League was still the only legitimately elected representative of the people. In addition there were two other factors which promoted the need for elections. Discipline in the army had collapsed, with mutinies and conspiracy in the garrisons an everyday occurrence. Zia probably reckoned that if he could win a general election, he would minimise the chances of yet another coup against his regime. It was also argued that by giving Bangladesh a democratic image abroad, it would enhance her prospects for obtaining more foreign aid. The regime's dependence on aid had made it particularly vulnerable to foreign opinion.

However, to rush into an election would have been foolhardy. The tactics and timing of the elections must be stage-managed to give the maximum advantage to the regime. Even though most of Awami League's top leaders had been killed and the party was in a state of disarray, it was possibly still the best organised party. To have taken the Awami League head on would have been suicidal. Zia needed to create a body of supporters who would be able to act as vote brokers. Borrowing yet another device from Ayub's political repertoire, he decided to reactivate the local councils (Ayub's basic democrats) who were known to be dependable supporters of previous military regimes. The local councillors were normally influential people who could be won over by official patronage and bureaucratic pressures. It therefore came as no surprise when Zia announced the changed election schedule. Instead of holding fresh parliamentary elections straight away, under revised arrangements the elections to local councils would be followed by a presidential election, and the parliamentary elections would come last.

The local elections were a tame affair, and did not evince much public interest. But immediately after that, Zia began preparing himself for the presidential election. His various policies mentioned earlier had already established his credentials as a middle of the road leader, and he toyed with the idea of forming an alliance with all those parties which might join him. It soon became clear that most of the leaders who were prepared to play ball with him were electoral nonentities, and the two major parties, Awami League and JSD, remained aloof. While still projecting his image as an impartial broker, non-partisan and above politics, Zia encouraged his Vice-President, Justice Sattar, to launch a new political party. In February 1978 the Jatiyabadi Gonotantric Dal (JAGODAL) duly came into being. Zia was not a member of the new party, but with few exceptions his entire council of ministers joined in. The party became the mouthpiece of the regime and prospered under official patronage. But as a party it remained essentially a conglomerate of second rate politicians and nondescripts of various sorts. It failed to attract a single national figure. Clearly this would not do as a platform from which to launch his presidential campaign.

If he was to win the election, Zia needed a wider electoral alliance. Here he was luckier. While the leaders of many of the parties he approached earlier were unwilling to merge with JAGODAL, they were more than willing to join in an electoral alliance which would help to keep out the Awami League. Bearing in mind the old maxim that your enemy´s enemy is your friend, the leaders of smaller political parties began to knock at the general´s door in almost unending queue. Thus emerged a Jatiyabadi Front (JF), with a minimum agreement that these parties would support Zia for the presidency, provided the Awami League candidate could be kept out. The JF consisted of JAGODAL, the pro-Peking faction of the National Awami Party, United People´s Party, Bangladesh Muslim League, Scheduled Caste Federation, Bangladesh Labour Party, Islamic Democratic League, the Sammobadi Dal, and the East Bengal Communist Party. Even the JSD and a coalition of parties led by Ataur Rahman Khan provided negative support for Zia by asking their supporters not to vote for the Awami League.

The Awami League did not put up a candidate of its own, and together with the pro-Moscow faction of the National Awami Party, agreed to support General M.A.G. Usmani, the candidate of the tiny Janata Party. Only one month was allowed for campaigning, and the Awami League, leaderless and for so long on the run, could not muster sufficient will to put up a fight. The result was a foregone conclusion. Zia polled nearly 75% of the votes cast and Usmani about 22%. But perhaps the real feelings of the electorate were expressed with their feet - only a little over 50% of the voters cared to turn up. Having acquired a formal legitimacy for his regime, Zia broadened his cabinet to include some representatives of the various parties who had helped him win the election. Of his 28 man cabinet, 19 were from JAGODAL, 3 from NAP (Peking), 2 each from Muslim League and UPP, and one from the Scheduled Caste Federation. Mashiur Rahman, the president of NAP (Peking), became Prime Minister.

Zia had won the presidential election handsomely, but organising and campaigning for a parliamentary election called for a different type of machinery. It was relatively easy for a wide-ranging group of parties to agree on Zia as a presidential candidate, but would not be so easy when it came to selecting candidates for 300 seats. This would require a party machinery which could match the Awami League´s network. The JF was dissolved in September 1978 and Zia thereupon launched his Bangladesh National Party (BNP), which essentially consisted of the various components of the JF, but in a single party rather than a coalition. Having forged a party, and assured of support from the local councillors, Zia announced parliamentary elections in January 1979.

The Awami League, which split following the defeat in the presidential election, was now more uncertain than ever about contesting elections to be held under Martial Law regulations. With considerable misgivings, and less than a month before polling day on 18 February 1979, the Awami League decided to join the campaign. The other parties to contest the elections were the JSD, ML-IDL, and the breakaway faction of the League. Zia once again capitalised on a divided opposition. Most of the parties hurled bricks at each other, and the BNP emerged as the only viable option. The result gave the BNP 207 seats out of 300, with Awami League a poor second at 39. Only 50% of the voters turned out, of which 44% went to the BNP and 25% to the League, the lowest turnout in any election held since 1970. Repeated military intervention and bureaucratic pressures to manipulate votes may well have eroded popular confidence in their efficacy.

The parliamentary election ostensibly completed the process of civilianisation and, it was claimed, a "transition to democracy". The real custodian of power continued to be the military. The elections and transition to civilian rule had taken place under military rules, and it remained a moot point whether the military would allow the continued growth of civil and democratic institutions. Threats and claims of a special ´role´ for the military continued to be voiced by senior officers, and open intervention in government was only held back by Zia´s personality and perhaps a realisation by the soldiers that he would protect their privileged position. In the administration, despite the appearance of parliament and politicians, the civil-military bureaucrats continued to play the decision-making role.

With the country once again under civilian rule, it seemed that if Zia could forge his BNP into a cohesive group, political stability might be achieved. But prospects for stability never seemed real. Zia had hastened the ´civilianisation´ and transition to ´democracy´ most importantly because he wanted to create a power base independent of the armed forces. Once he had cut his links from the army and began to rely on civilians and politicians, however, his survival would again depend on the goodwill and tolerance of the military commanders. At first he seemed to walk the tightrope well, and kept the armed forces contented with lavish budget allocations and by allowing them an important role in decision-making. But this was an uneasy equilibrium. As Zia turned his attention to building up his party, old tensions and conflicts surfaced. Many in the armed forces began to fear that he might become too powerful and less amenable to the military. The divisions within the army meant that Zia had to take sides, and in the process alienated the garrison commander of Chittagong, where he was killed during a visit in 1981. His murder split the army, and for a time it seemed that the army was locked in a war within itself. After several tense days the Chittagong garrison surrendered. The civilian Vice-President, Justice Sattar, took over as President to everyone´s relief. After Zia´s death, the army was far too divided and discredited to attempt to wrest power from the civilian government, but no sooner had it sorted out its immediate quarrels than the Chief of Staff demanded the creation of a ´National Security Council´ consisting of the three defence chiefs, which would have powers of veto over the decisions of the cabinet. In the struggle that ensued the outcome was almost inevitable. The army Chief of Staff dismissed the President and cabinet, appointed a new President, and imposed martial law. Zia´s attempt to institutionalise a civil-military bureaucracy was abuptly ended. The country´s political developent had turned full circle, and was back to where it had started after Mujib´s death in 1975. The military was in the saddle again.

CONCLUSION

The unhappy experience of Pakistan and Bangladesh
illuminates many of the themes with which this
volume is concerned. The failure of even such
broadly based electoral regimes as those of Bhutto
and Mujib to hold on to power for more than a few
years shows how tenuous is the hope of stable
civilian government once the military has taken
over, but the problems of military rulers have been
scarcely less acute. Coming to power as the
striking force of an unrepresentative
military-bureaucratic alliance, they have been
obliged to seek some colouring of popular backing
for both domestic and international purposes. They
have had two ways of going about it: either by
gathering a coalition of small parties and
unrepresentative politicians whose need for the
military has been every bit as great as its need for
them; or else by setting up its own clientele of
local notables who could be tied to government by
bureaucratic pressures and rewards. In either case
the strategy has been essentially clientelistic.
Where the regimes have differed has been in the
level of military unity, and hence in the much
greater capacity of Pakistani regimes (both before
and after 1971) to maintain an authoritarian
clientelist system, in contrast to the factional
clientelism of Bangladesh. In either case, even
popular civilian parties have been fairly weakly
organised, and this has helped to avert some of the
fury which may accompany a veto regime of the
Argentine or Chilean kind, though military regimes
in both countries have been prepared to resort to
the physical extermination of political rivals. The
basic dilemma remains the same: the clientelist
option is incapable of providing any long term
solution to demands for popular participation, and
the ´institutions´ so painstakingly created by an
Ayub Khan or a Zia ur-Rahman are liable to collapse
overnight in the face either of intra-military
factionalism or of a decline in patronage funds –
itself an eventually inevitable result of the
rapacious demands of the military. As support
diminishes, and the threat especially from urban
opponents increases, the military finds itself
forced to cling to power by the danger to its own
position implied by a handover to popular forces.
It is riding a tiger which it cannot dismount.

NOTES

1. Government of India, White Paper on Jammu & Kashmir (New Delhi, 1950) p.85.
2. W.W. Wilcox, "The Political Role of the Army in Pakistan", in S.P. Varma & V. Narain, eds, Pakistan's Political System in Crisis : The Emergence of Bangladesh (Jaipur, South Asia Studies Centre, 1972) pp.30-44, esp.31-9.
3. ibid., p.36.
4. M. Ayub Khan, Friends not Masters : A Political Autobiography (Oxford U.P., 1967) ch.11; L. Ziring, The Ayub Khan Era : Politics in Pakistan 1958-1969 (Syracuse U.P., 1971) pp.10-11.
5. Ayub Khan, op.cit., ch.6.
6. M. Ayoob, "The Military in Pakistan's Political Development", in Varma & Narain, op.cit.
7. H.A. Rizvi, The Military and Politics in Pakistan (Lahore, Progressive Publishers, 1974) p.111.
8. R. Jahan, Pakistan : Failure in National Integration (Columbia U.P., 1972) p.111.
9. H. Feldman, Revolution in Pakistan : A Study of the Martial Law Administration (Oxford U.P., 1967) pp.102, 124.
10. For an excellent discussion of the composition of the Basic Democracies, see Jahan, op.cit., ch.6.
11. ibid., p.124.
12. Rizvi, op.cit., pp.154-5.
13. Jahan, op.cit., p.125.
14. Pakistan Electoral Commission, Presidential Election Results, 1965.
15. Ayub Khan, op.cit., p.213.
16. C.M. Ali, in Dawn newspaper, 24.4.1963, cited in K.D. Sayeed, The Political System of Pakistan (Boston, 1967) p.105.
17. Jahan, op.cit., pp.127-32.
18. H.S. Suhrawardy, the formidable opponent of Ayub, had been arrested in January 1962 under the Security of Pakistan Act, and remained incarcerated without trial until shortly before his death in 1963.
19. Jahan, op.cit., p.58.
20. Wilcox, loc.cit., p.36.
21. Rizvi, op.cit., p.160.
22. Jahan, op.cit., pp.119-26.
23. F.A. Kochanek, Interest Groups and Development : Business and Politics in Pakistan (Delhi, Oxford U.P., 1983) pp.195-90.
24. ibid., pp.183-85.

25. Rizvi, op.cit., p.163.
26. ibid., p.213.
27. ibid., p.209.
28. G.W. Choudhury, The Last Days of United Pakistan (Hurst, 1974) pp.102-04, 147-48, 152-58.
29. Constitution of Pakistan (1975), Art.245, cited in Rizvi, op.cit., pp.254-55.

Chapter Ten

SUDAN: THE RETREAT TO MILITARY CLIENTELISM

Peter Woodward

INTRODUCTION

Sudan has long been noted as a country of paradoxes. A vast country of one million square miles, the largest in Africa, it yet has a very thin population of only twenty million. Noted for its heterogeneous society, from the nomadic Arabs of the north to the numerous African communities in the south, there is nevertheless a relatively homogeneous core located in the north and east of the country from which all national leaders have emerged. Though independent for less than thirty years, there has long been some kind of state - first Turco-Egyptian (1820-1885), then independent under the Mahdists (1885-1898), and finally British ruled (1898-1956) - in an area approximating to the present frontiers, while state formation along the Nile reaches back into antiquity. Yet in spite of the relative longevity of the state in Sudan, it has always been particularly influenced both by its regional position in north-east Africa, and by the vicissitudes of international politics, at least since the Fashoda crisis of 1898. The period since independence in 1956 has added another paradox: though noted internationally for political instability in the days from 1956 until Numairi's seizure of power in 1969, it has in a number of ways been more unstable in the fourteen years since then than it was previously. It is this final paradox, experienced under a military regime which has run the full gamut of its options, that this paper will endeavour to clarify.

ESTABLISHING THE NEW REGIME

Sudan's establishment of a new military regime in

1969 came after two periods of civilian parliamentary government (1956-58, 1964-69) and one previous period of military rule (1958-64). Yet as far as the new military regime was concerned, all that had gone before stood condemned together. It was not parliamentarianism as such that was condemned, but the sterile party struggles which rested unstable coalition governments on personal and party manoeuvres for temporary advantage. The understandable if nonetheless discreditable failures of domestic policy, especially the lack of economic growth and the neglect of the long civil war in the South, were not confined to the civilians but were an accusation levelled by the new rulers at the earlier military regime as well. In particular, it was an attack on a certain socio-economic structure which had been central to the workings of the system hitherto.

One leg of this structure, rooted in the Umma Party, had consisted of the Mahdists. In all, neo-Mahdism in the twentieth century had been virtually a state within a state, increasingly powerful, but never quite attaining the decisive role to which it appeared to lay claim. That the Mahdists should have been so highly organised, with private estates growing cotton along the White Nile, commercial activities and real estate in the capital and major towns, at least a private semi-army in the Ansar (the followers), and professional bearers of the religious message, especially among the peoples of the western Sudan, is unsurprising in view of the existence of the Mahdist state in Sudan from 1885 to 1898, and the ambition of Sayed Sir Abd al-Rahman to resurrect the movement even under British imperial rule. Subsequently the Mahdists were to be at the heart of two major armed clashes with the new military regime, in 1970 and 1976, and to be defeated in both.

The other leg consisted of an alliance of nationalist politicians led by Ismail al-Azhari, who appeared to feel that in leading Sudan to independence they had done their bit, and should be allowed to concentrate on enjoying their wealth and prestige as rulers - a view which, to judge from popular reaction at the time, was not strongly shared by the people at large. The nationalist politicians were ever more closely associated with Sudan's longstanding commercial community, whose origins lay mainly in Omdurman and the northern region, but whose commercial and to a lesser extent political tentacles reached out to the south and west of the country. Their main concern appeared to be that whatever the coalition of the moment, members of the Unionist Party should endeavour to control the ministries of finance and commerce. The other part of the coalition was the Khatmiyya sect. While far from opposed to commerce, the sect´s main purpose had been to maintain its own religious identity; and from past experience it determined that this required political organisation, particularly for the purpose of countering its old enemy, Mahdism.

The military intervention led by General Abboud in 1958 was seen as at best a moderator regime, and at worst as a continuance of factionalism. The moderating stance which the regime sought to project lifted it above the sterility of the factional deadlock into which parliamentary politics appeared to have fallen; while those critics who charged it with factionalism pointed to the close initial links between the Umma Party, hard pressed to hold power at the time of the coup, and the senior army officers involved. But whatever its origins, it soon appeared to confine itself to removing offending institutions (parliament and the political parties), while effectively acquiescing in the continuance of the socio-economic order on which the old system had rested. Not surprisingly the ousted politicians resented their treatment, especially so soon after their triumphant attainment of independence in 1956; while the more radical critics felt that little had changed, except perhaps for the worse in the southern Sudan where earlier hostility had led to sustained civil war from 1962. It was indeed protests about the south which triggered off the civil disturbances and strikes of October 1964. The Abboud regime had few options other than coercion, which it lacked the will (and possibly the means) to enforce. However, though the radicals appeared to play a leading role in the ´October Revolution´ and the transitional government which took power, they were soon out-manoeuvred by the sectarian based old parties, and the status quo ante was re-established in 1965.

In contrast the military interveners of 1969 were not closely associated with religious sects or commercial groupings. They were young middle rank officers from social backgrounds that in Sudanese terms approximated to those of Egypt´s Free Officer movement, which was indeed their inspiration and model. They too criticised the parties and the parliament for a ´false independence´, and their politicisation too had included involvement in war, although theirs was a civil war. They also claimed to have had past political experience and disillusionment, having sided effectively with the radical masses in October 1964 to prevent any possible coercion by Abboud, but having seen their hopes dashed in the return to the sterile old routines of ´traditional´ party politics. The way was open politically for a classic breakthrough regime, for which there was no shortage of enthusiasm amongst either the coup leaders or a large section of Sudan´s articulate and influential intelligentsia. But agreement on the manifest shortcomings of the past does not necessarily mean agreement on the all important question, ´what is to be done?´ The new leader Ga´afar al-Numairi was essentially of Nasserite character. The Free Officers movement had been modelled on Egypt´s experience of an army-led revolution whose instruments were the young middle-rank army officers, overthrowing not only the old political system but the former politicians´ previous collaborators at the top of the armed forces as well. Sudan´s Free Officers, it was claimed, had sided crucially with the civilians in October 1964, to remove the Abboud regime from power, and now needed to do the job again as a result of the failure of the civilian parties from 1965 to 1969. The May Revolution of 1969 was proclaimed as the completion of the aborted popular October Revolution of 1964. The People´s Armed Forces, as they were now renamed, would continue the work which radicals in the transitional government of 1964 had been unable to push through. In order to ensure popular participation, a new mass movement - not a party with its implications of faction - would be created. Nasser had established the Arab Socialist Union, the Revolutionary Command Council (RCC), as the Free Officers had now become, would establish the Sudan Socialist Union (SSU).

A second major strand of the new regime was provided by the most influential organisation among those radical civilians who had actively criticised the deposed parliamentary system, the Sudan Communist Party (SCP). The SCP had been in existence for over twenty years, it had developed considerable influence not only amongst the intelligentsia but in the larger trade unions and tenants´ associations, and was generally regarded both inside and outside Sudan as the largest and best organised communist party in Africa and the

Arab world. Never short of ideological opponents from the old Islamic sectarian parties, it had had plenty of critical publicity, but persecution in the tolerant atmosphere of northern Sudanese politics had been comparatively mild, and these circumstances had provided a fairly fertile soil for the party to grow even in an Islamic society.(1) The SCP, especially its Secretary General, Abd al-Khaliq Mahjub, had produced sophisticated analyses of Sudan in class and developmental terms. It did not believe in a swift revolution, but was committed to the coming of socialism in a series of stages. It had an inherent suspicion of military coups, which were regarded as opportunistic and potentially unreliable: Abd al-Khaliq in particular was aware of their limitations, and regarded Numairi especially as no more than a progressive petty bourgeois. Nevertheless, the coup had taken place; it could be regarded as progressive; and the SCP was represented among the seven-man RCC.

The first stages of the breakthrough were set in motion without serious disagreement. The old parties were outlawed and their leaders detained; and when the wing of the Umma Party led by the Imam al-Hadi al-Mahdi challenged the new regime with force in March 1970, it was vigorously suppressed in the most violent incidents in the northern Sudan since the Battle of Omdurman in 1898. The commanding heights of the economy were nationalised: the banks, larger companies and industries, and the large private farms which were mainly Mahdist-owned.

Ironically, the backbone of the Sudanese economy, the Gezira cotton scheme, had been nationalised near the end of the period of British imperial rule. But on other crucial policy and organisational issues, disputes grew. The Nasserites were keen to promote a union with Egypt and Libya, where another group of radical young officers had also seized power in 1969. This new union was formally announced, and was expected to play a positive pan-Arab role. The SCP recalled with horror Nasser's brutal suppresson of the communist party in Egypt (of which the SCP was itself an offshoot), while reflecting that pan-Arabism had led to clashes with communists elsewhere in the Arab world as well. Organisationally the main issue was that of the relationship between the SCP and the new projected SSU. Numairi and his supporters wanted the SCP to dissolve itself, with members committing themselves fully to the SSU. Though a section of the SCP agreed with this, Abd al-Khaliq and the majority

241

felt that what had been built up over years should not be carelessly committed to what was still a somewhat dubious enterprise. Relations rapidly deteriorated, resulting not only in the detention of Abd al-Khaliq but also in the dismissal of the three most prominent SCP supporters in the RCC in November 1970. They in turn led a coup in July 1971, but swiftly lost to a counter coup which resulted in Numairi´s return to power. He had survived only with a large slice of luck and some outside assistance; and this had represented the worst clash within the armed forces that had ever taken place.(2)

In the wake of these events, Numairi retained power but effectively lost the impetus to pursue a breakthrough strategy, and soon fell back on pragmatic actions designed to strengthen his very exposed position. Nasserism, though a strong emotional appeal, represented only a limited number of immediately tangible objectives for the predominantly dispersed, rural and illiterate society of Sudan; while Nasser himself died, and his successor Anwar Sadat (though he had a Sudanese mother) never struck the same emotional chord, any more than he ever did with Egypt´s more discernible masses. Meanwhile Numairi, the crusher of the old politicians, and now bereft of the only experienced supporters of his May Revolution, the SCP, was left with the extension of the state´s economic role which was unpopular with those who had benefitted from the previous set up, while the inevitable disruption produced no significant body of clients instantly attached to the regime. Economic policies were soon to change, with the encouragement of both western backers and Sudanese businessmen. But any advantage here was offset by further repeated evidence of political instability in the armed forces, where there were numerous attempted coups.

One action, perhaps the greatest success of the regime, was to negotiate a peaceful end to the long civil war in the south in 1972, and to create a largely autonomous regional government there. Ironically, Numairi´s exposed position in the north made this easier than it had been in the past. There were no prominent political figures to make capital from criticising the concessions made to the south, which had hindered progress in the past, while the regime needed a substantial success as well as the support of new allies. For their part, the southerners had also attained a rare degree of unity, and thus conditions in both north and south

assisted the difficult achievement of a negotiated
settlement of a civil war.(3) The next stage was to
create the new national civilian institutions which,
it was hoped, would bring the regime popularity with
the people such as previous regimes had lacked, and
might at the same time act as a balance to the
unstable armed forces which had brought the regime
to power.

CREATING NEW INSTITUTIONS

Sudan´s lack of political consensus had prevented
the establishment at any time of a permanent
constitution, but the vacuum and dangers which
existed after July 1971 encouraged the introduction
for the first time of a Permanent Constitution in
1973. Numairi, who had like Nasser come to power
only as primus inter pares, now stood formally at
the top as President, and was given the power to
appoint ministers to execute his policies. There
are on paper certain checks which the People´s
Assembly can exercise over the President, but in
practice it has become a system in which Numairi has
acquired great personal powers, and strengthened his
position politically as a result of the various
challenges which have beset his path since 1969.
There are a number of significant dimensions to
the way in which he has exercised power. He has
been active in external relations over important
political and economic developments. Especially
significant here have been the relations with Egypt,
the Gulf states, and the West. Egypt and Sudan for
obvious reasons have long held a unique position in
each others´ external relations, and Numairi´s
support for Nasser has been noted. After an initial
suspicion this opened out into an even closer
relationship with Sadat which, after slight
hesitation, survived even Sadat´s policy towards
Israel. Its most obvious manifestation was the
military relationship, culminating in the Mutual
Defence Treaty of 1976 which implied Egyptian
military support for Numairi´s regime. But the
relationship also encouraged Sudan to follow Egypt
in an economic policy of an open door to the West.
The Western powers, most notably Britain and the
United States, for their part encouraged Numairi´s
new-found anti-communism after July 1971, especially
following the Ethiopian revolution with its
subsequent Soviet backing, and Libya´s military
involvement with the Soviet Union and evident

regional ambitions. Western business activity also increased dramatically after 1973 as Arab funds, accumulated as a result of the OPEC price rises, became available for new agricultural schemes in particular. Much of the introduction of these schemes involved Numairi himself in dealing with both Arab financiers and Western businessmen, as well as endeavouring to push the plans through Sudan´s inadequate planning authorities.(4) For their part, the Gulf states welcomed both the pro-Western character of the regime and an apparent opportunity to develop a food supplier which would prevent their ´oil weapon´ being matched in the future by a Western ´food weapon´.

Domestically Numairi´s presidential power, forged initially by his success in withstanding armed challenges from both outside and within the regime, was nurtured on a continuing ability to deploy political and financial resources to continue to avoid dangers from both. Numerous attempted military coups were survived with increasing ease as the army was repeatedly purged and the internal security apparatus improved - with Western help.(5) Any potential challengers from within the regime, including all the remaining Free Officers, were removed at various times, and vice-presidential shuffles were particularly important in this respect. But, true to the Sudanese style, those departing were rewarded through their banks rather than by the bullet, and new enmities were thus generally avoided. Meanwhile opposition from the old political parties was at least partially neutralised, especially after their narrow failure to succeed with their own coup in 1976. The subsequent process of National Reconciliation with those who attempted the overthrow, begun only a year later, left Numairi no less firmly at the helm, but seriously compromised his most important opposition challenger, former prime minister Sadiq al-Mahdi. At the same time disbursement of financial rewards and opportunities, and an increasing reconciliation with a variety of Islamic forces, helped to contain the appeal of the opposition, which in any case was led from outside rather than inside the country. The Presidency thus arose as by far the most important institution of government, but it has been held only by one man. Potential successors have been discouraged, and the power of the Presidency has greatly restricted the opportunity for other institutions to thrive, as exemplified by the fact that none has ever seriously challenged the

President.

The SSU had preceded the Permanent Constitution, but was fully incorporated into it. It was intended that the SSU would be a crucial institution promoting radical change, and in particular that it would seek to undo the socio-economic order which had underpinned the old parliamentary system. While it was established as a mass rather than a cadre party, persons associated prominently with the banned parties, not just as parliamentary figures but as leaders in the rural areas as well, were excluded from membership. The SSU was intended to guide both central government and the newly reformed local government in the restructuring of society. Ten years later, it was being admitted from all quarters, including the President, that the SSU was not functioning as intended, and was in need of further substantial reform. It was much less clear where the dynamism, let alone the model, for reform was to be found. One independent survey based on data from the mid-1970s pointed to some of the reasons for the weakness.(7) Membership of the SSU was often more ambiguous than the initial intentions suggested. It became clear that in some rural areas at least the families connected with the old parties saw it as desirable to penetrate the new organisation, indirectly if not directly; while after the start of National Reconciliation in 1977, former opponents of the regime were to be found in national positions as well.(8) In some areas it became clear that though local people were willing to respond to the opportunities for improvement in their social conditions which the SSU wished to bring about, for various reasons it was unable to fulfil their expectations. Closely related to this was a lack of clarity as to the role of the SSU in relation to the structure of regional and local government, especially when a number of officials were also SSU figures. Finally the spread of corruption also ate its way into the SSU, leading to growing cynicism on the part of the public, for by its nature it was the last institution capable of combining its supposed role with graft.

The People´s Assembly, established under the 1973 Constitution, is supposed to be interwoven in its powers with the Presidency. In practice, however, it has never worked as the check on the President apparently permitted by the Constitution. A major formal limitation on its critical role arises because Assembly candidates are themselves selected by the SSU, though a controlled choice is permitted. In practice the elections of 1981, the first following National Reconciliation, did see the return of some representatives from those who had hitherto been opponents of the regime, but this did not serve to greatly enhance the credibility of the Assembly. In spite of criticism, it is possible that if President Numairi were to leave power in circumstances which permitted a smooth handover to his successor, the SSU and the Assembly might survive in some form; but if he were to depart in circumstances which gave rise to at least a period of instability, the inherent weaknesses of the institutions themselves, coupled with the probable wish of new rulers to sweep away the trappings of the old regime, would lead to their unlamented demise.

One other institution, not discussed here, also deserves mention as a result of its importance to the regime's effectiveness - the civil service. The bureaucracy in Sudan, as in many new states, is the oldest established governmental institution. Under Numairi the civil service and parastatal organisations took on new responsibilities, especially with the initial nationalisation programme, the reorganisation of local government, and the development schemes begun in the mid-1970s. The size and cost of government rose substantially, and conditions for most employees improved as well. However, the better opportunities in the private sector and abroad tempted many of the more able and ambitious away, seriously affecting the performance of what was in any case an inefficient and increasingly corrupt institution.

SOCIAL SUPPORT

The institutions mentioned above have all attracted a variety of different participants, sometimes at different times. There were those who, out of general dislike for the social bases of politics before 1969, supported the new military regime with enthusiasm. Mention has been made of two ideologically based groups, the SCP and the Nasserists, but there were also other pan-Arabists and Baathists, as well as a number of 'technocrats' noted for their opposition to 'ideological' politics. In addition there were some who joined the People's Assembly and the SSU because of opportunism. The old system had put significant social obstacles in the way of upward mobility and these eased considerably, as was to be expected in a regime in which the President himself (like his hero Nasser) came from relatively humble origins. Political openings also gave rise to a variety of financially rewarding opportunities, greatly enlarged in the mid-1970s by Sudan's own version of an Open Door policy, when a flood of new schemes were established. Commerce, real estate, and mechanised agriculture offered particularly rich pickings, and the scale of corruption rose dramatically.

From 1977 the regime's initial supporters were joined by at least some of their former opponents identified with the banned parties. Some of these regretted the violence of July 1976, and felt that the attempt at National Reconciliation begun in 1977 offered a new opportunity to broaden the regime, which might in time be changed from within; some perhaps wanted to participate in what still appeared as good opportunities to prosper, since the regime was happy to make amends for earlier sequestration. But the broader popular base for the new institutions remained weak. The SSU, as noted, remained something of a political shell, while the Assembly was perceived as working essentially on sufferance from the President. However, support for the regime had come not only from those who participated in the institutions it created, but from a variety of other interest groups. Those in commerce unaffected by the initial nationalisation found opportunities to make higher profits, especially in partnership with Gulf Arab enterprises in the mid-1970s. They were joined by others from a variety of backgrounds - artisans, ex-military officers, civil servants and others - who soon became known as the 'new class', sometimes helped on the way by presidential patronage. Though little researched, popular discussion depicts a group somewhat similar to the growth of Egypt's Fat Cats under Sadat, and observation shows the rapid proliferation of new mansions, more and bigger cars, and very public demonstrations of ostentatious living.(9)

National reconciliation in 1977 also marked the beginning of an attempt to harness Islamic revivalism to the regime. The most obvious manifestation was the attempt to make peace between the regime and the Mahdists, and also to include another of its former enemies, the Moslem Brotherhood. The exercise was a substantial success for Numairi, for while there were those in both movements who were reluctant to participate, they at least did so sufficiently to weaken the opposition, as well as showing cracks in their own organisations from which the regime sought to benefit. At the same time Numairi behaved encouragingly enough to the traditional sufi orders, including the Khatmiyya, to ensure at least their neutrality if not active support. Muslim support, like commercial support, was being sought very similarly by Numairi to the way in which Sadat was using it in Egypt. Some regarded it as a sign of nascent pluralism in both countries, but in neither was it permitted to challenge presidential power.(10)

However, there was one further body of support for Numairi´s regime which had no parallel in Egypt - the southern Sudan. Numairi himself was seen as the peacemaker and the originator of regional self-government, and no other northern Sudanese political regime commanded any comparable support. The recognition of Numairi´s unique position provided both support for him from the region, and a foothold in national politics which the southern Sudan had never previously held. The importance of this has been magnified with the discovery of oil in the region. But southern and Islamic interests in the regime were strongly suspicious of one another, and hence the balance between them needed careful presidential handling.

The social bases of support not only involved careful balancing, but were developed at a time when an air of economic optimism reigned, a situation which placed substantial resources in the hands of the regime for distribution as it saw fit. This situation faltered seriously in the late 1970s. Economic and financial problems meant that the rich had to struggle to maintain their businesses, while many of the poor grew poorer.(11) As criticism grew, it became more difficult for supporters to remain associated with a regime which itself appeared neither to accept responsibility for its shortcomings, nor to offer any way out other than collaboration with international institutions which in turn demanded measures which further undermined living standards, in the short run at least. The decline in living standards also gave rise to social tension. While ethnic disturbances proliferated in the rural areas of west and south, the towns also manifested the greatest unrest that many of them had ever seen. The regime survived 1981 and 1982 only by resorting to sticks and whatever carrots it could

Sudan: The Retreat to Military Clientelism

muster.   But it had become clear that Numairi, who
had once commanded a degree of respect, albeit
grudgingly from some, would now probably be no more
lamented by his people than their cousins in Egypt
lamented the assassination of his friend Anwar
Sadat. It appeared also that for all their
institutional experiments and pluralistic dabbling,
the summing up of P.J. Vatikiotis following Egypt´s
food riots of 1977 applied equally to Sudan at the
end of 1983: "real power, as in Nasser´s time,
rests with the military - police or complex
security, not civilian, institutions".(12)
     This leads directly to the continuing need to
assess the military itself.   Once a threat to
Numairi, it has been brought increasingly under his
control, and it has remained the domestic backbone
of the regime. Features already mentioned include
the improvement of military intelligence, and the
purging of many officers, who were then placated by
enjoying profitable opportunities in retirement.
Those remaining were also well provided for, with
defence a growing item in the national budget, and
the armed forces expanded.(13) For the country as a
whole the military has continued to pose two major
issues.   The first is the likelihood of significant
change resulting from a successful coup, and though
the chances appear to have diminished, a threat
still remains particularly in worsening economic
circumstances.   The second issue has been the
preparedness of the security forces to confront
spontaneous popular disturbances in a country which
prided itself on the civilian-led overthrow of a
military regime in 1964. While confrontation was
long avoided, events in 1982 suggest an ultimate
readiness of the present security forces to use
force, though so far generally in a relatively
restrained manner when compared with a number of
Middle East and African states.   Whatever the
political order established after Numairi leaves
office, it seems unlikely at present that the
civilian institutions or the possible future
civilian politicians will be in a position to
prevent the military continuing to be a significant
force in national politics.
     However, the political order is not only a
product of the domestic scene.   For most of its
history as a state Sudan has been significantly
shaped by regional and world politics. Western
interest has already been mentioned and in the 1970s
may have contributed to keeping Numairi in power,
while at the same time becoming increasingly

249

important in view of Sudan´s parlous financial position. In regional terms concern has focussed on neighbour states, especially Egypt and the Gulf states. These have not only economic but also strategic interests in Sudan. Their involvement has been linked to repeated schemes for integration. Though the prospect of union between Sudan, Egypt and Libya, raised in 1969, quickly receded, it was followed by plans for integration of Egypt and Sudan first launched by Numairi and Sadat in 1974, and in 1982 revived in a revised form by Numairi and Mubarak. The Gulf states have not only been important financially, but have themselves sought to develop a direct interest by the cultivation of the Muslim Brotherhood, which has sought since 1977 to benefit from working within the regime. There is nothing in the development of Egypt and the Gulf States, or of great power manoeuvring in the region, to suggest that their interests will not be sustained. To a lesser extent the more narrowly domestic arrangements in other neighbouring states may also have an influence. Uganda has in the past had some influence on affairs in the southern Sudan. Idi Amin, as leader of a regime which had links with the south, largely kept Ugandan politics out, but his replacement by Milton Obote has contributed to the creation of magnified internal problems in the region. Though peaceful for ten years, the south remains a dimension of Sudan´s domestic politics, and could again cause problems for a new order, especially one in which Egypt and Saudi Arabia continue to wish to play a role.

Relations between Sudan and another of her neighbours, Ethiopia, are not only of growing importance in themselves, but also derive from divergences in the development of two initially rather similar military regimes. The governments of both Numairi in Sudan and Mengistu Haile-Maryam in Ethiopia originated from breakthrough military regimes seeking to overthrow immobilist political structures which had apparently proved incapable either of producing radical development policies or of solving long secessionist wars. However, from these comparatively similar beginnings, their responses to the three main political issues confronting them took the two regimes in significantly different directions. Firstly, in the area of central political control, the Ethiopian regime both suppressed its main civilian allies and maintained its revolutionary course, while Numairi in Sudan, after his traumatic break with the

Communists and the execution of three of his former
fellow Free Officers, turned to other and less
radical social and political groups. Secondly,
whereas the struggles for control of peripheral
areas were tackled in Sudan through a policy of
reconciliation with the South which brought with it
a measure of regional autonomy, the Derg in Ethiopia
sought a coercive and centralising solution which
has proved particularly unsuccessful in the northern
provinces. Thirdly, both regimes have also
constructed new external alliances. Sudan, after
the break with the Communists, turned to Egypt, the
oil rich Gulf states and the West, in search of
economic benefits; Ethiopia's revolution, with its
overwhelming need for military support, led to an
alliance with the Soviet Union assisted by Cuba, as
well as a local pact with Libya and South Yemen.
These differences have had serious implications for
the relations between the two countries. In Sudan
the regime's policy towards oil discoveries in the
South has provoked fresh outbursts of opposition in
the region which may deteriorate once more into
sustained civil war, and might threaten not only the
regime's political and economic policies, but its
survival as well. At least a section of the
Southern guerillas receive military support from
Ethiopia, and Sudan may seek the assistance of her
external backers if a military solution to the
renewed Southern problem is attempted. Meanwhile
Sudan and Saudi Arabia support the guerillas in
Eritrea and elsewhere in northern Ethiopia, on
grounds of both cultural solidarity and strategic
concern. There are several possible outcomes.
Growing conflict in both peripheries may prove
damaging to the two regimes; an arrangement might
be reached between Sudan and Ethiopia, of the kind
made tacitly in 1972 when the Addis Ababa agreement
ended the war in Southern Sudan; or mutual
hostility over their respective peripheries might
lead to open conflict, possibly involving also their
external backers.

CONCLUSION

This paper has sought to suggest that both political
and economic developments have helped to make the
civilianisation of Sudanese politics and the
creation of a new political order hard to
contemplate. Politically the exercise of the office
of the presidency by Ga'afar al-Numairi has been

such as to enhance his own powers at the expense of others, making uncertainty surround not only the other institutions created by the Permanent Constitution of 1973, but also the position of anyone who might succeed to his office. Indeed it is possible that in the future it might be regional governments which are the institutions capable of strengthening themselves spontaneously in the wake of his departure, for he would inevitably leave, at least temporarily, something of a vacuum. And if this were to happen some regions at least might threaten the territorial integrity of the present state. At the same time the distribution of resources by the President has encouraged the emergence of Sudan's equivalent of Egypt's Fat Cats, sometimes referred to as the 'new class'. Some are in reality not so new, but there is still a substantial number of nouveaux riches, whose success, seen as deriving ultimately from the regime, is regarded with increasing dislike as, for both internal and external reasons, Sudan's economic circumstances decline. Hope for the regime of recovery here rests heavily on measures of reform, in conjunction with the IMF and the World Bank, which may at last permit the attainment of Sudan's undoubted agricultural potential, and on the growth of oil exports in the years to come. If these do not transform the economic and social character of the country, the prospects for sustained civilian institutions around which a new political order could be built appear bleak.

NOTES

The following books are suggested for general reading: P.M. Holt & M.W. Daley, The History of the Sudan (London, 1979); P.K. Bechtold, Politics in the Sudan (New York, 1976); H.D. Nelson, ed, Sudan: a country study (Washington, 1982).
    1. The fullest account of the SCP is contained in Gabriel Warburg, Islam, Nationalism and Communism in a Traditional Society (London, 1978).
    2. There is some evidence of British, Egyptian and Libyan assistance to Numairi.
    3. M.O. Beshir, The Southern Sudan: from conflict to peace (New York, 1975); in the late 1970s the experiment with regional governments was repeated in the northern Sudan as well, and in 1983 the south was redivided into three regional

governments, Bahr el Ghazal, Equatoria, and Upper Nile; see D.A. Rondinelli, "Sudan´s Experiment with Devolution", <u>Journal of Modern African Studies</u>, Vol.19, 1981.

4. It was said at this time that only two men could see the President without an appointment: Asnam Khashoggi of TRIAD and ´Tiny´ Rowlands of LONRHO; see P. Woodward, "Sudan´s Domestic Politics and Relations with Neighbouring States", in <u>Post Independence Sudan</u> (Edinburgh, 1981).

5. A catalogue of attempted coups is contained in D.M. Wai, "Revolution, Rhetoric and Reality in the Sudan", <u>Journal of Modern African Studies</u>, Vol.17, 1979.

6. Hundreds of thousands of Sudanese left their country, mainly to work in the Gulf states; while the incentives were generally financial, it has been suggested that the departure of many of the more enterprising and poltically critical has given the regime an easier time domestically than it might otherwise have had - though it has also had a negative effect on economic performance.

7. T.C. Niblock, "The Role of the SSU in Sudan´s System of Government", in <u>Post Independence Sudan</u>, op.cit.

8. There are of course parallels, especially before 1977, in the weaknesses of the SSU and Egypt´s ASU; even ex-prime minister Sadiq al-Mahdi was invited to join the Politbureau, though he soon left it, rebuking the organisation as he went.

9. It is easy to recognise Sudanese equivalents of the Fat Cats described in the recent book by D. Hurst & I. Beeston, <u>Sadat</u> (London, 1981), Chapter 5, "An Uprising of Thieves; see F.B. Mahmoud, <u>The Sudanese Bourgeoisie: vanguard of development?</u> (forthcoming, London, 1984).

10. A.S. Cudsi, "Islam and Politics in the Sudan", in J.P. Piscatori, ed, <u>Islam in the Political Process</u> (London, 1983); in September 1983 Numairi also introduced Islamic law, ceremonially committing gallons of alcohol to the Nile.

11. Sudan´s rapidly deteriorating economic position resulted from several interlocking factors: the new schemes proved difficult to implement successfully, and ran up huge debts ($7.2bn in 1982); old schemes were neglected and deteriorated, reducing real export earnings; and world recession lowered the real value of exports, while imports continued to rise.

12. P.J. Vatikiotis, <u>Egypt</u> (London, 1979), p.420.

Sudan: The Retreat to Military Clientelism

13.   The   armed   forces   now   total   68,000,
compared with 50,000 in 1969 when a   civil   war   was
raging.

Chapter Eleven

ETHIOPIA : THE INSTITUTIONALISATION OF A MARXIST
MILITARY REGIME

Christopher Clapham

INTRODUCTION

This paper explores two general questions, within
the specific context of Ethiopia. Firstly, why
should a military regime explicitly adhere to a
Marxist-Leninist ideology? Secondly, what are the
implications of this ideological commitment for the
process of institutionalisation or demilitarisation
which the regime then undertakes?

So far as the first question is concerned, the
Ethiopian case is rare, and may possibly be regarded
as unique. Marxist-Leninist regimes
characteristically result either from domestic
revolution guided by an existing Communist party,
from occupation by another Communist regime, or from
a process of armed decolonisation by a nationalist
party which forms a guerilla movement and espouses
Marxism-Leninism for reasons both of internal
control and of external support. In third world
countries such as Cuba or Vietnam, the domestic
revolutionary and external anti-imperial elements
are often very closely linked.

Military regimes - those based on an
established national army rather than a rural
revolutionary force - fairly regularly take a
radical nationalist and anti-imperial form, despite
the persistence of the stereotype which sees them as
inherently conservative and allied with the West.
Nasser's Egypt is the classic case, and this and
other examples may usefully be ascribed to the
Breakthrough type examined in the introductory
chapter, in which the army serves as spearhead of a
new educated urban group opposed to a tottering
traditionalist regime. Ethiopia too, of course, may
be placed in the Breakthrough category. But in

255

almost every case, while espousing some form of 'socialism', such regimes remain chary of both the domestic and the international implications of Marxism-Leninism. There are a number of military regimes apart from Ethiopia which have attached to themselves a Marxist-Leninist label, but in every case of which I am aware the claim is fairly clearly specious, in that quite apart from the genuineness of the leaders' ideological commitment, there has simply been no domestic revolution, surely the essential precondition for the establishment of a convincingly Marxist-Leninist government. The cases I have in mind here are Benin, Congo, Madagascar, and the Somali Republic. In Ethiopia, though it is always open to critics to query the leadership's belief in its own Marxist-Leninist slogans, the revolution itself is unquestionably real.

My concern for the Marxism-Leninism of Ethiopia is due not simply to the interest of such regimes in their own right, or to its relevance to global political alignments, but to its implications for the processes of institutionalisation and demilitarisation with which this volume is concerned. The particular interest of Marxism-Leninism in this respect is that it appears to exclude either of the two commonest and most familiar forms of institutionalisation or demilitarisation. The first of these is the Handback option, exemplified by Ghana in 1969 and 1979, and by Nigeria in 1979, whereby the army creates a new constitutional structure and transfers power to those who win the elections held under it, then returning to barracks. In addition to the obvious point that Marxists have no belief in the validity of Liberal elections in any event, this form of demilitarisation comes up against two further problems. First, the revolutionary process must necessarily involve the overthrow and destruction of the existing ruling class, with the result that there is no existing group of party politicians to whom power can be transferred; those who succeed to power must be brought up within the revolutionary experience itself. Secondly, this transfer of power model assumes a relationship between the political process and the armed forces which is quite foreign to Marxism. The army cannot 'return to barracks' in the sense of acquiring a postion insulated from (or, as its officers would say, 'above') the political arena. There is no room for the myth of apoliticality. The army must be an integral part of the revolutionary process, while remaining subordinated to it.

It is this last requirement which excludes the commonest form of institutionalisation of military regimes: the transformation of the military leadership into a government which maintains itself in power, on the one hand by copious rhetorical appeals to nationalism and good government, on the other by the establishment of clientele relationships of either a factional or an authoritarian kind. This appears to be the experience of Zia´s Pakistan, of Brazil since 1964, or, carried to its extreme, of Mobutu´s Zaire. This is much harder than the liberal constitutionalist model to distinguish from ´genuine´ Marxist-Leninist demilitarisation, in that it can be combined both with Marxist (or, as some would say, Marxoid) rhetoric, and with a single party claiming to be the vanguard party which Lenin prescribed. The position is further complicated by the problem that vanguard parties - most obviously the CPSU - themselves readily become permeated by clientelist relationships.

Nonetheless, there is a distinction, and this distinction is critical to understanding the problems of demilitarisation in Ethiopia. ´Being Marxist-Leninist´ is not just a matter of believing in an ideology, nor of doing certain things which follow from it, such as nationalising the means of production and collectivising agriculture. It is a matter of creating a system, and the problem lies in reconciling such a system with the attitudes, organisation and personal power bases implicit in a military regime. At the centre of the system is of course the Party, and it will thus be no surprise that conflicts about demilitarisation in Ethiopia in large measure take the form of conflicts about what kind of party there should be, and how it should be controlled. This party must, first of all, be autonomous; it should not simply be the expression of the political power of any pre-existing group, whether personal (like the current head of state and his supporters) or institutional (like the army). It has to incorporate centres of social and economic power within the country, and while drawing on these for support, control them within the bounds of a single organisation. The way in which this is to be achieved is through strict controls on party membership, through the inculcation of its ideology, and through the organisation of democratic centralism. This requires, as already noted, the subordination of the armed forces. One of the

principal dangers against which the vanguard party
is intended to guard is indeed that of
'Bonapartism', the hijacking of the revolution by a
personalist regime led by a successful general.

A further problem implicit in the
institutionalisation of a Marxist-Leninist system is
that of its relationship with other Marxist-Leninist
regimes, and notably the Soviet Union. One of the
main reasons for the reluctance of Nasserist
militaries to embrace Marxism-Leninism is that it
threatens to commit them permanently to the Soviet
bloc, in a way that endangers not only national
independence, but also the individual leader's
freedom of action and tenure of power. No domestic
revolution, least of all in third world states
today, can be divorced fom its international
ramifications; in Ethiopia, these play a
significant part both in the regime's willingness to
embrace Marxism-Leninism initially, and in the
subsequent difficulties of institutionalising it. In
the next section, I shall examine the nature of the
Ethiopian military regime, before going on in a
later section to discuss the question of
institutionalisation.

ETHIOPIA: ARMY AND REVOLUTION

The Ethiopian armed forces seized power from the
regime of the Emperor Haile-Selassie in September
1974, as the culminating point of a 'creeping
revolution' which first got under way in February of
that year. The committee of the armed forces which
took over control of the government, known as the
Derg (the Amharic word for committee) came
increasingly to be dominated by Lieutenant-Colonel
Mengistu Haile-Maryam, who became head of the
government in February 1977, after the execution of
his two predecessors. Since that time, and
especially since the 1977-78 war against the
Somalis, which was won by the Ethiopians with
overwhelming Soviet and Cuban military support,
Mengistu has consolidated his position. In the
process, the Derg and Mengistu personally have
identified themselves and refined their options by
reference to five critical groups of political
actors, and in order to account for the peculiar
nature of the Ethiopian military regime, it is
necessary to look at its relationships with each of
these in turn. They are firstly the ancien regime,

secondly the army itself, thirdly civilian political groups, fourthly the 'nationalities', or ethnic and regional movements within Ethiopia, and fifthly the regime's external allies and opponents.

The Ancien Regime

Despite the label of 'feudal' which was readily applied by the new regime to its predecessor, Haile-Selassie's government, at least by the time it fell, was in reality nothing of the kind. The old Ethiopian Empire, which was indeed based on the control of land and the economic and military resources which followed from it, had been eaten away from within long before it was toppled from without. The primary agent in this process was Haile-Selassie himself, who, though continuing a process initiated by his immediate predecessors, could justifiably be described as his own gravedigger. Haile-Selassie was a modernising monarch, for whom modernisation was largely synonymous with the creation of mechanisms for central control of a traditionally unruly periphery: a cash-crop economy, whose products were channelled through the capital and government controlled ports, whence they could be sold to raise government revenue; a communications network which radiated from Addis Ababa; a central bureaucracy and the educational system necessary to man it; and most obvious of all, a large standing army.

This centralising process was unaccompanied by any creation of effective political institutions. These were indeed discouraged as potential threats to imperial authority. There was for instance a partially elected Parliament, but this had no political parties. Government became increasingly concentrated on the palace, and on a group of courtier bureaucrats who owed their advancement to the Emperor's favour rather than to any political backing in the country as a whole, or even within its modernising sector. The whole process comes very close to that described by Huntington as 'the king's dilemma: success vs survival'(3), and amounts in terms of the basic variables outlined in the introduction to this volume to a very low level of autonomous political organisation.

The effect was to create an educated elite group necessary to man the new machinery of the state, on which the Emperor depended, but which, outside the small court circle, had no reason to depend on him. Instead, the court became the object of a deep and pervasive contempt: not because it was ´traditional´, nor even, by African standards, particularly corrupt, but because it was inward-looking, immobilist, undynamic. This contempt was most dramatically expressed on 24 November 1974, when fifty-two leading members of the court elite, many of them senior army officers, were machine-gunned in cold blood. The first way in which the Derg identified itself was negative: it was not like the old regime, and has never shown any wish to return to it.

The Armed Forces

One of the most important features of any military regime is its relationship with its own armed forces, and in this respect the Derg was highly peculiar. Its initial membership comprised three representatives (a junior officer, a non-commissioned officer, and an ordinary soldier) from each of the forty-two main units in the armed forces. It was a parliament rather than a junta, formed to co-ordinate the armed forces´ response to the attempts made by the old regime to maintain its position in early 1974, and in particular to guard against the divisions within the military which Haile-Selassie had been adept at manipulating. It indicated a low level of unity within the military command structure, soon to be confirmed not only by the killing of senior officers, but also by intense conflict and bloodshed within the Derg itself. The repesentative functions of the Derg did not last long. Units soon found that they could not recall and replace the delegates whom they had initially chosen, and the number of members steadily declined as a result of internal divisions and purges, until by 1980 probably between 60 and 80 were left. Another distinctive feature of the Derg (again partly the result of the conditions in which it was formed, though also of an inbuilt Ethopian secretiveness) was that the names of its members have never been made public.

The political programme of the Derg during its early period, up to November 1974, was characterised by an inchoate radicalism and the nationalism commonly associated with military regimes. It had a motto (´Ityopya tikdem´, or ´Ethiopia First´) rather than a policy, though into this should be read both a measure of xenophobia and, more important, a determination to sustain central state control against the various peripheral secessionist movements threatening it, especially in Eritrea and the Ogaden. The first Chairman of the Provisional Military Administrative Council (PMAC), a general of Eritrean origin named Aman Andom, was killed in November 1974 after advocating a policy of reconciliation with the rebel groups in Eritrea. Any articulation of policy or ideology beyond this rather simple initial series of reactions depended on the injection of ideas from civilian political groups.

Civilian Political Groups

As already noted, the takeover of power by the PMAC in September 1974 was not so much a military coup in the classic sense as a stage in a broader process, not unlike that which was to take place in Iran a few years later: a series of strikes, riots, demonstrations and mutinies, accompanied by desperate and eventually unsuccessful attempts by the monarchical regime to keep things under control.

It would be misleading to see this as a democratic civilian revolution which was subverted and betrayed by the military;(4) the armed forces had been involved from the very start, and the various civilian groups had at this stage little more coherent policy and much less coherent organisation than the military. Nonetheless, the role of civilians was critical. They demonstrated the existence of widespread opposition which first encouraged and then enabled the army to supplant the entrenched imperial regime; they constituted a force within the urban political arena which the PMAC had to take into account, whether by co-opting or controlling them; and consistently the army took over their policies, even while suppressing the groups themselves. The autonomy of civilian political organisation, in terms of the criteria suggested in the introduction to this volume, was extremely weak; such power as they were able to exercise depended on their relations with the military. But it was no less important for that.

What were these civilian groups ? Broadly speaking, they can be divided into the intelligentsia and the urban workforce. The 1974 disturbances started with a strike by taxi drivers, and continued with a general strike called by the Confederation of Ethiopian Labour Unions (CELU), which claimed a membership of 120,000. CELU had ambivalent relations with the Derg from the start, as the army first sided with the imperial government to crush strikes in mid-1974, and then joined the trade union movement in pressing for anti-corruption measures immediately before Haile-Selassie's overthrow. It never became fully reconciled to the army takeover, and continued to press for an elected civilian government. The PMAC responded by banning strikes, killed trade union demonstrators calling for civilian rule in May 1975, and dissolved CELU the following December, eventually replacing it by the All-Ethiopia Trade Union (AETU) in 1976. This too proved difficult to control.

The intelligentsia consisted of a leadership group of student radicals, mostly educated in the United States, with their sympathisers in the bureaucracy and the Addis Ababa student population. These, like the trade unions, faced a choice between collaborating with the PMAC and holding out for a civilian regime, and characteristically split. One group, later to become the All Ethiopia Socialist Movement (Meison) opted for collaboration; the other, which was to form the Ethiopian People's Revolutionary Party (EPRP), for opposition. I will look at the fate of these parties and their successors in the next section. The Meison group had substantial successes, in late 1974 and early 1975, in turning the PMAC's vaguely defined 'Ethiopian socialism' into a series of specific and far-reaching measures which established the economic basis of the revolution: the nationalisation of banks, insurance companies and major industrial and commercial enterprises; of urban land, the house rents on which, especially in Addis Ababa, had formed a major source of income for the officials gathered round the throne; and most important, of rural land, peasants being allowed only usufructory rights over land which they could till as a family unit, up to a maximum of ten hectares. In southern Ethiopia, where large areas had been owned by central government officials and their families, this was immediately popular, and in some areas landlords were killed or driven out. In the north, where peasants often had effective traditional land rights, it met with much greater suspicion. The Addis Ababa rentier class was destroyed.

To replace both rural and urban landlords, the PMAC formed what are still its only local level revolutionary institutions: the Peasants' Associations in the countryside, and the Urban Associations (generally known by their Amharic name, Kebelles) in the towns. The politicisation of the countryside was intensified by despatching some

60,000 students to help organise the Peasants'
Associations (of which there were 28,500 by 1978)
and spread literacy. This campaign, the Zemecha,
had very mixed results, radicalising the students as
much as the peasantry, often in opposition to the
government.

Ethnic and Regional Movements

Ethiopia is no more ethnically homogeneous than most
other African states, the major exception in this
respect being its neighbour and enemy, Somalia.
Unlike most African states, however, it does have a
historic national core, composed of the central
Amhara people who, with the related Tigreans to the
north, have formed a single state whose history
stretches back over the past two thousand years.
The present boundaries of Ethiopia were established
in the late nineteenth and early twentieth centuries
by the extension of core (and especially Amhara)
control over peripheral peoples, especially to the
east, south and west. The principal opposition to
the Ethiopian state has taken the form of peripheral
secessionist movements, by far the most important of
which have been in the Somali-inhabited territories
in the south-east and in Eritrea in the north.
Eritrea is an ethnically and religiously mixed area,
much of it lying within 'traditional' Ethiopia,
which was united with Ethiopia in 1952 after over
sixty years under Italian and briefly British
administration.
    The historic function of the Ethiopian army has
been the creation and enforcement of a centralised
state, and by its motto 'Ethiopia First' and by
killing its first Chairman, the PMAC demonstrated
that this was still a function which it took
seriously. At no time has the Derg wavered in its
determination to maintain the integrity of the
Ethiopian state within its existing boundaries. The
Brest-Litovsk solution, a settlement with external
enemies involving the abandonment of territory in
order to create a breathing space to build a
socialist state within a truncated national
territory, has consistently been ruled out. Rather,
the regime hoped in its early days that socialism
might serve as a formula for maintaining national
unity. The main threats to unity came from
movements, the Somali government of Mohammed Siyad
Barre and the two main Eritrean liberation fronts,
which themselves claimed to be Marxist-Leninist. It
was easy to surmise that regional opposition to the

263

Haile-Selassie government was but a disguised form of class conflict, prompted by the 'feudalism' of the old regime and the alienation of land to a landlord class dependent on central government, coupled with the cultural trappings of Amhara hegemony in the form of Orthodox Christianity and the Amhara language. Land reform, a literacy campaign conducted in ten of the principal national languages, a secular state combined with a recognition of Islam as having a status equivalent to that of Christianity, and above all a common ideological outlook, should all combine to do the trick.

They didn´t, because none of these measures tackled the central problem of political control, and neither Somalis nor Eritreans were prepared to abandon their long-sought autonomy for subordination to a government drawn from their old enemy, the Ethiopian army, merely on the ground that this had now seen the light in ideological terms. They were, in their own terms, perfectly correct. They had little to gain from a body so uncompromisingly centralist as the Derg, and instead took advantage of the slackening of central control caused by the upheavals in Addis Ababa. At the same time other regionalist movements appeared. In the north of the country, especially in Tigre province which bordered Eritrea, peasants feared that the Derg´s land reform threatened their traditional inheritance rights in land. In the south, there was some growth of political identity among the majority ethnic group, the Oromo, which not even the local popularity of the new regime´s land reform policy was enough to prevent.

The deteriorating political and military position in many areas of Ethiopia between 1974 and 1977 did not lead the Derg to change its ideological stance. Instead, it reinforced it, by drawing on it to provide the basis for the vast increase in coercive capacity now needed to preserve national unity. One form which this took was the raising of peasant militias, whose first attempts at mass invasion of Eritrea in 1976 were catastrophic, but which improved in effectiveness with better arms and training from 1977 onwards. As in the French and Russian revolutions, much of the mobilisation undertaken by the regime was thus a direct reaction to an intense sense of threat, initially from competing factions at the central level, but subsequently and chiefly from challenges to the regime´s control of the national periphery. Equally important, this threat promoted the use of Marxism-Leninism not only as a mechanism for domestic mobilisation, but also as a means of promoting and legitimising the Derg´s access to external military support.

The External Factor

Under Haile-Selassie, Ethiopia was, despite its formal non-alignment, closely linked with the West and especially with the United States. In particular, the United States supplied by far the greater part of its weaponry and military training, while Ethiopia in turn accounted for most of the United States´ military aid to sub-Saharan Africa. This connection did not lead to a reaction as intense as that in Iran, but nonetheless led easily enough to an association of the United States with the forces of feudalism and reaction. The impression was intensified during the period 1974-76, during which U.S. arms supplies to Ethiopia paradoxically increased (though in the form of cash sales rather than grants), but were subject to disruption in response to American disapproval of Ethiopian domestic policies, especially in the field of ´human rights´ in which the Derg´s record was by any standard appalling.

The shift in international alignment to the Soviet Union, which in retrospect may seem natural or even inevitable, was delayed at the time by the fact that the Russians were already (in response to American support for Ethiopia) arming most of the Derg´s principal enemies, either directly as in Somalia (where the Siyad regime had emerged since 1969 as the most faithful Soviet client in black Africa), or indirectly as in Eritrea. The Russians, like the Derg, hoped to get over their difficulties through the panacea of socialist unity, and tried through the good offices of Fidel Castro in early 1977 to set up a confederation of socialist states in the Horn which would guarantee the essential interests of all three contestants. When this failed and the Russians had to come down on one side or the other, they opted decisively for Ethiopia, a policy which had the advantages of putting them on the side of the largest and most powerful state in the region, as well as of supporting the principle of maintaining existing states and boundaries, in agreement with the Organisation of African Unity. The main costs were the loss of their naval and air base facilities in Somalia, and the charges of opportunism arising from their abandonment of longtime allies.(5)

The enormous injection of Soviet and Cuban military assistance which followed, estimated at some $2,000m in cash terms and up to 20,000 Cuban troops, enabled the Ethiopians to defeat the Somali invasion of 1977-78, and sharply reduce the area of Eritrea controlled by the guerilla movements. In the process, this not only encouraged the Derg to trumpet the virtues of Marxism-Leninism, but also gave the Russians considerable influence and prestige within domestic politics. Ethiopia still falls some way short of a full process of Soviet satellitisation, and the process of demilitarisation itself displays the difficulties and ambiguities of the Russian position in the country, but the establishment of Marxism-Leninism in Ethiopia (as in every country in the world save the Soviet Union itself and possibly China) cannot be divorced from its external support.

To summarise, Ethiopia might in any event have been expected to produce a radical military regime of the Breakthrough type, because of the nature of the regime which it displaced. This tendency was reinforced by the peculiar structure of the Derg, the leadership of which was drawn from young officers who, during the critical period of seizing and consolidating power, had to appeal directly to the representatives of the non-commissioned officers and the rank and file. Senior officers by contrast were excluded, and in many cases executed. However, the critical feature which converted the regime from a radical to a revolutionary stance was the temporary alliance between the military leadership and civilian intellectuals, by far the most important achievement of which was the nationalisation of rural land. The nationalisation of urban land, and of capitalist enterprises both indigenous and foreign owned, were significant but subsidiary measures. These destroyed both the economic and political base of the old regime, a mixed traditional ruling class and new educated urban elite which relied on its control of the central state apparatus and its access to new forms of wealth, especially the export cash crop growing areas of southern Ethiopia. Their place was taken by new institutions, the peasants and urban associations, within each of which sharp and ofen violent power struggles took place. What did not change, but rather intensified, was the centralising mission of the state apparatus, strengthened by the attachment to territory entrenched in the values of an agrarian society. Yet this too could be reconciled with a Leninist belief in democratic centralism, reinforced by a more Stalinist approach to the problem of ´nationalities´, and a readiness to resort to terror. And on top of that, the supremacy of the centre could be guaranteed by the overwhelming military support of the Soviet Union and its allies.

THE DILEMMAS OF DEMILITARISATION

As the Introduction suggests, the political organisation of a Marxist-Leninist regime is, in principle at least, extremely straightforward. There is not much doubt about what you need to do. You need to create, and transfer power to, a party which is strictly and hierarchically organised, held together by bonds of discipline and ideological agreement, which provides the only acceptable channel for personal advancement, and which at the same time, encompasses all of the permissible subordinate institutions of the society. The problem is how you get there.

In Ethiopia, while the end has been generally accepted, the means have given rise to intense dispute, resulting at times in the most savage outbreaks of violence. The picture is a murky one, by no means yet complete, but three broad patterns can be distinguished, each primarily associated with a particular phase in the development of the regime. The first derived from parties established by the civilian intelligentsia, the second from the organisation of factions within the army, the third from an attempt to incorporate the surviving civilian elements into a new party dominated by the military leadership.

The Civilian Parties

Ethiopia has no tradition of political party organisation and activity, either legitimate or underground. Under the imperial regime, though there was a popularly elected House of Representatives, its members ran for election on a personal basis, and it was always tacitly accepted, though never formally decreed, that parties would not be permitted. Perhaps more surprisingly, the opposition to the regime which developed from the early 1960s onwards never took a party form either, in sharp contrast for example to the well-organised clandestine Communist Party in neighbouring Sudan. This absence of parties is generally ascribed by Ethiopians to cultural traits, especially a pronounced lack of interpersonal trust and the difficulty of maintaining any co-operative institution in a very hierarchically structured society. It may also in part be accounted for by the urban and government centredness of the opposition groups concerned. Mostly in or seeking government employment, despising the elected parliament as a set of ignorant countrymen, they had neither the motivation nor the opportunity to create any organisation going beyond their own small circle. The effects in producing a low level of autonomous political organisation have already been noted.

Some of the most effective and articulate opposition to the imperial government was organised through Ethiopian student movements abroad, especially in the United States, and these returned students provided the leadership of two main political organisations which sprang up in the wake of (i.e. followed, and did not cause) the upheavals of 1974. These were the All Ethiopia Socialist Movement (generally known by its Amharic acronym, Meison) led by Haile Fida, and the Ethiopian People's Revolutionary Party (EPRP) led by Berhane-Meskal Redda. They shared a common rhetorical stance, a 'socialism' derived more from Western Marxism than from the USSR, but differed partly in membership (Meison seems to have had a larger proportion of southerners, especially Oromo, EPRP of northern Tigreans), and most importantly in tactics. While each regarded itself a the rightful vanguard of a socialist Ethiopia, Meison recognised the need for a tactical alliance with the Derg which EPRP consistently rejected. The difference became all the sharper when, from May 1975 onwards, the PMAC started to resort to repression against rivals within the revolutionary movement, banning strikes and killing some demonstrators who were demanding a return to civilian rule.

Since the EPRP was never part of the military regime, it has only a marginal relevance to a case study of demilitarisation, but it was nonetheless extremely important in the development of the military government's attitudes. First, it helped to foment a breach with organised labour in the form of the CELU, which took a broadly EPRP line, and launched a series of strikes in favour of civilian rule in September 1975. Secondly, from August 1976 onward it launched a campaign of urban terrorism against the PMAC and its supporters, several hundred of whom were assassinated, most of them civilians. During the Red Terror of the following eighteen months, which was at its most intense in late 1977 and early 1978, several thousand real or alleged EPRP supporters, mostly students, were killed by government execution squads, and some 30,000 more imprisoned.(6) The shattered remnants retreated to northern Ethiopia, where they attempted without much success to form a rural guerilla force. If it is a characteristic of revolutions to devour their own children, Ethiopia certainly qualifies.

The second movement, Meison, while also seeing the future of the revolution as lying with the transfer of power to a civilian vanguard party (itself), nonetheless recognised the short term advantages of collaboration with the PMAC. In the short term, it achieved a great deal. Its leading members (though the party itself was not formed until later) took probably the most critical role in converting the inchoate nationalist radicalism of the Derg into a set of revolutionary measures, notably land reform, backed by a reasonably articulate Marxist ideology. Under the military's protection, they also worked their way into leading positions in most of the organisations which linked the government to civilian political forces. At the top level, they took part with several minor political groups in the Provisional Office of Mass Organisation Affairs (POMOA), which from late 1975 onwards provided an umbrella organisation for the government's supporters. This founded an ideological training school, and in July 1977 established the Union of Marxist-Leninist Organisations (Imalered) which was intended to develop into a national Communist Party. Once CELU was banned for supporting the EPRP, Meison supporters dominated its successor, the All-Ethiopia Trade Union (AETU), the first three presidents of which were all assassinated by the EPRP. As this suggests, Meison joined enthusiastically in the liquidation of its fellow intellectuals in EPRP during the Red Terror, in the process building up its position in another important source of power, the kebelles or urban associations.

Unfortunately for Meison, while the PMAC was quite happy to use it as a subordinate ally, it had no intention of handing over to it as a successor.

At its crudest, it was simply a matter of power. The PMAC had it, and would not voluntarily relinquish it. Indeed, in a revolution in which being on the winning side was literally a matter of life or death, they could scarcely be expected to. A number of factors precipitated the eventual breach. First, Mengistu Haile-Maryam's assassination of his predecessor as Chairman of the PMAC, Teferi Bante, in a shoot-out in the old imperial palace in February 1977 replaced an uneasy balance of factions in the Derg with a single strongman, a process reinforced when Mengistu's deputy was executed the following November. Meison's freedom of manoeuvre was thereby restricted. Second, the PMAC distrusted Meison's political influence, and especially it seems an attempt to gain control over the militia forces formed to combat the Somali and Eritrean threats in mid-1977.(7) Perhaps most important, the Somali invasion in July 1977 raised the national question in an intense form. Neither Meison nor the EPRP had entirely shared the Derg's intense dedication to the maintenance of the state and its territory. Drawing much of their experience from student politics, and much of their support from members of peripheral ethnic groups in northern or southern Ethiopia, they were prepared to consider the possibilities of regional autonomy or even secession, and to compromise the immediate needs of national integrity in the interests of ideological purity. The break came in August 1977, without posing any serious challenge to the PMAC, and Meison's leading members were killed, went underground, or made their peace with the regime. The question of the relationship between military and civilian political forces had been settled in favour of the military.

The Army as Vanguard

On a visit to Moscow in November 1978, Mengistu Haile-Maryam stated that "the historical uniqueness of the Ethiopian revolution" consisted in the fact that the army had assumed the vanguard role which was normally reserved for the Communist Party.(8) What the Russians thought of this contribution to the Leninist theory of revolution, they were too diplomatic to say, though they nonetheless made it clear enough by the consistency with which they pressed the PMAC to establish a Communist Party. Despite their urging, for a period of over two years

up to December 1979 there was no civilian political
organisation through which the PMAC (which by this
time had become the PMGSE, or Provisional Military
Government of Socialist Ethiopia) could either
demilitarise or institutionalise its power. In
part, of course, this was because it had decisively
broken with the only existing civilian political
groups through which it could operate. In part
also, it reflected the fact that from mid-1977 to
the end of 1978 was a period of bitter warfare, at
first in the Ogaden and subsequently in Eritrea,
which simply preoccupied the PMGSE's attention. But
the war, with its injection of Soviet and Cuban
military support, also raised for the first time the
problem of the external implications of
demilitarisation.

There is no doubt about the Soviet Union's
belief in the need for a Communist Party. In its
clearest form, this was expressed in a paper on
"National Democratic Revolution in Ethiopia"
delivered by two Soviet scholars at an Ethiopian
studies conference as early as December 1977:(9)

> Equally important for the creation of a
> people's democratic republic is the correct
> solution of the party question. Our conception
> of this question is that a vanguard party is
> indispensable, a party which is equipped with
> the revolutionary theory of scientific
> socialism and guided by the Leninist idea of
> the union between working class and peasantry,
> and embraces within its ranks all progressive
> members of the working class, the peasantry, and
> the intelligentsia. Such a party should cement
> the unity of its ranks and maintain friendly
> ties with other vanguard communist parties.

Intriguingly, this passage says nothing whatever
about the role of the army, while its references to
the intelligentsia and to ties with other communist
parties might suggest, to the proverbially
suspicious Ethiopian mind, the possibility of an
alliance between the Russians and the remnants of
Meison and/or the EPRP behind the backs of Mengistu
and his colleagues.

Such suspicions were reinforced by an incident
in May 1978 when an exiled Meison leader, Negede
Gobeze, was smuggled back on a South Yemeni passport
into the Cuban embassy in Addis Ababa;(10) when
this was discovered, Negede, the Cuban ambassador
and his deputy, and the South Yemeni charge

d´affaires were all rapidly expelled. Henze also suggests that the EPRP may have been funded by the Soviet Union, though allowance must be made for his position as a staff officer to the US National Security Council.(11) The only political organisations to maintain themselves during this period seem to have been largely or entirely military in membership and control, the most prominent being <u>Abyot Seded</u> (Revolutionary Flame), a party formed with Mengistu´s approval by a group in the Derg in order to combat Meison influence in the urban <u>kebelles</u>. Groups such as this however were, in addition to their own endemic factionalism, too restricted in support and limited in goals to serve as a base for a national Marxist-Leninist party.

COPWE: Party Formation from Above

No further attempt to institutionalise the regime was made until 18 December 1979, when Mengistu announced the formation of the Commission for Organising the Party of the Working People of Ethiopia, generally known as COPWE. The first point to be made about COPWE is that it is not itself a party, merely the commission for organising one, and more than four years after its inception the party has yet to emerge. It does however have many of the attributes of a party, including an Executive Committee of seven members, a Central Committee of ninety-one, a number of subject committees devoted to various fields of party organisation and ideology, and representatives stretching down to the lower levels of the regional administration. It was made clear from the start that the party would have only individual members, unlike other bodies from POMOA onwards which had served as umbrella organisations for existing political groups. This would give the leadership of the party much greater control over its composition and activities. Though COPWE is not confined to the military, it is overwhelmingly dominated by it. The seven members of the Executive Committee all belong to the inner group of the Derg, and most of the members of the Central Committee come from the armed forces and police.(12) This army (and more specifically Derg) representation spreads down at least to the upper reaches of the regional COPWE organisation, though it is said that some ´re-educated´ Meison and even EPRP members have positions lower down. Some of the civilian members of the Central Committee were previously involved in POMOA or the ideological

272

school which it established, and party cadres have been sent for training to the Soviet Union and other socialist states. The national trade union, peasants', women's and youth organisations are associated with COPWE, but appear to have little if any direct representation in it.

It is nonetheless difficult, however tempting, to dismiss COPWE as a mere facade for continuing military rule. For one thing, there would in that case have been no difficulty in converting the PMAC directly into the executive of the new party, perhaps with token civilian participation, and then formally transferring government functions to it, just as Mohammed Siyad Barre did when he formed the Somali Socialist Revolutionary Party in 1976. A purely cosmetic operation could have been carried out long ago. Part of the difference between Somalia and Ethiopia in this respect goes back to the fact that whereas the Somali 'revolution' of 1969 was little more than a military coup, the Ethiopian one of 1974 was indeed a revolution, from which a level of civilian political consciousness arose which (despite the failure of Meison and EPRP) cannot now be disregarded. The dangers of an unrepresentative political structure are most strikingly demonstrated by the proliferation of regionalist movements, into which opposition to the regime has progressively been diverted. The wars of 1977-78 appear to have marked the consolidation of centralist Amhara strength within the PMGSE, in place of the earlier belief that national unity could be built around the programme of the revolution itself. Following the purge of some of its Oromo elements, the Derg, like the COPWE Central Committee, now appears to be heavily Amhara in composition, though it still includes some Oromo such as its chief of security, Teka Tulu. The question of 'nationalities' remains one of the most difficult which any effective party structure must tackle, and an Institute for the Study of Ethiopian Nationalities was established in May 1983 to examine the issue.

A further problem implicit in the conversion of COPWE into a fully fledged Marxist-Leninist ruling party remains that of the relationship with the Soviet Union. The Soviet intervention in Afghanistan, coming precisely one week after the formation of COPWE, provided a dramatic example of the vulnerability of a Communist Party government to Russian penetration. Though the PMAC eventually came out in support of the intervention, it took

longer to do so (over a fortnight) than the Soviet
Union would have wished. The major problem here
concerns the division within the PMGSE between those
who are first and foremost Ethiopian nationalists,
viewing the Soviet alliance as a tactical necessity
to preserve Ethiopia's territorial integrity, and
ideologues seeking a permanent Cuban-style
relationship with the USSR. Mengistu Haile-Maryam
himself is generally regarded as favouring the
nationalist group, but nonetheless finds it
necessary or desirable to retain in the inner circle
of the government a number of officers, trained in
the Soviet Union, who appear to be much more deeply
committed to the Soviet alliance. The full
institution of a party would not only increase the
possibility that party organisation could be used to
mount or legitimise a putsch against Mengistu. It
would also create the conditions for party-to-party
links with fraternal parties, through which Soviet
penetration could be extended down to a low level.
Military rule helps to insulate domestic politics
from such penetration, by providing a single
hierarchical channel through which the Soviet Union
and its allies have to work. Their frustration at
this insulation, and the swiftness of Mengistu's
reaction to any activity on their part which might
threaten it, is most clearly illustrated by the
Negede Gobeze incident referred to above. It is
also reflected in a pattern of appointments within
COPWE and the PMGSE, most clearly indicated in the
Second COPWE Congress in January 1983 and a cabinet
reshuffle the following April, which suggested that
personal loyalty to Mengistu was the primary
criterion for promotion. The pre-eminence at an
equivalent stage of Stalin in Russia, Mao in China
and Castro in Cuba indicate that a high level of
personalism is no necessary bar to the development
of an entrenched party structure, and may indeed be
essential to it. It does however lengthen the
period during which the nature of the regime might
be altered by a dominant individual, and thus delay
the entrenchment of the Soviet connection.

Beyond the specific problems of ideology and
organisation which beset COPWE, and the practical
difficulties of the representation of nationalities
and of relations with the Soviet Union, there is
another more basic issue which will be familiar to
all students of military regimes: the enormous
difficulty which such regimes have in establishing
effective political institutions. Implementing
specific policies, even the most revolutionary ones,

and co-opting individuals are a very different matter from creating structures, by their nature very different from military ones, which if they are to count for anything must subject the military leadership to influence if not control from people with political power bases in the society as a whole. In principle, the Ethiopian combination of low unity, autonomy and differentiation, coupled with a sense of threat which in this case leads to intensified mobilisation and the reinforcement of the regime´s revolutionary aspirations, offers an unrivalled set of preconditions for the creation and institutionalisation of a military party state. In practice, the outcome also depends on the fortunes of particular individuals, on decisions made in conditions of high uncertainty and personal stress, and on the difficulties of institutionalising any kind of political order in a state as riven as Ethiopia both by personal distrust and by centre-peripheral tension. While much of the revolutionary process is now irreversible, the ultimate character of the post-revolutionary regime is still in doubt.

NOTES

1. P. Wiles, ed, The New Communist Third World (London, Croom Helm, 1982), chapters 6-9.
2. On the whole the best account is F. Halliday & M. Molyneux, The Ethiopian Revolution (London, Verso, 1981).
3. S.P. Huntington, Political Order in Changing Societies (New Haven, Yale, 1968), chapter 3.
4. See for example, M. Chege, "The Revolution Betrayed", J. Modern African Studies, 13, 1979; and J. Markakis & N. Ayele, Class and Revolution in Ethiopia (Nottingham, Spokesman, 1978).
5. C. Clapham, "The Soviet Experience in the Horn of Africa", in E.J. Feuchtwanger & P. Nailor, eds, The Soviet Union and the Third World (London, Macmillan, 1981), chapter 9.
6. Amnesty International, Human Rights Violations in Ethiopia (London, 1978).
7. Halliday & Molyneux, op.cit., p.132.
8. P.B. Henze, "Communism and Ethiopia", Problems of Communism, 30, 1981.
9. A. Kokiev & V. Vigand, "National Democratic Revolution in Ethiopia", in J. Tubiana, ed, Modern

Ethiopia (Rotterdam, Balkema, 1980).
    10.   The Times, London, 29 May 1978; Henze, loc.cit.
    11.   Henze, loc.cit.
    12.   Halliday & Molyneux, op.cit., p.142.

INDEX

Index